MPLS-BASED VPNs

ISBN 0-13-028225-1

Prentice Hall Series in
Computer Networking and Distributed Systems
Radia Perlman, Series Editor

Kaufman, Perlman & Speciner	*Network Security: Private Communication in a Public World*
Dayem	*Mobile Data and Wireless LAN Technologies*
Dayem	*PCS and Digital Cellular Technologies: Accessing Your Options*
Greenblatt	*Internet Directories: How to Build and Manage Applications for LDAP, DNS, and Other Directories*
Kadambi, Kalkunte & Crayford	*Gigabit Ethernet: Migrating to High Bandwidth LANS*
Kercheval	*DHCP: A Guide to Dynamic TCP/IP Network Management*
Kercheval	*TCP/IP Over ATM: A No-Nonsense Internetworking Guide*
Mancill	*Linux Routers: A Primer for Network Administrators*
Mann & Mitchell	*Linux System Security: The Administrator's Guide to Open Source Security Tools*
Skoudis	*Counter Hack: A Step-by-Step Guide to Computer Attacks and Effective Defenses*
Solomon	*Mobile IP: The Internet Unplugged*
Tomsu & Schmutzer	*Next Generation Optical Networks*
Tomsu & Wieser	*MPLS-Based VPNs: Designing Advanced Virtual Networks*
Zeltserman	*A Practical Guide to SNMPv3 and Network Management*
Zeltserman & Puoplo	*Building Network Management Tools with Tcl/Tk*

PRENTICE HALL SERIES IN COMPUTER NETWORKING AND DISTRIBUTED SYSTEMS

MPLS-BASED VPNs

Designing Advanced Virtual Networks

Peter Tomsu · Gerhard Wieser

PH PTR

Prentice Hall PTR
Upper Saddle River, NJ 07458
www.phptr.com

Library of Congress Cataloging-in-Publication Data
Tomsu, Peter.
    MPLS-based VPNs: designing advanced virtual networks / Peter Tomsu and Gerhard Wieser.
        p.   cm. -- (Prentice Hall series in computer networking and distributed systems)
Includes bibliographical references and index.
ISBN 0-13-028225-1
    1. MPLS standard. 2. Extranets (Computer networks) I. Wieser, Gerhard.
   II. Title. III. Series
TK5105.573 .T66 2001
004.6'2--dc21
                                                                2001053088

Technical Editor: *Thomas D. Nadeau*
Editorial/production supervision: *Donna Cullen-Dolce*
Acquisition Editor: *Mary Franz*
Editorial Assistant: *Noreen Regina*
Marketing Manager: *Dan DePasquale*
Manufacturing Manager: *Alexis Heydt-Long*
Cover Design: *Talar Boorujy*
Cover Design Director: *Jerry Votta*
Interior Design: *Gail Cocker-Bogusz*

© 2002 Prentice Hall PTR
Prentice-Hall, Inc.
Upper Saddle River, NJ 07458

All rights reserved. No part pf this book may be reproduced, in any form or by any means, without permission in writing from the publisher

The publisher offers discounts on this book when ordered in bulk quantities.
For more information, contact:
Corporate Sales Department
Prentice Hall PTR
One Lake Street
Upper Saddle River, NJ 07458
Phone: 800-382-3419; FAX: 201-236-714
E-mail (Internet): corpsales@prenhall.com

Printed in the United States of America

10 9 8 7 6 5 4 3 2 1

ISBN 0-13-028225-1

Pearson Education LTD.
Pearson Education Australia PTY, Limited
Pearson Education Singapore, Pte. Ltd.
Pearson Education North Asia Ltd.
Pearson Education Canada, Ltd.
Pearson Educatión de Mexico, S.A. de C.V.
Pearson Education–Japan
Pearson Education Malaysia, Pte. Ltd.

To our families and friends

ACKNOWLEDGMENTS

There are many people we would like to thank. First, this book would not have been possible without the patience and support of our families. They provided sustained encouragement during the entire period, from the very beginning of planning this book through the final edits.

A special thanks goes to Radia Perlman, who provided valuable input in structuring the book, as well as defining the final format. Additional thanks to the outstanding professionals at Prentice Hall, especially Mary Franz, who was a significant help in all phases of the project.

Very special thanks to our employer, Cisco Systems, for providing tremendous assistance over the past two years, especially Jane Butler and Rob Lloyd, who supported this book from the very beginning.

We would also like to acknowledge a long list of individuals with whom we worked directly or indirectly throughout the writing process. They all encouraged, facilitated, and inspired the exploration of many different topics, namely: Christian Schmutzer, Stefano Previdi, Jim Guichard, and Bruce Davie. Many thanks also to Thomas D. Nadeau, who in endless hours did an excellent and patient job as technical editor. And to all the others who helped us finalize this book and are not listed here, thank you as well.

Many of the figures were adapted from Cisco Systems presentations, as well as from the ITU, IETF, ATM Forum, and other standardization bodies.

Contents

Acknowledgments *vii*

Chapter 1

About This Book 1

Introduction 2
Integrating Switching and Routing 3
Advantages of BGP/MPLS VPNs 4
    Privacy and Security 5
    Customer Independence 6
    Scalability and Stability 6
    Management 7
Who Should Read This Book 7

Chapter 2

Label Switching Alternatives 9

Overlay Models 9
- Classical IP over ATM 9
  - Scalability 10
- Integration Models 13
  - IP Switching 13
  - Data-Driven IP Switching 14
  - Topology-Driven IP Switching 15
    - Multiprotocol Label Switching (MPLS) 16

Chapter 3

MPLS Architecture and Operation 17

- Simplicity of Operation—Labels 17
- Decoupling Control and Forwarding 18
- Forwarding Equivalency Classes (FECs) and Label Imposition 19
  - Advantages of MPLS over Legacy Network Layer Forwarding 21
- MPLS Architecture Examples 23
  - MPLS Data Structures 26
  - Penultimate Hop Popping 30
- Label Encapsulation 31
  - The Label Stack (Generic Label Encapsulation/Shim Header) 32
    - Encoding the Label Stack 32
    - Label-Switched Paths (LSPs) 34
      - Tunnels and Hierarchy 34
      - Determining the Network Layer Protocol 36

Processing the TTL Field   37
   IP-Dependent Rules   38
   Translating between Different Encapsulations   38
      Case 1 (Figure 3–12):   38
      Case 2 (Figure 3–13):   39
      Case 3 (Figure 3–14):   40
Fragmentation and Path MTU Discovery   43
Transporting Labeled Packets over PPP   46
Transporting Labeled Packets over LAN Media   47
Alternative Label Encapsulation Techniques   48
   Overlay vs. Label-Encoded   48
Encapsulating Top Labels with ATM   50
   Using the VPI/VCI Field on Different Connection Types   51
   Direct Connection   53
   Connection via a VP Tunnel   54
   Connection via SVC   54
   Label Binding Procedures with ATM-LSRs   55
   Encapsulation   55
   VC-Merge   57
   Manipulating the TTL Field   58

Labels and Label Distribution Methods   59
   LDP—The Label Distribution Protocol   59
      LDP Operation   61
         LDP Protocol Structure   61
      Label Distribution—Downstream vs. Downstream-on-Demand   65
      Ordered vs. Independent LSP Control   67
      Loop Detection   69
      LDP Extended Discovery   71

Label Distribution Protocols for TE   71
Why Use MPLS TE?   71
Distributing Labels with RSVP   73
Introduction to RSVP   73
Augmenting RSVP with MPLS Features (MPLS-RSVP)   74
Summary of RSVP Attributes   77
Extensions to LDP (CR-LDP)   77

Chapter 4

Introduction to Virtual Private Networks   81

It's All about Connectivity ...   81
A Taxonomy of VPNs   86
Hub-and-Spoke vs. Fully-Meshed   86
IPSec   88
Other VPN Technologies   88
MPLS VPN   88
Feature Matrix   89
Overlay Model—Layer 2 VPNs   90
The Peer Model—Layer 3 VPNs   95

Chapter 5

Components of MPLS VPNs   101

Introduction to the Border Gateway Protocol (BGP-4)   101
Why Use Multiprotocol BGP-4 for MPLS VPNs?   105

Chapter 6

Details of MPLS VPNs   107

    Definition of BGP/MPLS VPNs   107
    Terminology   109
    Route Distribution   115
       RDs and the VPN-IPv4 Address Family   115
       Route Targets (RTs)   118
       Route Distribution among PE Routers   122
       Route Exchange between PE and CE Routers   129
    Topologies   132
       VPN Sites with Optimal Inter-VPN Routing   133
       VPN Sites with Hub-and-Spoke Routing   133
       Internet Routing   137
           Internet Access at Customer Site   137
           Internet Access handled by Service Provider   137
           Network Address Translation (NAT)   140
    Scalability   141
       Route Reflectors (RRs)   141
       Adding New Sites to a VPN   145
       BGP Update Filtering   145
       Outbound Route Filters (ORFs)   146
    Carrier's Carrier (CsC)   147

Chapter 7

MPLS VPN Applications   153

    Enterprise VPN Services   153
    ADSL VPNs   154
        DSL Technology Overview   154
        Connection Paradigm   156
        ADSL IP VPNs   156
        Routing   159
    Cable Access VPNs   160
        Cable Technology Overview   160
        Connection Paradigm   162
        Cable IP VPNs   163
    Mobile Wireless VPNs   166
        GPRS Technology Overview   166
    Dial Access IP VPNs   172

Appendix A

LDP Protocol Structure—Examples   177

Glossary   187

Notes   193

Index   197

1
About This Book

This book concentrates on the functionality of Internet Protocol-based Multiprotocol Label Switching Virtual Private Networks (IP-based MPLS VPNs). It will strive to explain in detail the basic definition, terminology, and techniques of how BGP/MPLS-based VPNs operate. This includes route distribution, possible VPN topologies, as well as scalability issues surrounding the deployment of this technology. This book will also explain potential problems with the deployment of this technology, which can be solved through advanced Border Gateway Protocol (BGP) design.

We will also visit some useful applications of BGP/MPLS such as Asymmetric Digital Subscriber Line (ADSL), cable, mobile, and dial access VPNs. Additionally, we will examine some background on Layer 3 switching technologies and will compare the benefits of the peer model against the overlay model. We will look at the differences between data-driven IP switching and topology-driven IP switching. This comparison will end in a discussion of MPLS. We will learn in detail about the salient components of MPLS and their operation. Examples of these topics are encapsulation techniques and label distribution. Finally, we will concentrate on BGP/MPLS VPN architectures.

To get a better understanding of the topic, this book divides the discussion of MPLS into two parts. In Chapter 2, we discuss some alternatives and predecessors to MPLS. The architecture and operation of MPLS are explained in detail in Chapter 3. Chapters 4–6 discuss BGP/MPLS VPNs in detail. We further enhance the description of MPLS VPN operation by listing and explaining some popular current and future applications in Chapter 7.

Introduction

The success of intranets within businesses and the success of the Internet as a means for interconnecting different intranets to form a single, global network have generated an unforeseeable demand for highly flexible, reliable, and secure network architectures that go beyond the simple LAN architectures available to businesses only a few years ago. These new types of network architectures are based primarily on the IP and form the foundation for deploying value-added services within these new networks such as application and data hosting, network commerce, and telephony services, as well as the ability to arbitrarily interconnect these services.

The IP-based intranet phenomenon has fundamentally changed the way companies conduct internal business operations. Due to the vast increase in productivity and reduction in overhead cost, companies are increasingly moving their mission-critical business applications from centralized, manual entry (i.e., paper-based) systems to their intranets. Business users can now access these services quickly and securely from virtually anywhere on the globe. However, for this to be possible, the internal networks of businesses must be extended over a wide area to encompass telecommuters, branch offices, and mobile users. Companies may also wish to further leverage the success of their intranets by including their customers, suppliers, and partners via extranets. Extranets are secure access points between intranets that allow information to flow between them, usually in a controlled and secure fashion. Extranets can further reduce business process costs by enabling supply-chain automation, electronic data interchange (EDI), and other forms of networked and automated commerce. For businesses to take advantage of these opportunities, service providers that are typically contracted to interconnect branch offices, telecommuters, and business partners must have some form of infrastructure in place to facilitate this mode of operation. It is important that this infrastructure be easy to install and maintain *private* network services to businesses over a *public* infrastructure.

MPLS was originally developed to integrate the best qualities of the most widely used routing protocols from the IP suite and frame and cell switching technologies such as Asynchronous Transfer Mode (ATM). Over the past few years, it has grown and been adapted to facilitate many advanced applications such as traffic engineering (TE), differentiated services (DiffServ), and VPNs. MPLS VPNs enable service providers as well as enterprises to fulfill their ever-growing needs for private network infrastructure deployment with unprecedented elegance, efficiency, scalability, and security. This text is devoted to the explanation of this new and innovative technology.

Integrating Switching and Routing

Ordinary IP routing is based on the exchange of network reachability information. This information is utilized locally at each node in the network to build a forwarding database that can then be used to determine how to handle (i.e., forward, drop, or reclassify) any given packet. Typically, when a node receives a packet, it compares the destination address with routes it has programmed in its forwarding database. From this lookup, it can make a decision as to where (if at all) to forward the packet. Other fields in the IP packet may be considered when forwarding packets as well. The effect of ignoring the other information contained in the IP packet is that maximum forwarding performance can be achieved by forwarding nodes since they generally only interrogate one fixed-length field in the packet—the destination address. On the other hand, investigating other fields is sometimes necessary, and unfortunately does add additional overhead to the processing time of the packet, as well as adding to the delay it takes to ultimately deliver the packet to its destination. Further adding to the overhead of traditional packet routing is the fact that packets are of a variable length, and hence impose additional overhead during processing.

Pure packet switching is concerned with the act of setting up a static path through a network and programming a forwarding table that is typically implemented in hardware. An entry in the forwarding table almost always contains a short, fixed-length identifier that can be used to quickly and efficiently make a decision as to where to forward a packet. Traditionally, packet, cell, and frame switching have seen performance orders of magnitude higher than in typical routing. This is due to the fact that the simple forwarding algorithm required to switch short, fixed-length fields is able to be implemented in the hardware of these devices, which obviates the need to interrupt a CPU every time a packet is received. Examples of traditional packet switching technologies are ATM and Frame Relay.

MPLS was developed to integrate the best qualities of pure packet, frame, and cell switching with the best qualities of IP routing. Like frame and cell switching, MPLS is based on the use of short, fixed-length labels in a fixed-length packet header. These fixed-length labels are assigned to route destinations by various mechanisms such as the IGP forwarding algorithm, or through static, explicit, or constrain-based routing TE. The label summarizes the following information about how to direct the packet throughout the MPLS network, including:

- Destination
- Precedence
- VPN membership
- QoS information from the Resource Reservation Protocol (RSVP) or DiffServ
- The route for the packet, as chosen by TE, RSVP, or Constraint-based Routing—Label Distribution Protocol (CR-LDP)

Because forwarding decisions are based on some or all of these different pieces of information, forwarding decisions based on more than just the destination address are feasible with a single table lookup from the destination label without imposing additional processing overhead on the lookup process. The result is that the MPLS-based network forwarding engines are both highly flexible and highly scalable.

Advantages of BGP/MPLS VPNs

VPN services are an excellent example of how MPLS takes advantage of packet switching, while at the same time supporting a hierarchy of routing knowledge. This combination of information with the help of the Multiprotocol Border Gateway Protocol (MP-BGP, or just BGP) allows MPLS to support VPNs within an MPLS domain. The combination of MPLS and MP-BGP makes MPLS-based VPN services relatively manageable, with straightforward operations to provision and monitor VPN sites as well as VPN membership. MP-BGP is used exclusively as the inter-domain routing protocol by Internet nodes today. The reason why it is used is simple: Its scalability properties continue to prove that it is suitable for a network with as many nodes as the Internet. For this reason, it also follows that since MPLS-based VPNs are based on MP-BGP, it too is extremely scalable.

Another important application of routing hierarchy and the integration of MPLS with MP-BGP is the isolation of Internet routing tables in service provider network cores. MPLS allows the Internet routing table to be constrained to being present only in edge nodes in the MPLS network. All transit traffic entering at the edge of the provider's autonomous system (AS) can be given labels that are associated with specific exit points on the other side of the MPLS domain. Furthermore, these labels may be used to aggregate all of the destination routes that will use the same egress point in the network, thereby collapsing hundreds or thousands of routes into a single label. As a result, internal transit routers and switches only have to understand and provide connectivity between a provider's edge routers. This effectively shields the core devices from the high routing volume exchanged in the Internet. This separation of interior routes from full Internet routes also provides better fault isolation, improved network stability, and increased security.

Privacy and Security

BGP/MPLS VPNs afford the same level of privacy as Frame Relay and ATM-networked circuits that are interconnected to form a full or partial mesh private network between customer sites. In a Frame Relay and ATM network, each packet carries a label called a data link connection identifier (DLCI) or virtual channel identifier (VCI), respectively. In either case, the use of this short, fixed-length label along with the packet switching employed by both network technologies ensures correct delivery of the packet. This of course assumes that the network is configured properly.

In the case of ATM and Frame Relay, circuits between customer sites traverse the public Frame Relay or ATM networks via shared switches.

BGP/MPLS VPNs label each packet with similar destination information, guaranteeing that a packet will be switched locally throughout the network until it reaches its ultimate destination, similar to Frame Relay and ATM networks. The result is that MPLS VPNs achieve the same level of privacy as Frame Relay and ATM networks. In addition, like ATM and Frame Relay, MPLS packets traverse the service provider's common infrastructure of switches. Furthermore,

BGP/MPLS VPN services keep routing information separated on a per-VPN basis. This separation of routing information has the added consequence that a separate route distinguisher controls route distribution. This results in the separation of each customer's routing information, and ensures that customers can reach only legal addresses that have been programmed *a priori* for their VPN.

Customer Independence

One of the major advantages of MPLS VPNs is the flexibility with which service providers have to assign addresses to customers. Due to the closed nature of address space management and advertisement inside of and between VPNs, customers may be assigned any valid registered, invalid test network, or unregistered IP address ranges. Addresses are kept separate with the help of route distinguishers, as well as through the use of network address translation (NAT). In fact, customer address ranges may overlap or be the same; the only restriction is that route distinguishers be unique. Network address translation is really only necessary in case the customer wishes to have Internet access. Furthermore, equipment within the customer network is not required to run MPLS or any other special features other than IP. Any IP-capable equipment can be used at customer sites. The customer sites do not need to run "VPN routers with IPSec," or any other special equipment, although they are free to, and in some cases, may wish to.

Scalability and Stability

In an MPLS VPN network, a single set of BGP peerings between provider edge (PE) devices (MPLS edge routers or switches) is used. This is irrespective of how many different VPNs are supported, or which VPN deployment model is used (i.e., hub-and-spoke versus fully-meshed). In addition, existing BGP techniques such as route reflectors can be used to help VPN route distribution scale when the number of supported VPNs and routes becomes large. Today, service providers are typically capable of supporting hundreds of thousands of VPNs, where each VPN contains thousands of routes. Some VPNs may even contain full Internet routing tables. At the present time, there is no known reason besides the cost of hardware that would hinder future increases in these figures. In addition, MP-BGP has techniques such as route flap damping that prevent badly behaving customer sites from affecting BGP stability on a global scale within the service provider network. Finally, since MPLS VPNs do not alter the forwarding of MPLS packets, forwarding characteristics will remain the same as with typical MPLS packet flows.

Management

BGP/MPLS VPNs have significant and distinct management advantages over other VPN technologies. In particular, the provider network uses only one set of BGP peerings, no matter how many VPNs it supports. This results in very simplified administration of the routing within the network. Furthermore, the addition of new VPNs or sites (instances of VPNs) is a straightforward task that only needs to be done on the new site's router. Other VPN technologies require operators to not only configure the new site, but also to reconfigure every other device in the network to which it will be connected. This is especially laborious where the VPN is configured in a fully-meshed topology.

Who Should Read This Book

Those wishing to learn about MPLS VPN technology should read this book. We provide a thorough and comprehensive explanation of the technology, its origins, and its evolution at a level acceptable for those who possess an introductory grasp of routing and switching technology. Those with an advanced understanding of the technology may wish to skip some of the introductory sections at the beginning of the text, as they may be redundant. However, we invite advanced readers to look at these sections, as they may provide a refreshing look at the technology. In general, those wishing to understand how and why this technology might be better than competing technologies and under which circumstances will want to read this text.

We have assumed that our readers are already familiar with the basics of networking and have some experience with router and switch configuration. In particular, it is not imperative to understand IP, TCP, UDP, ATM, or Frame Relay intimately, but that will certainly aid the reader in the speed at which the material can be covered and assimilated.

Those wishing to gain an understanding of how MPLS VPNs are configured or deployed on a specific vendor's device should look elsewhere for this information. We have strived to keep the presentation and discussion of MPLS VPNs in terms that should apply to almost any deployment of MPLS VPNs. The advantage of this is that our text will apply to most deployments. This format also lends itself well to academic and corporate educational programs, which will benefit greatly from the use of this text for their courses.

2
Label Switching Alternatives

Overlay Models

In the following sections, we will briefly describe the overlay model for networks, which was the precursor to MPLS. We will also explain why this model was eventually not adopted by the larger Internet community.

Classical IP over ATM

The Classical IP (CLIP) over ATM architecture was proposed by the Internet Engineering Task Force's (IETF's) IP over ATM Working Group around 1998 (see Figure 2–1). The architecture is described in RFC 1577 [IETF-3]. In a nutshell, the CLIP architecture specifies a scheme by which a group of ATM stations can be divided into logical IP subnets (LISs). Subsequently, these LISs can then be interconnected via routers to allow traditional IP connectivity between end stations. Each LIS has an ATM Address Resolution Protocol (ATM_ARP) server that is employed for the translation between IP and ATM addresses. Nodes within different LISs have to communicate via routers, even if they are directly connected.

Each edge node on the ATM network must maintain logical connections, or virtual circuits (permanent or switched), with all other edge nodes on the network.

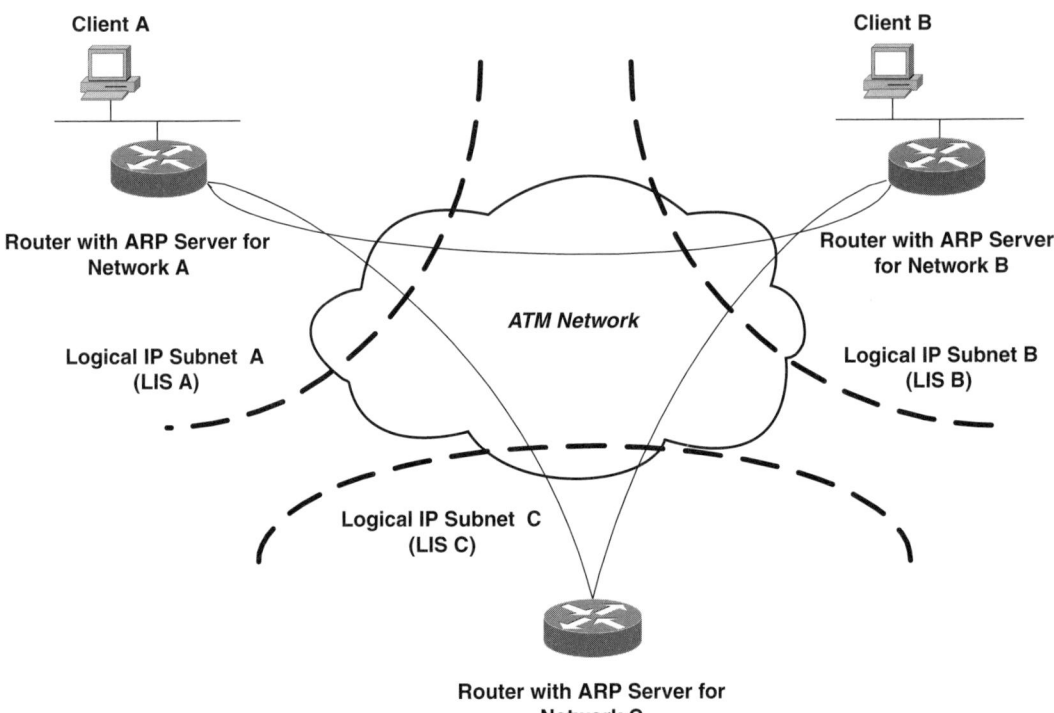

Figure 2-1 Example of CLIP over ATM architecture.

SCALABILITY

NOTE

Scalability problems occur if the complexity of the network grows much faster than the number of attached nodes and/or users!

The main disadvantage of combining the connection-oriented approach of ATM with the connectionless approach of IP within the architecture of CLIP over ATM is that the number of virtual circuits (VCs) (permanent or switched) required to maintain a full mesh of connectivity between all nodes increases by the square of the number of routers attached to the ATM cloud.

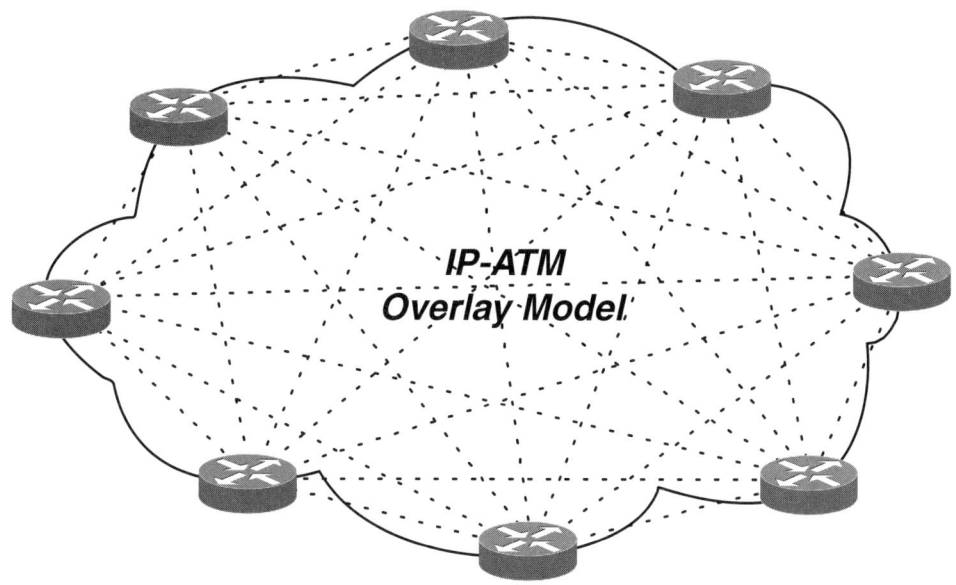

Figure 2–2   IP-ATM overlay model.

The number of connections in the model shown in Figure 2–2 increases according to the following formula:

Equation 2–1
```
N = (n*(n-1))/2 ≈ n²
```

In the above equation, N is the total number of connections required to maintain a full mesh of connectivity between all routers, and n is the number of routers attached to the ATM cloud. This is commonly known as the *n-square problem*, and it becomes unwieldy to maintain in many dimensions when the number of routers exceeds about 20. The most problematic characteristic in terms of scalability is the number of routing updates required in the case of a link failure or the addition of a new router. This number could be as high as n^4 in a fully-meshed topology [DAVIE-1]. Routers could become overloaded with routing information, and the actual data throughput may become unsatisfactory due to routing traffic. Another problematic area in terms of scalability in this architecture is the sheer amount of work required to configure new routers added into such a network. Of course, one of the worst problems is one that combines aspects of both of these areas just described—that is, the case where a router possessing multiple links is removed from the network.

Typically, the administrator of an ATM network that supports switched virtual circuits (SVCs) will choose to utilize the SVCs as the primary connection type between ATM clients as well as between ATM clients and the ATM ARP server. The reason why is that the use of ATM SVCs decreases the configuration effort on the routers because only the ATM address of the ARP server has to be configured. For each packet with an unknown IP address, the client sends an ATM ARP request to the server. When the ARP server responds, the client opens a connection via an SVC to the new destination. Any additional packets to that same destination will be directly routed to it via the already established SVC.

By contrast, when the switches within an ATM network only support permanent virtual connections (PVCs)—that is, SVCs are not supported—the configuration effort on each router will increase by n^2 as described above. The cost involved in adding a new edge node in a topology where PVCs are the predominant connection is proportional to the number of PVC endpoints in a fully-meshed network. This is because all edge routers have to be reconfigured. That is, when a new edge router is added, all routers in the existing network will need to be configured with a new PVC that connects to the new edge node.

As we will see later, MPLS is not subject to the scalability problems described above simply because it leverages the peer model instead of the overlay model (see Figure 2–3). That is, all devices in the network, including the ATM switches, act as IP routers and perform label forwarding.

To achieve this, ATM switches are augmented with Layer 3 routing capability and are visible to the edge routers. Instead of maintaining fully-meshed virtual connections like in the CLIP over ATM overlay model, routing adjacencies can be formed directly between edge routers and ATM switches. Thus, MPLS minimizes the number of logical connections in the network and peerings between edge nodes drastically.

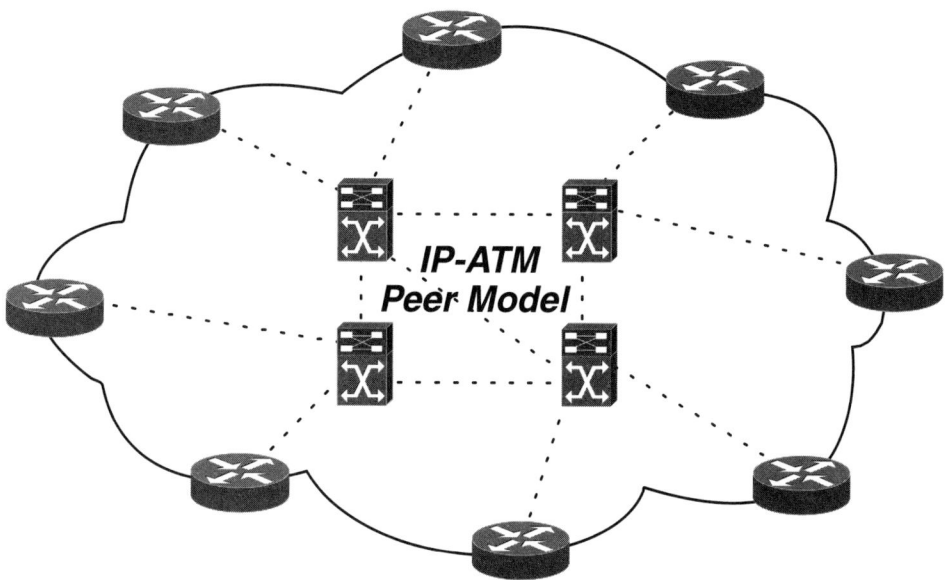

Figure 2–3 IP–ATM integration peer model.

Integration Models

IP Switching

The term "IP switching" was initially coined by Ipsilon Networks Inc. to describe the functions of their then new IP switch. This term has since taken on a more general meaning that defines IP switching as a solution that enables selected IP traffic to be forwarded separately from traditional router-based processing to hardware-based switching to achieve switch-level performance, while maintaining the scalability of routing-based approaches. In short, an IP switching solution enables routers to accelerate the IP forwarding process while retaining the standard functions of traditional routing such as default packet forwarding, broadcast containment, filtering, topology and reachability exchange, and so on [IETF-9]. Figure 2–4 shows an example of an IP switching architecture.

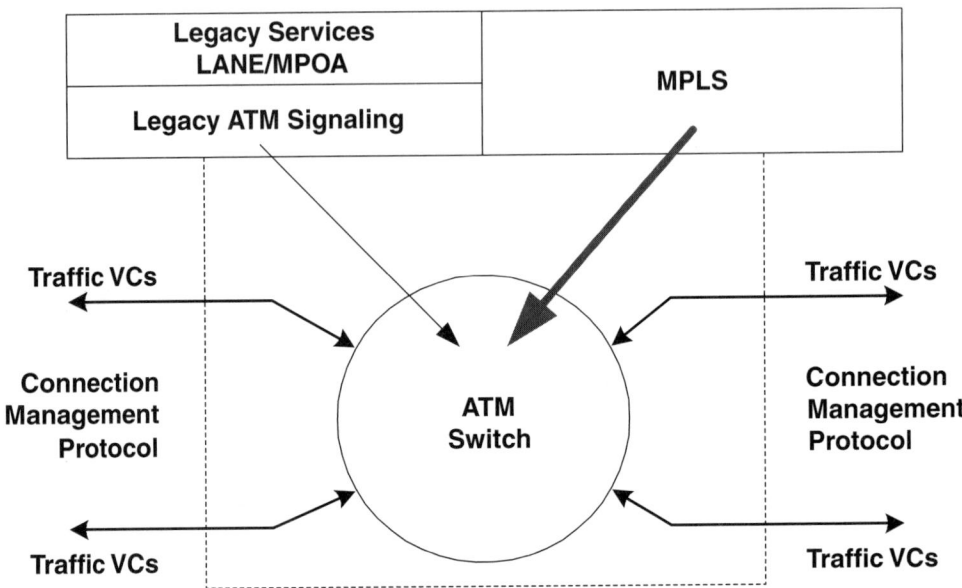

Figure 2–4   IP/ATM switch.

Data-Driven IP Switching

IP switching by Ipsilon Networks, cell-switched routing (CSR) by Toshiba, and various other approaches like Ipsofacto are all in essence similar proposals for accomplishing the same thing: All use data_driven label assignment and all utilize the binding of a label to a flow. This binding is initiated by the arrival of traffic from that flow. *IP switching* and the *CSR* proposal forward packets on a new flow on a hop_by_hop basis until a switched path is established. IP switching requires a point_to_point ATM link between IP switches. This link may be a permanent virtual path (PVP) across an ATM network, but not a permanent virtual connection or switched virtual circuit (PVC or SVC). This is because IP switching expects to manipulate the VCI itself.

The CSR proposal permits the use of PVCs or SVCs across an ATM network between cell-switched routers. This allows cell-switched routers to be interconnected across an ATM network—that is, a CLIP over ATM subnet (RFC 1577) or LAN emulation (LANE) subnet. The drawback with this approach is that CSR is required to implement ATM signaling. It is possible for switched virtual circuits to be established on-demand between cell-switched routers using ATM signaling. However, the typical high delay accompanied by ATM connection establishment implies that a pool of ATM connections is likely to be pre-established between cell-switched routers and activated upon traffic arrival. A further drawback to this approach is that these pre-established connections are expensive resources, which unfortunately might never be used.

For a proposal with centralized IP processing and unannounced VCI selection, such as *Ipsofacto*, all inactive VCIs would need to be mapped to a single ATM switch port leading to the IP processor (IP switch controller). By contrast, IP switching and the CSR proposal both use a protocol to bind a flow to a VCI; therefore, only those switched flows in the process of being established need a unique VCI to the switch controller.

The apparent disadvantage of these approaches is their restricted suitability for short-lived data flows like http, email, and ftp traffic. Thus, short-lived data flows can never truly benefit from fast switching using the aforementioned approaches. Traffic patterns on the Internet today are mostly short-lived; hence, the flow-based approaches to switching data traffic just described will never really enjoy wide deployment in large networks such as those backbone routers that connect to the Internet and carry large numbers of flows. This was truly a huge roadblock to their extensive adoption by the service provider industry. The flow-based approach might be more suitable for smaller enterprise backbones, where the total number of flows is typically lower than in Internet core devices and the percentage of longer-lived flows such as videoconferences is more prevalent. However, it is still questionable whether they would be sufficient in these areas, since many enterprise networks still carry high percentages of short-lived flows that would not benefit at all from these approaches.

Topology-Driven IP Switching

Tag Switching from Cisco and *ARIS* from IBM are two approaches for IP switching that were proposed at roughly the same time. These approaches differ from those described previously because they are based on topology-driven label assignment rather than being data-driven. Labels are allocated based on information available from the routing protocols, and virtual connections are established in advance of traffic being received. These approaches have the advantage of not requiring packets to be forwarded by the processor while establishing a virtual connection. Thus, there is no or very little delay in establishing the link layer connection, and no possibility for packet misordering when traffic is cut through to the new connection. Even very short flows can benefit from Layer 2 switching because flow classification is not required to distinguish between short- and long-lived flows.

The ARIS proposal differs from tag switching in that it builds a sink tree rooted at the egress node back throughout the network. This requires VC-merge capability in the switches or the use of both the VPI and VCI for label assignment. This guarantees that VC loops are prevented, even in the presence of transient IP routing loops. The disadvantage of offering such a strong guarantee of loop prevention is that this approach requires a more complex label assignment protocol. It also implies that the label assignment process will take longer to converge.

MULTIPROTOCOL LABEL SWITCHING (MPLS)
Seeing several competing approaches for IP switching, the IETF decided to converge on a standard approach to promote interoperability among vendor devices. This task was and still is being worked on primarily in the MPLS Working Group, but has now also spread to the Common Control and Measurement Plane (CCAMP), Provider-Provisioned Virtual Private Networks (PPVPNs), TE, and Pseudo-Wire Emulation Edge-to-Edge (PWE3) working groups. Companies like Cisco Systems, Inc., Nortel Networks Corp., Lucent Technologies, and Juniper Networks, just to name a few, and service providers like UUNet, AT&T, and others are working together in these working groups with the common goal of building a set of standards that describe a deployable MPLS architecture. These groups are also working on specifying applications such as TE and VPNs that can utilize this basic architecture to provide additional services and value to those deploying the technology. A description of the basic MPLS architecture can be found in "Multiprotocol Label Switching Architecture" [IETF-11].

NOTE

Although "Multiprotocol Label Switching" contains the term "Multiprotocol" and does so because its techniques are applicable to a multitude of network layer protocols and also to many data link technologies, IP is the protocol of choice for a wide variety of applications. Therefore, all subsequent discussions in this book will focus on IP (version 4, or IPv4) as the network protocol used with MPLS.

3
MPLS Architecture and Operation

Simplicity of Operation—Labels

Multiprotocol Label Switching (MPLS) is a technology that uses an additional fixed-length information element inside each packet header, a so-called label. Each hop along a packet's way will make its forwarding decision based on this label. Hence, the forwarding decision is no longer a function of the Internet Protocol (IP) address of the packet header and/or the other elements in the header; instead, it is entirely based on the label value.

Two of the major aims of MPLS are to reduce the complexity in the core network nodes and to introduce flexible new routing services in the network. The reduction of complexity can be achieved because the core nodes only have to forward packets based on labels. Complex decisions, such as those that are required when processing packets to determine which VPN or service class they belong to, are performed exclusively at the edge of the MPLS network. All subsequent hops will perform their forwarding decision based solely on the label value present in the MPLS packet header.

A further advantage to MPLS is that the introduction of new services or applications is almost always implemented at the edges of the network—typically only at the ingress—while the core nodes remain unaffected and simply swap labeled packets between their interfaces.

> **NOTE**
> In the MPLS architecture, packets are forwarded only based on the label information, not on the IP information.

Decoupling Control and Forwarding

In legacy-routed networks, each packet received at a router must have its packet header examined for a forwarding decision to be made about that packet. Each hop makes its own independent forwarding decision based on a lookup it makes in its forwarding database. This forwarding database contains reachability information, which is used when a router needs to make a decision as to which interface it should forward a newly received packet on to. To create this forwarding database, routing information must be gathered and assimilated. The forwarding database is then created from this information. Routers accomplish this by distributing network reachability information through the use of one or more Layer 3 routing protocols. These routing protocols are employed between all nodes that belong to a certain routing domain, or between nodes that border different routing domains. Routing information is subsequently used to build the forwarding database in each router. Upon receipt of a packet, the router will consult its forwarding database in an effort to determine the interface (i.e., next hop) to which to forward the packet.

What should be clear from the description above is that legacy routers commingle forwarding and control information within the same protocol processes. A major advantage of MPLS is that it decouples the routing/control process completely from the forwarding process as shown in Figure 3–1.

A label switch router (LSR) contains separate forwarding and control processes. The advantage of making this separation is that it enables the deployment of new routing services without having to change the actual packet forwarding process. That is, new types of routing information can be distributed and used to build the forwarding database, but the label in a packet is still exclusively used to forward the packet throughout the MPLS network. A routing service can be, for example, Border Gateway Protocol/Multiprotocol Label Switching Virtual Private Networks (BGP/MPLS VPNs) or traffic engineering (TE), where packets are assigned a path through the network based on additional information found in the IP header. This additional information can be

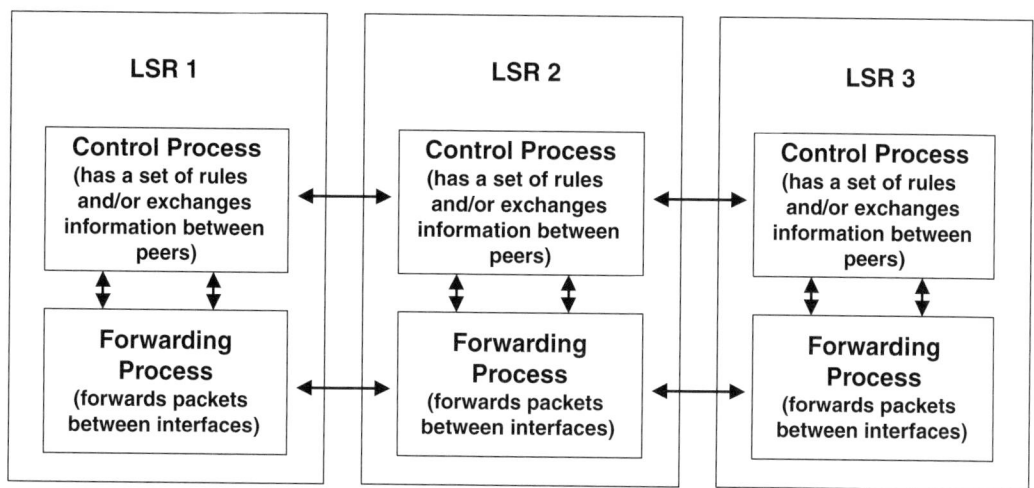

Figure 3–1 MPLS separates the control process and forwarding process.

membership in a VPN or a classification as part of a flow of packets that are destined to travel on a particular predetermined path through the MPLS domain. Despite the use of any of these mechanisms, once a packet enters the MPLS domain and has an initial label imposed on it, it will be forwarded through the MPLS domain regardless of how it entered.

NOTE

A router that runs both the MPLS control process and MPLS forwarding process is called a label switch router (LSR).

Forwarding Equivalency Classes (FECs) and Label Imposition

We have alluded to the fact that once a packet enters the MPLS domain, it must carry a fixed-length label. This label is used subsequently to forward the packet throughout the MPLS domain. What has not been explained yet are the details of this process.

When a non-MPLS packet is received by an edge LSR, the LSR must decide whether or not to forward this packet into the MPLS domain and whether or not to forward the packet in its native form. A decision is made based on whether or not the packet is part of what is referred to as a forwarding equivalency class (FEC). An FEC is a group of destination routes, services (i.e., VPN), Quality of Service (QoS) parameters (i.e., Type of Service [TOS] bits), or a combination of these attributes, which share a common path through the MPLS domain. That is, once any packet in this class enters the MPLS domain, it will have the same label imposed upon it. The result is that it will travel through the MPLS domain along the same label-switched path and will exit the domain at the same point. Thus, without loss of generality, any packet in the same FEC can use the same label-switched path (i.e., same initial label) to enter the MPLS domain, and can be switched along the same path until it has the MPLS header removed and exits the domain. All packets belonging to the same FEC will travel via the same hops in the network as long as the topology is not changed or no link failure occurs. No network layer lookup will be done until the packet leaves the MPLS network at the egress point.

NOTE

The packet-to-FEC assignment is done once, at the ingress point of the network. This procedure is called label imposition.

As was explained earlier, the major advantage of MPLS is that it is topology-driven. That is, forwarding entries are established using topology information instead of dynamically when packet flows arrive. Topology information is provided in one of two ways. The most obvious method is static programming. This is accomplished when an operator wants to explicitly route certain types of traffic based on certain criteria through the MPLS domain. This traffic typically takes an explicit path through the network and is done to accomplish TE. We will focus on this topic later. The second method is what is commonly referred to as "autorouting." This is a mechanism whereby the interior gateway protocols such as Open Shortest Path First Protocol (OSPF) or Intermediate System-to-Intermediate System Protocol (IS-IS) determine FEC entries using their destination next hops or other routing metrics and automatically program FEC entries for the LSR. This allows the LSR to be ready to forward traffic to those destinations as soon as it arrives. It also allows MPLS to automatically adjust to network conditions such as link outages without operator intervention.

When a packet is determined to be a part of an FEC, the packet will then have an MPLS packet header pushed onto the front of the packet. This is referred to as label imposition. The MPLS packet header is composed of several items, including the fixed-length label. We will delve into the MPLS header in greater detail later in this chapter in the section titled "The Label Stack (Generic Label Encapsulation/Shim Header)." What is important to understand is that the packet will carry the MPLS label throughout its journey through the MPLS network once the MPLS label has been imposed on the packet.

Advantages of MPLS over Legacy Network Layer Forwarding

In the MPLS forwarding paradigm, once a packet enters the MPLS domain, no further network header analysis is done by subsequent routers; all forwarding is driven by the top-most label in the packet. This has a number of advantages over conventional network layer forwarding.

In [IETF-11], the MPLS architecture is described in the following way:

- The ingress router can use additional information when it is assigning packets to an FEC, like incoming port, ToS bits, source address, or any arbitrary information the operator of the LSR may want to use. Different packets with the same destination address can be assigned to different FECs, which could result in different processing and forwarding of these packets at subsequent hops in the network. Conventional forwarding can only consider information that travels with the packet in the packet header.
- Since LSRs only have to perform a relatively simple fixed-length label lookup once the packet is inside the MPLS domain, this technology can be used with switches that are not capable of analyzing network layer headers, like ATM and/or Frame Relay switches.
- Other even more complicated combinations of attributes that determine the assignment of a packet may be found in the future, but the processing overhead in the network will not change since the assignment to a certain FEC is only done once, at the ingress LSR of the network. This implies that the MPLS architecture will scale for future demands.
- In large service provider environments, there is often a need for predicting certain routed paths for certain kinds of traffic or at certain times of

the day (e.g., voice traffic at busy hours). The predominant aims are to reduce the overall cost of operations and use bandwidth resources more efficiently by preventing a situation where some parts of a service provider network are over-utilized (congested), while other parts are under-utilized. This technique is called traffic engineering (TE). Another application is policy routing. A possible method is to apply a given routed path to every packet header (explicit or source routing) at every hop through the network, though this produces overhead at every hop. MPLS solves this problem by determining a fixed routed path that can be derived from the applied label at the ingress point of the MPLS network.

- The DiffServ model allows us to derive the service class of a packet from the type of service (ToS) bits in the packet header. MPLS allows the precedence, or class of service, to be inferred from the label header. The class of service information can be inferred either from the value of the label or from the value of the EXP/QoS field in the label header. In this case, one may say that the label represents the combination of an FEC and a precedence, or class of service [IETF-11].

In the early drafts of MPLS, its main application was simply to integrate IP and ATM. However, later drafts focused on more clever applications of MPLS such as VPNs and TE. The reason for the change of focus from integrating IP and ATM to more advanced applications was simply because it was thought that these could be used as real differentiators between legacy-routed networks and MPLS. This differentiation of MPLS from legacy routing technologies was and continues to be an important factor that drives service providers to adopt MPLS. Simply put, MPLS gives service providers additional tools and services to sell to customers. It also gives them tools with which to differentiate themselves from other service providers. For example, the opportunity to offer VPN services based on IP, which would be implemented using BGP/MPLS VPNs, makes this technology very attractive for certain segments of the service provider market.

The basic concept of MPLS brings us some benefits indeed, but the applications of MPLS are the real drivers behind this technology.

MPLS Architecture Examples

Figure 3–2 demonstrates how four packets enter, traverse, and then exit an MPLS network. Each packet destined for B, C, D, and E, respectively, first enters the MPLS network from some IP network (network A) at ingress LSR 1. At LSR 1, a label that belongs to the same FEC is assigned to each packet. Packets with the newly imposed MPLS header and corresponding label are sent to the next hop in the network as MPLS packets. In this case, all packets are sent to LSR 2.

At LSR 2, the decision to forward an MPLS packet is based solely on the incoming packet's top-most MPLS label.

Each LSR maintains a number of databases and caches that enable it to perform the mapping of FECs to labels. It is this mapping that also allows them to switch labeled packets or cells between their interfaces. A detailed description of the data structures that the LSR uses can be found in the section titled "MPLS Data Structures."

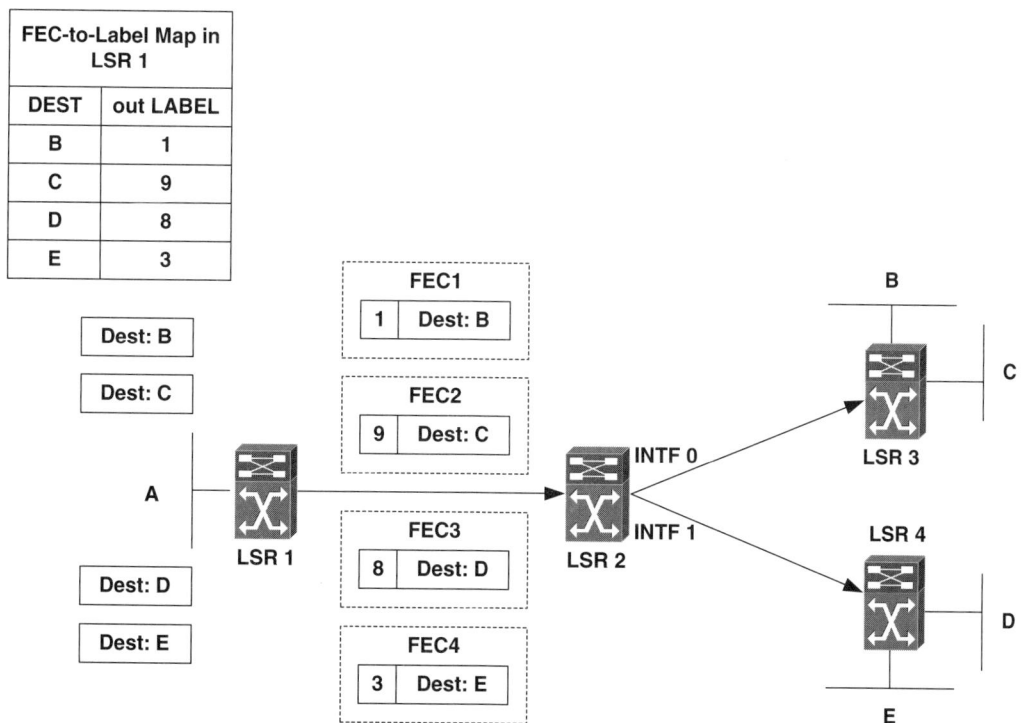

Figure 3–2 Mapping FECs to labels.

Next, using the top-most label found in the MPLS header, LSR 2 performs a cache lookup in its label forwarding information base (LFIB). If the LSR locates an outgoing label and interface for this incoming label, it will replace the top-most label in the MPLS header with the new label, and then transmit the packet to the next-hop LSR via the appropriate interface. In the example in Figure 3–3, it should be clear that LSR 2 will transmit packets with incoming labels of 1 and 9 to LSR 3 using labels 5 and 7, respectively. Additionally, packets that are received and contain labels 8 and 3 as their top-most labels will be transmitted to LSR 4 with labels 1 and 6, respectively.

It is important to observe that since the label values change from hop to hop, the label used only has local significance between the two LSRs. The only exception to this rule is multicast MPLS, where labels may have subnet significance.

In Figure 3–4, LSR 3 and LSR 4 are referred to as egress LSRs. They are named as such because it is their primary function to remove the MPLS header from MPLS packets before they exit the MPLS network. Once packets have the MPLS header removed, they are forwarded using whichever routing technology lies underneath the MPLS header. In the example above, the egress LSR first removes each packet's MPLS header. It then looks under the MPLS header to find an IP header, from which it obtains a destination address and any other IP forwarding information it deems necessary. It then uses this information to look up the IP next hop for each of the final destinations, B, C, D, and E.

If we look more closely at LSR 3 and LSR 4, we see that each LSR actually has to perform two lookups. This is quite different from the single lookup required within the core of the MPLS domain. The first entry in the LFIB tells the LSR to strip the label off and pass the packet to the second routing process. The second process in this case is the legacy IP routing lookup, which determines which next-hop router or switch the packet should be forwarded to, as well as the appropriate interface via which to reach the next hop. It is important to note that each of the two aforementioned lookups are completely separate, and in many implementations, actually occur in different processes. So within the context of the second lookup, the only pertinent information used in the forwarding decision is based solely on the IP header. That is, there is no MPLS-related information involved in this lookup. It might be desirable to avoid this double lookup, which may degrade the performance of the LSR. One technique used to reduce the number of router lookups along any given

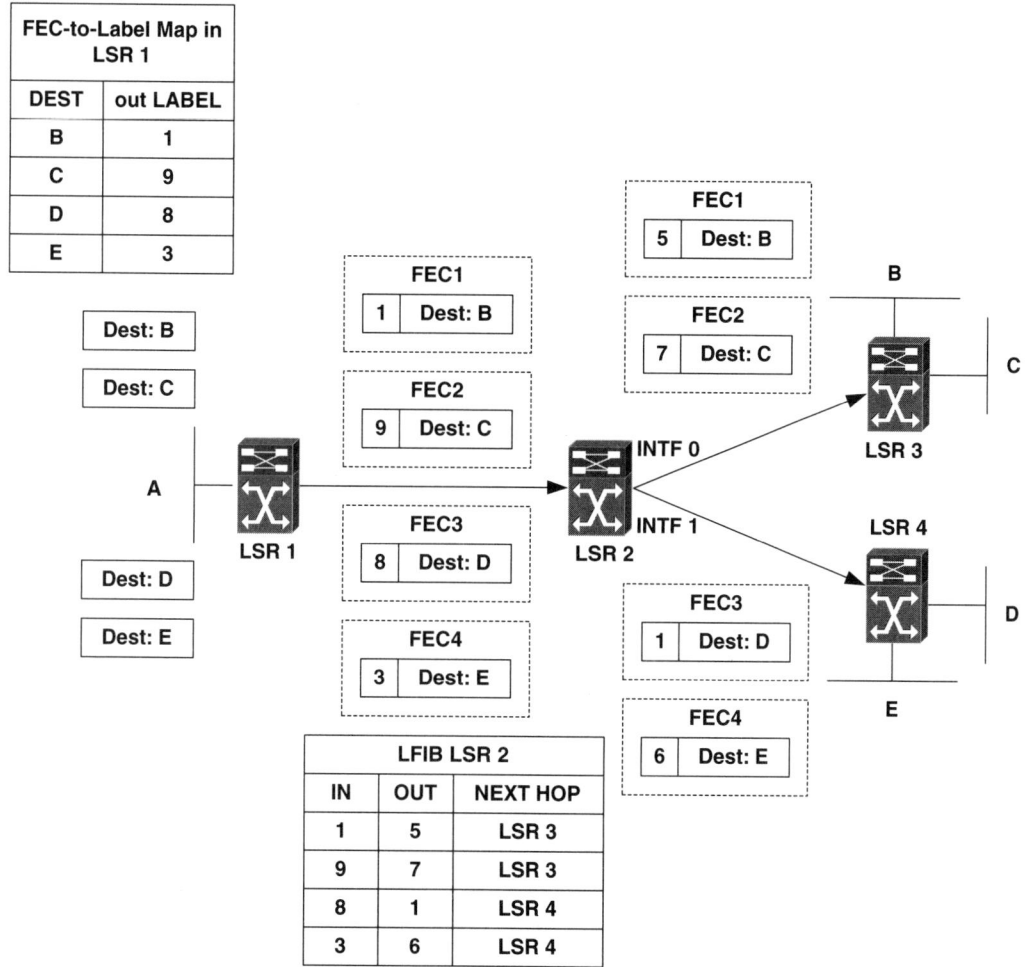

Figure 3-3   Forwarding labels.

path in an MPLS network is called "penultimate hop popping." This is a process whereby the MPLS header is removed by the second-to-last, or penultimate, LSR along the packet's path. In this case, the egress LSR would receive an unlabeled packet that can be passed to the IP routing lookup process directly, without having to first remove the MPLS header. This is also useful since edge routers are typically of lower horsepower than core routers. You can find more information on penultimate hop popping in the subsequent section titled "Penultimate Hop Popping."

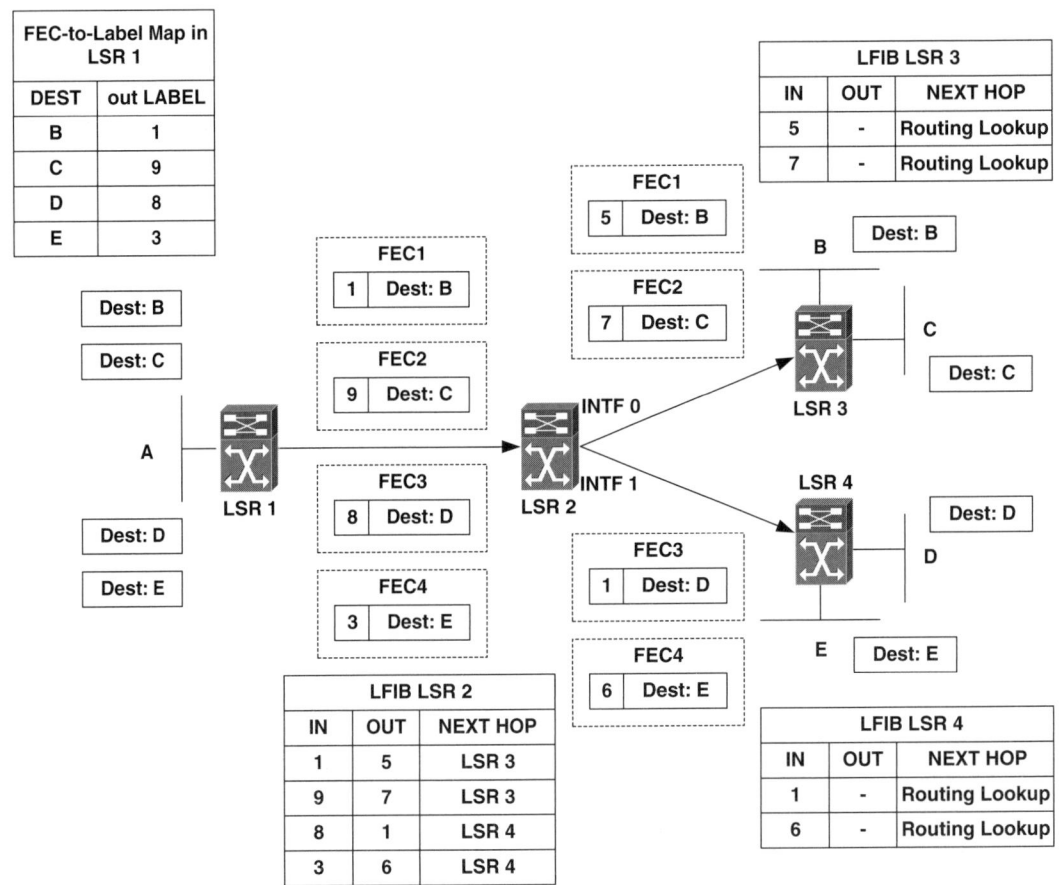

Figure 3-4 The MPLS header is removed at the egress LSR.

MPLS Data Structures

An MPLS LSR maintains three important data structures. The first is a database called the label information base (LIB). The LIB stores all labels that have been advertised by other LSRs in the MPLS network. LSRs need to exchange the mapping of labels to their associated FECs. This is achieved using a variety of label distribution protocols. Examples of label distribution protocols include the Label Distribution Protocol (LDP), the Resource Reservation Protocol (RSVP), and the Multiprotocol BGP (MP-BGP). A detailed description of label distribution can be found in the section titled "Labels and Label Distribution Methods."

The second structure is a cache called the label forwarding information base (LFIB). The LFIB cache is used by the actual packet forwarding process, and is analogous to the IP forwarding database used when routing IP packets except that it contains MPLS-related information instead. The LFIB contains information such as the incoming label value, outgoing label value, prefix/FEC, outgoing interface and its associated encapsulation type, and the next-hop address. An MPLS LSR that wants to forward a packet will consult this cache to determine which label to swap onto the packet (if any) as well as which next-hop interface it must forward the packet on to. Once all labels are distributed correctly, the LFIB cache contains all the information required to switch the packet through the LSR.

The third data structure that all MPLS LSRs maintain is the normal IP routing table. It is used to determine the next-hop forwarding information for the LFIB. The contents of the IP routing table are of course the result of exchanging reachability information among all routing protocol peers within the network via some routing protocol, and then executing some routing algorithm over that information. The result computed by the routing algorithm is then stored in the IP routing table.

The information in the LFIB is the result of examining the IP routing table and the contents of the LIB and determining which IP destinations can be mapped to which MPLS labels. The process of how the LFIB table is built can be described in the following way, and is further illustrated in Figure 3–5.

After the IGP (i.e., OSPF or IS-IS) has completed exchanging reachability information with all network peers, it will run a shortest path computation over the reachability information. When this process is complete, the routing protocol is said to have converged. At this point, the routing table will reflect the current Layer 3 topology of the network, as well as the shortest path(s) to reach any given network node. The routing table holds information about the destination prefix, the metrics associated with this destination, the next-hop address, and the interface on to which the packet must be sent to reach the next hop. All of the routers shown in Figure 3–5 know how they can reach the destination networks (networks A, B, and C) connected to each of the routers. For example, LSR 1 has an entry in its routing table for network B, where LSR 2 is listed as the next hop to network B. The metrics are 10 to reach network B from LSR 1. We can also see that another route to network B via LSR 3 exists and is present

28   Chapter 3 ▸ MPLS Architecture and Operation

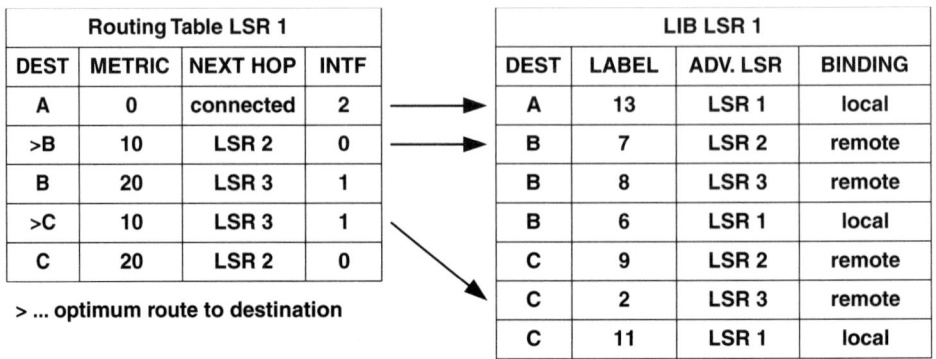

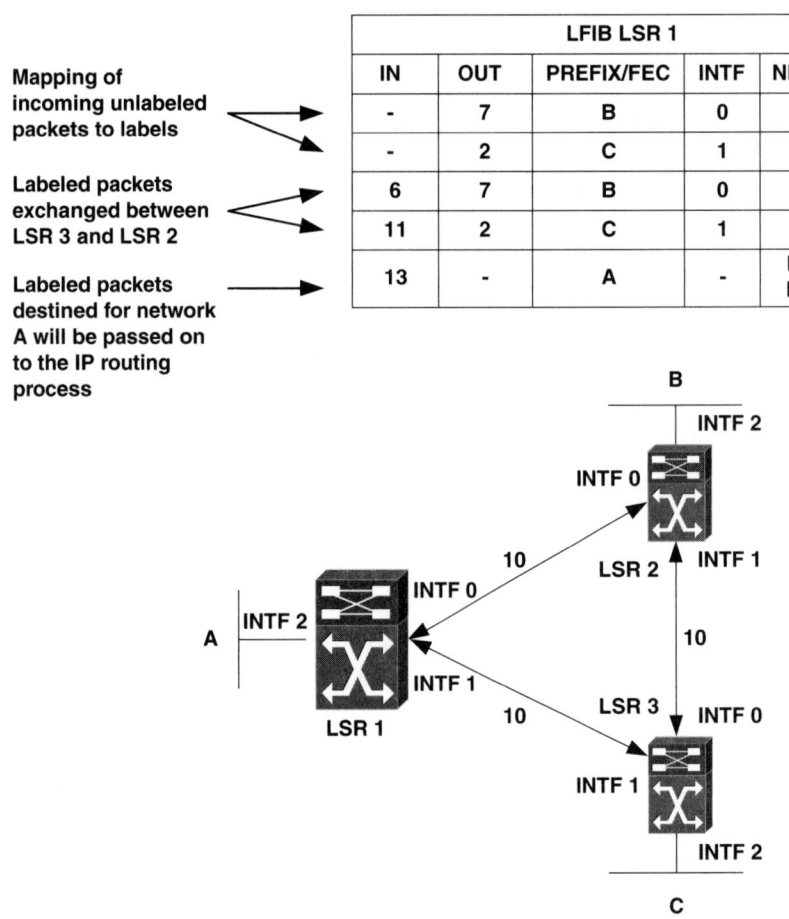

Figure 3–5   MPLS data structures.

in the routing table as well. This path has a metric of 20 that is of course higher, and therefore less preferable, compared to the other route to network B. As long as we do not use any unequal metric load balancing mechanisms, LSR 1 will always choose LSR 2 as the optimum next hop to network B.

After the routing process has converged, the LDP will build a session between all LDP neighbors, or LDP "peers," that are directly reachable via that LSR. Each LDP session is established using TCP port 646, and label mapping information is exchanged with the LSR and all of the appropriate Label Distribution Protocol (LDP) peers. The downstream LSR must then define which label is mapped to a particular FEC/prefix. The label distribution procedure is called *downstream-on-demand* label allocation and is explained further in the section titled "Labels and Label Distribution Methods."

LSR 2 will next inform LSR 1, "When sending packets destined for network B to this LSR, use label 7." LSR 1 will subsequently install a remote binding in its LIB that says, "When sending packets destined for network B to LSR 2, use label 7." At the same time, LSR 3 will also announce to LSR 1, "When sending packets destined for network B to LSR 3, use label 8." LSR 1 will then install a corresponding entry in its LIB which effectively says, "If LSR 1 sends packets destined for network B to LSR 3, use label 8."

The LIB will eventually be populated with all possible destinations to networks A, B, and C using this process. The LIB now contains all the required mappings between prefixes/FECs and labels. However, it does not yet contain any information about the next-hop address a packet classified within a particular FEC-to-label mapping should take. The next-hop information can only be found in the IP routing table. The next-hop information in the IP routing table defines which label from the LIB should be used to forward the packets. In our example, the routing protocol has chosen LSR 2 as the optimum next hop to network B. Therefore, LSR 1 will choose the label advertised by LSR 2 to forward packets to network B.

The next-hop information and related label information are then put in the LFIB. The LFIB is used exclusively by the forwarding process when forwarding traffic in the data path. In our example, we show how the first two entries in the LFIB of LSR 1 are present without an incoming label. This indicates that the packets arrived from outside the MPLS domain and will have to have labels imposed on them by LSR 1. This also indicates that LSR 1 is taking on the role of an edge, or ingress, LSR.

To show how an MPLS network deals with a node failure, imagine that the link between LSR 2 and LSR 3 breaks. It should be clear that every packet that would under normal circumstances travel between these two LSRs via the now-broken link must now instead be switched by LSR 1. In this situation, the next two entries found in the LFIB are essential for the MPLS network to remain resilient to failure. In this case, LSR 1 would receive labeled packets at interface 0 or 1 and would then re-label the packets and forward them to their destination. LSR 1, in this case, would act as a pure label switch without examining the IP header of the packets at all.

The last entry of the LFIB in our example shows an entry for network A. It indicates that if a packet arrives with label 13, the label should be removed and the IP packet should be passed on to the routing process in LSR 1.

TROUBLESHOOTING TIP!

If you have to troubleshoot an MPLS network, it is very important that you understand these procedures and the contents of these data structures. A good place to start is to always examine the contents of the routing table. The routing table must be correct and complete. Second, the information in the LIB will tell you if all LSRs are announcing labels for all required FECs/prefixes in the routing tables. Lastly, you should verify that the LFIB contains the correct labels, and where appropriate, that these labels are mapped to the correct IP destination prefixes.

Penultimate Hop Popping

A labeled packet will have its label examined at each hop if it travels along a label-switched path and reaches the egress LSR. The egress LSR must perform a lookup in its LFIB to determine to which next-hop destination the original packet must be forwarded as an unlabeled packet. This procedure requires two lookups at the egress LSR. The first lookup determines that the label of the packet has to be popped and the second lookup determines the Layer 3 next-hop address for the packet. To avoid this double database lookup, it is desirable to perform the pop operation at the penultimate LSR. This avoids a second lookup at the egress edge LSR, speeds up the forwarding process, and allows the designers of the LSR code to calculate a certain fixed-time budget for the whole forwarding operation. This procedure is called *penultimate hop popping*.

Penultimate hop popping is an optional procedure that must be requested by the egress LSR (see Figure 3–6). If the egress LSR requests penultimate hop popping from the penultimate LSR, the penultimate LSR must perform hop popping for that particular FEC. The ability of an LSR to perform penultimate hop popping must be negotiated in the initial capability negotiations if the label distribution protocol (i.e., LDP, TDP, MP-BGP, RSVP, PIM) supports it.

Label Encapsulation

To ensure interoperability between different implementations of MPLS, the implementations must agree on a certain set of standard procedures to encode the MPLS label stack. Each LSR must support this encoding technique when emitting or forwarding a labeled packet. The procedures for encoding the label stack are defined and explained in [IETF-12].

KEY CONCEPT!

LSRs using different data link technologies may use different techniques to encode the first or second label of the stack; however, every LSR wishing to encapsulate additional labels on the label stack [IETF-12] must use the standard technique outlined in the section titled "Encoding the Label Stack."

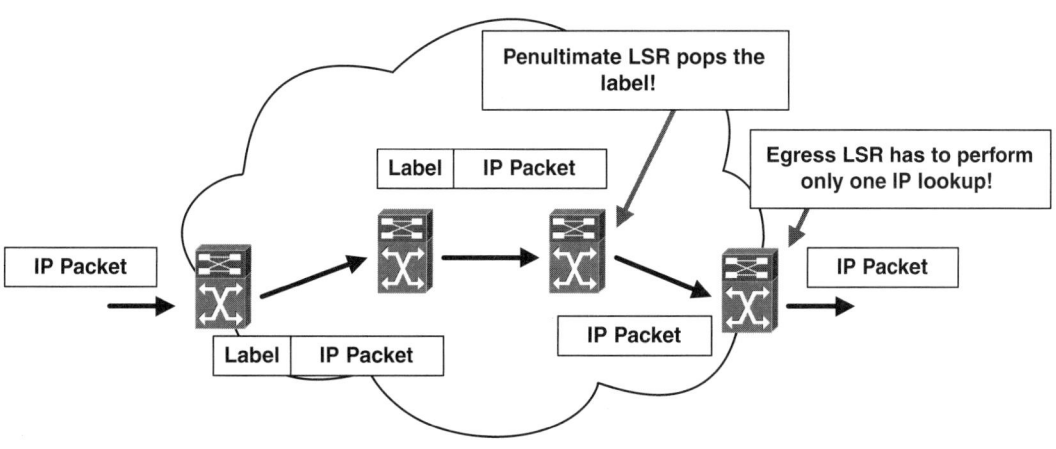

Figure 3–6   Penultimate hop popping.

The standard encapsulation proposed in [IETF-12] is referred to as a "shim header." The term "shim header" comes from the fact that MPLS defines an additional header that is placed, or shimmed, between the Layer 2 and Layer 3 headers. The term "generic label encapsulation" has the same meaning as "shim header." It is important to note that there are other ways to encode the first one or two labels of the label stack. For example, when ATM is used, the VPI/VCI field is used to carry the label information. Also, in Frame Relay, the DLCI field is used to encapsulate the first label of the stack. Label stacks can be used only at the edges of ATM or Frame Relay networks since the label stack is encoded into the payload of the cells or frames, respectively. All encapsulation types will be discussed in greater detail in the next chapter.

The Label Stack (Generic Label Encapsulation/Shim Header)

ENCODING THE LABEL STACK

Thus far, we have referred to the label contained in the MPSL header as a one-dimensional field—as a single label only—when in reality it is viewed as a stack of potentially many labels. It is therefore better to view the MPLS label stack as a two-dimensional field with a depth of m labels: L(m). An unlabeled packet has a depth of 0; the label on the bottom of the stack has a depth of 1; and the label on the top has a depth of m.

KEY CONCEPT!

Every packet must carry at least one label, but can contain more than one. All forwarding decisions are based exclusively on the label on the top of the label stack, L(m). If the label is swapped at an LSR, typically only the top-most label on the label stack, L(m), is altered and exchanged with a new outgoing label.

The label stack is represented as a sequence of label stack entries. Each label stack entry is represented by four octets, which are shown in Figure 3–7.

The format of the label stack entry is defined in [IETF-12].

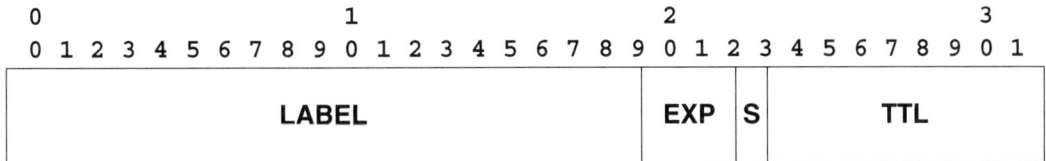

Figure 3-7 MPLS label stack entry.

Each label stack entry is broken down into the following fields:

- **Bottom of stack (S)**—This bit is set to 1 for the last entry in the label stack (i.e., for the bottom of the stack), and 0 for all other label stack entries.
- **Time to live (TTL)**—This eight-bit field is used to encode a time-to-live (TTL) value.
- **Experimental use (EXP)**—These three bits are commonly used to encode either Type of Service (ToS) values or DiffServ Code Point (DSCP) values. A detailed discussion of how the EXP field can be used is presented in [IETF-13].
- **LABEL value**—This 20-bit field carries the actual value of the label. When a labeled packet is received, the label value at the top of the stack is looked up. As a result of a successful lookup, one learns:

  i. The next hop to which the packet is to be forwarded.

  ii. The operation to be performed on the label stack before forwarding. This operation may replace the top label stack entry with another, pop an entry off the label stack, or replace the top label stack entry and then push one or more additional entries on the label stack.

  In addition to learning the next hop and label stack operation, one may also learn the outgoing data link encapsulation and possibly other information that is needed to properly forward the packet.

Label values from 0 to 15 are reserved. Further details on reserved labels can be found in [IETF-12].

Label stack entries appear after the data link layer headers, but before any network layer headers. The top of the label stack appears earliest in the packet, and the bottom appears latest. The network layer packet immediately follows the label stack entry that has the S bit set. This is illustrated in Figure 3-8.

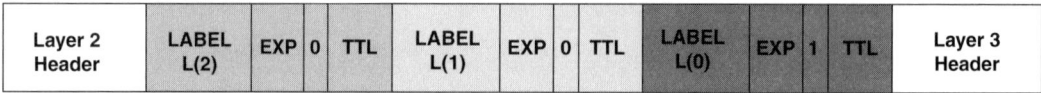

Figure 3–8   MPLS label stack.

LABEL-SWITCHED PATHS (LSPs)

A label-switched path (LSP) can be defined as a sequence of n LSRs that are traversed by a packet with a label of depth m.

`<R₁(m),…,Rₙ(m)>`

This can be generalized if we assume a label stack instead of only one label.

`<R₁(m), R₂(m), R₁(m+k), R₂(m+k)…, Rᵢ₋₁(m+k), Rᵢ(m+k), Rₙ₋₁(m), Rₙ(m)>, while k>0`

TUNNELS AND HIERARCHY

In certain situations, it may be useful to send a packet from one router to another, even though they are not consecutive routers on a hop-by-hop path and the receiving router is not the packet's final destination. This situation may occur if an ISP acts as a transit carrier for another ISP. We call this scenario "Carrier's Carrier" (CsC). It is possible to achieve this by encapsulating the packet inside a network layer packet. For example, this can be accomplished using generic route encapsulation (GRE). This creates a tunnel between two edge routers and allows packets to be "tunneled" through the network.

There are two types of tunnels:

i. Hop-by-hop routed tunnel
ii. Explicitly routed tunnel

In case i, packets will follow a hop-by-hop path; hence, the routing decision must be performed at each hop. In case ii, encapsulated packets might be source-routed, which means that the routing information is already processed at the source of the tunnel and applied to all subsequent hops, thus obviating the need to make a routing decision for the packet at each hop. Case ii is used with TE, where the LSP of the traffic-engineered tunnel is determined at the head of the tunnel *a priori*. The traffic flowing through this tunnel is therefore source-routed.

It is possible to implement a tunnel as an LSP and use label switching rather than network layer encapsulation to force the packet to travel through the tunnel.

The tunnel would be an LSR defined as <R1, ..., Rn>, where R1 is the transmit endpoint of the tunnel and Rn is the receive endpoint of the tunnel. This is called an "LSP tunnel."

Consider the following scenario where a packet travels from one LSR to a neighbor LSR. Neither of the LSRs is directly connected, but they are still reachable via a hop-by-hop tunnel through another MPLS network.

The resulting LSP would, for example, appear as follows:

```
< R_1(1), R_2(1), R_1(2), ..., R_n(2), R_3(1), R_4(1)>
```

All label values shown in Figure 3–9 correspond to the outgoing interface of the LSRs.

As the packet enters network AS V (autonomous system V), label "1" is applied to the packet on label level 1.

LSR $R_2(1)$ and LSR $R_3(1)$ are neighbors and maintain an LDP session, though they are not directly connected. LSR $R_2(1)$ also maintains an LDP session with $R_1(2)$. LSR $R_2(1)$ exchanges label information with its non-directly connected neighbor, $R_3(1)$, regarding a label binding with the label value "3" for FEC A. This binding is learned from its non-directly connected neighbor, $R_3(1)$. It then pushes on a new label containing a value that is meaningful to $R_1(2)$.

- As the labeled packet enters AS U, a new label, "8," is assigned by LSR $R_1(2)$. Switching is done on the level 2 label by $R_1(2)$, $R_2(2)$, ..., $R_n(2)$. $R_n(2)$, which is the penultimate hop in the $R_1(2)$—$R_n(2)$ tunnel, pops the label stack before forwarding the packet to $R_3(1)$.
- When $R_3(1)$ sees the packet, it has only a level 1 label, having now exited the tunnel.
- Since $R_3(1)$ is the penultimate hop in the packet's level 1 LSP, it pops the label stack and $R_4(1)$ receives the packet unlabeled. LSR $R_3(1)$ does not have to know the packet has traversed another network, and performs its forwarding decisions entirely on label L(1).

The label stack mechanism allows LSP tunneling to nest to practically any depth, and is only limited by the maximum packet size.

From the perspective of the Level 2 LSP, the label distribution peer of $R_2(1)$ is $R_1(2)$. From the perspective of the Level 1 LSP, the label distribution peers of $R_2(1)$ are $R_1(1)$ and $R_3(1)$. One can have label distribution peers at each layer of

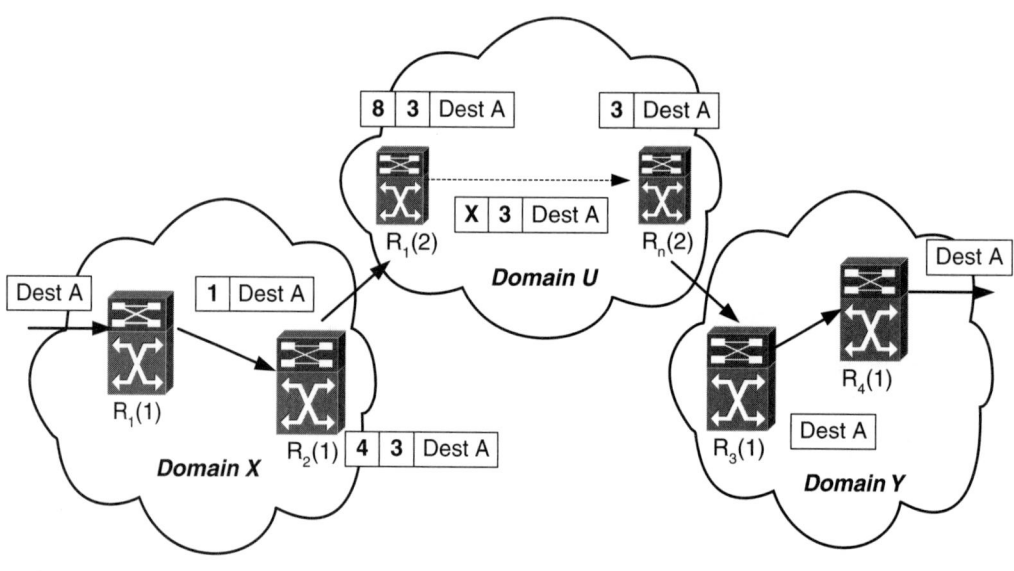

Figure 3–9 LSP hierarchy.

the hierarchy. $R_2(1)$ maintains three LDP sessions, namely with $R_1(1)$, $R_3(1)$, and $R_1(2)$. Note that in this example, $R_2(1)$ and $R_1(2)$ must be eBGP neighbors since they do not belong to the same AS. However, $R_2(1)$ and $R_3(1)$ need not be, since they belong to the same AS.

DETERMINING THE NETWORK LAYER PROTOCOL

It might be surprising to find that there is no protocol identifier field in the MPLS shim header, but one was omitted because MPLS is capable of functioning without one. The reasons for this omission are two-fold. First, the protocol type can be inferred from the label value itself. The software must also be able to determine which protocol is carried after the label header when, for example, an edge LSR must remove the shim header and forward the packet using its original network protocol. In addition, each hop has to know which protocol is encoded within a certain label range so that it can choose an appropriate outgoing label within that particular label range for that particular network protocol.

Since it is likely that IPv4 will be carried in the first implementations of MPLS, it may not seem obvious to think about this problem. However, there are certain error conditions under which it may be necessary to know which network layer protocol is used under shim encapsulation. For example, one such condition occurs when a packet is undeliverable. In this case, it might be useful to send an error message back to the sender. However, this is not possible without knowledge of the network protocol. In such a multiprotocol environment, it would be useful to assign certain label ranges to certain network protocols. In doing so, this would allow intermediate nodes to reach the sender of a packet in case there was an error at some intermediate node. If no such label ranges are defined and the network protocol used cannot be derived from the network header, the packet must unfortunately be silently discarded. An unfortunate side effect of this is that the network operator will learn nothing of the error condition.

PROCESSING THE TTL FIELD

To prevent network layer packets from looping endlessly in a network, the TTL field was invented. This field maintains a counter that is gradually decremented from some initial value down to zero. When this value reaches zero, the packet is discarded. Forwarding loops may occur during transitions of the routing protocol or because of network element configuration errors.

A similar field is present in the MPLS shim header. Since the possibility of encountering multiple network layer protocols within MPLS exists, there is a set of rules and definitions for how this field is to be treated when traversing the MPLS network.

The TTL field is used by some applications for reasons other than loop prevention and detection. The best-known application is "traceroute." Traceroute sends packets with a TTL value of 1 to their next-hop neighbor and resolves the ICMP error message to determine the IP address and/or Domain Name Server (DNS) name of the router. Traceroute will then send subsequent packets with a TTL value increased by 1 to that router's neighbor and wait for the answer of the subsequent hop in the network. This procedure is performed iteratively until the final destination of the network layer packet is reached. The final destination is discovered through the "Port Unreachable" Internet Control Message Protocol (ICMP) message. This works because the originating router sends a User Datagram Protocol (UDP) datagram to a bogus port (this UDP packet is in fact the traceroute packet itself). By using this technique, traceroute is able to determine the entire Layer 3 path of the packet and the address and/or name of all the routers along this path.

This feature is important for troubleshooting the network and should also be present in MPLS implementations. To provide network operators with such a feature, certain definitions have been made:

> The "incoming TTL" is defined to be the value of the TTL field of the top label entry when the packet is received. The "outgoing TTL" is defined to be the larger of one less than the "incoming TTL," or zero.

IP-DEPENDENT RULES
When an IP packet enters an MPLS network at the ingress LSR, the IPv4 TTL value is optionally copied into the TTL field of the label stack entry. When a packet is received by MPLS, it is assumed that IP processing has already occurred and that the IP TTL field was decremented when the IPv4 TTL field value was copied into the label TTL field of the label stack entry. Packets with an initial TTL value of 0 are not forwarded; instead, they are discarded and an ICMP message is returned to the sender. One method can be applied when the packet leaves the network: The egress LSR can simply copy the decremented label TTL field into the TTL field of the outgoing IPv4 packet. This method results in the hop count of the MPLS network being visible to all clients hanging off the LSRs at the edge (see Figure 3–10).

Since there are certain situations where one would not wish to make the MPLS hop count visible to all clients, there is another possibility in which clients will see the MPLS network as a single hop (see Figure 3–11).

TRANSLATING BETWEEN DIFFERENT ENCAPSULATIONS
Since there is more than one encapsulation technique used in MPLS (see the section titled "Alternative Label Encapsulation Techniques"), there is a need for translating between these different encapsulation types when encoding TTL values. Alternative label encapsulations may use different methods to propagate the TTL value other than to encode the TTL value in a dedicated TTL field in the header of a packet. An LSR may receive a packet with an encapsulation technique that differs from the one that is used to send the packet out the outgoing interface. To make sure that the TTL value is interpreted and processed correctly, three different cases must be distinguished.

CASE 1 (FIGURE 3–12):
- Incoming packet: unlabeled, labeled with shim header, or labeled with shim header and alternative encapsulation for the top label(s).

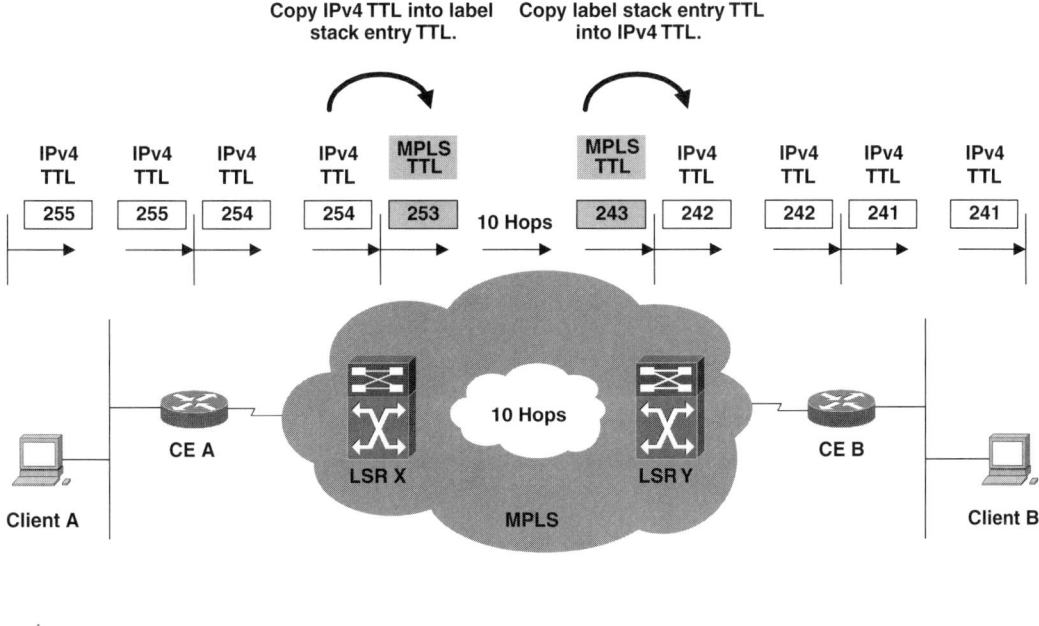

Figure 3–10 MPLS hop count visible to the clients.

- Outgoing packet: unlabeled.
- Incoming TTL is either inferred from the TTL value of the network layer field (e.g., IPv4) or from the TTL value of the top label stack entry.
- Outgoing TTL is encoded in the TTL field of the network layer header (e.g., IPv4 TTL field).

CASE 2 (FIGURE 3–13):
- Incoming packet: unlabeled, labeled with shim header, or labeled with shim header and alternative encapsulation for the top label(s).
- Outgoing packet: labeled with shim header.
- Incoming TTL is either inferred from the TTL value of the network layer field (e.g., IPv4) or from the TTL value of the top label stack entry.
- Outgoing TTL is encoded in the TTL field of the top label stack entry.

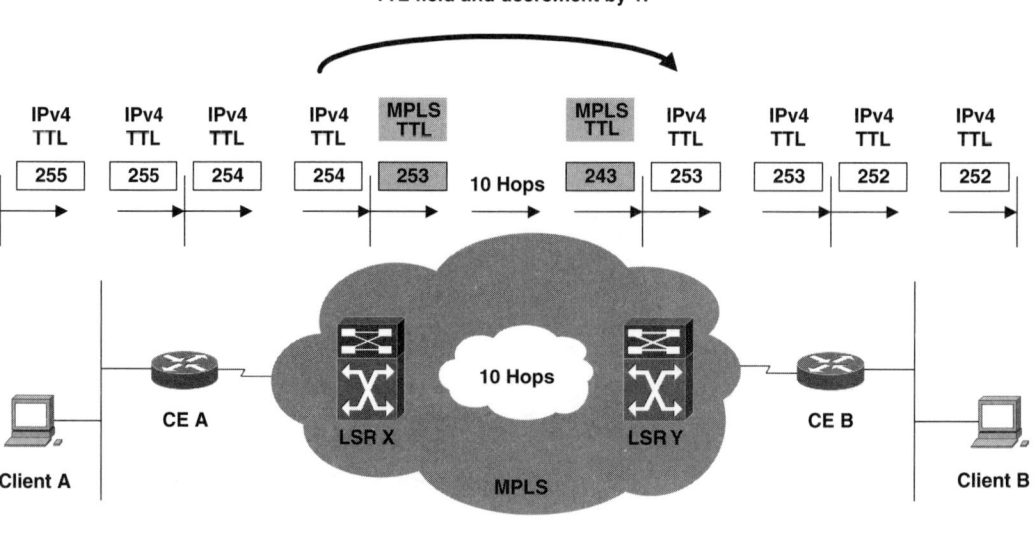

Figure 3–11 MPLS hop count not visible to the clients.

CASE 3 (FIGURE 3–14):
- Incoming packet: unlabeled, labeled with shim header, or labeled with shim header and alternative encapsulation for the top label(s).
- Outgoing packet: alternative encapsulation (ATM, Frame Relay) with additional shim header.
- Incoming TTL is either inferred from the TTL value of the network layer field (e.g., IPv4) or from the TTL value of the top label stack entry.

Since ATM-LSRs cannot process the TTL field of the shim header, the TTL value has to be copied into the TTL field of the packet, either at the ingress ATM-LSR or at the egress ATM-LSR. The ingress ATM-LSR is the more efficient device to perform the TTL processing, since the packets with a TTL field less than or equal to the hop count of the path would not be sent through the whole path down to the egress LSR, where these packets would be discarded. The ingress ATM-LSR has to know *a priori* the hop count of the path.

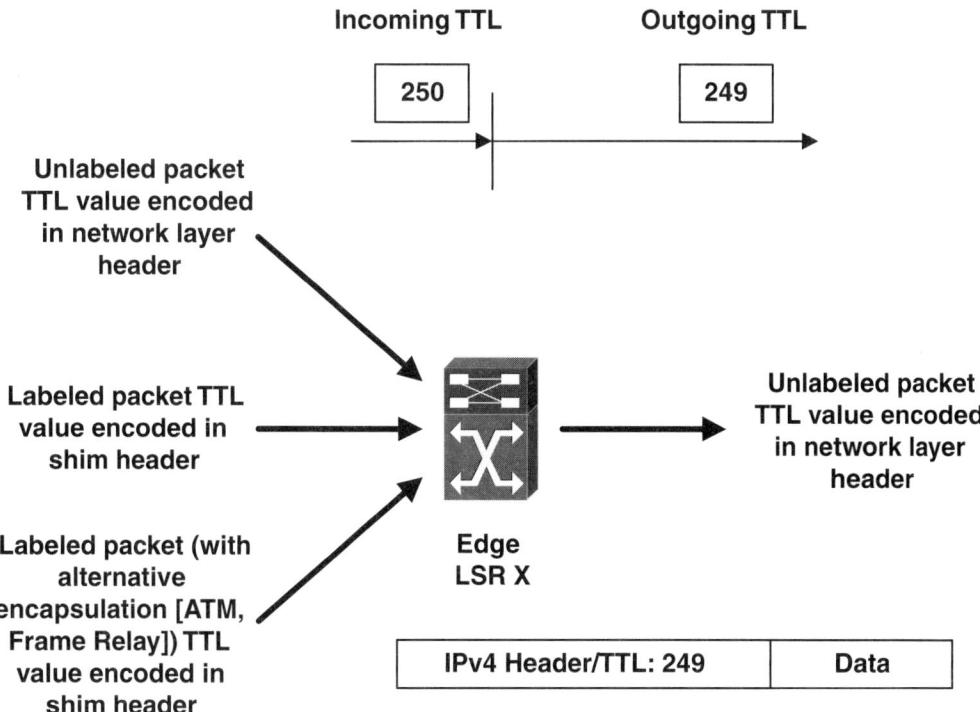

Figure 3-12 Case 1: outgoing packet unlabeled.

This is achieved during the label binding process between the adjacent LSRs down the LSP. The outgoing TTL is derived from the incoming TTL value minus the hop count associated with the LSP. Since ATM-LSRs make their forwarding decisions solely based on the information in the VPI/VCI field, these devices cannot process any TTL fields. Another technique must be used with ATM-LSRs to guarantee loop-free paths and to provide the same level of troubleshooting capability.

A practice used with ATM-LSRs is the loop detection via path vectors (LDPV) procedure. This procedure is able to detect loops more quickly and effectively than other procedures that process the TTL field. Loop detection can already be done at LSP setup, without any traffic circulating in this path.

A path vector contains the IDs of all LSRs that are setting up an LSP through the MPLS network. If an LSR detects its own ID in the path vector, it has detected a loop, since it must have already been involved in the setup of this path. A label binding can be associated with a hop count for this path down to

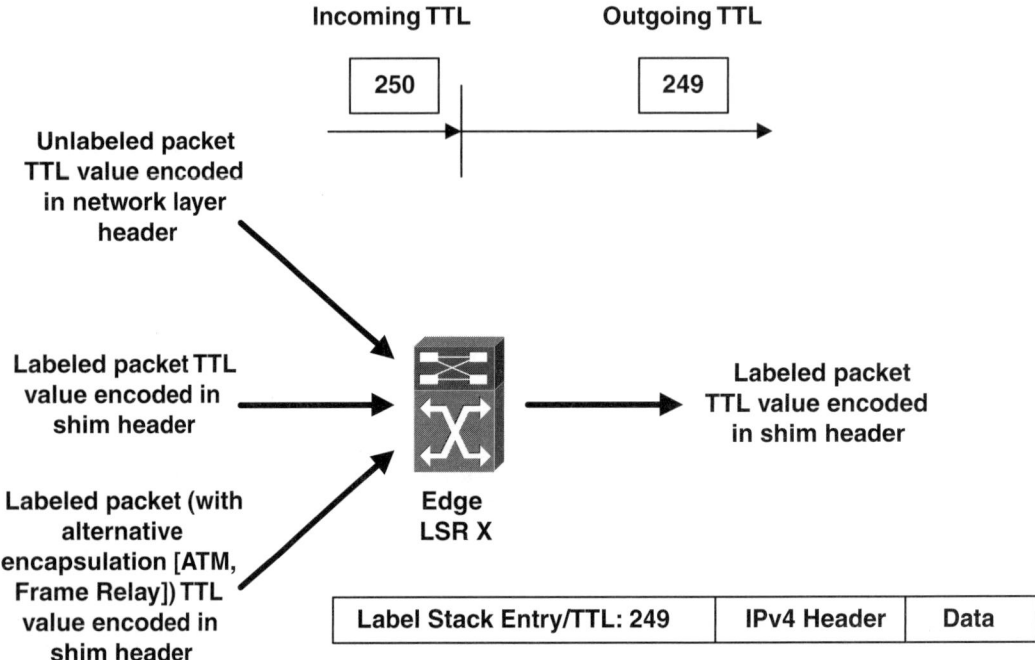

Figure 3-13   Case 2: labeled packet with shim header.

the egress LSR of the MPLS domain. The edge ATM-LSR is aware of the hop count to the destination edge ATM-LSR if it uses the LDPV procedure. If a hop count was associated with the label binding that was used when the packet was forwarded, the outgoing TTL will be set to the difference between the incoming TTL and the hop count. If a hop count was not associated with the label binding that was used when the packet was forwarded, the outgoing TTL will be set to one less than the incoming TTL. If this procedure causes the TTL field of the packet to become zero, the packet will be discarded and an ICMP message will be sent to the source of the packet if such a source can be derived from the labeled packet. When an edge LSR receives a labeled packet over an LC-ATM interface, it obtains the incoming TTL from the top label stack entry of the generic encapsulation, or if that encapsulation is not present, from the IP header. The edge LSR forwards the packet and uses the top label stack entry to encode the outgoing TTL value.

Label Encapsulation 43

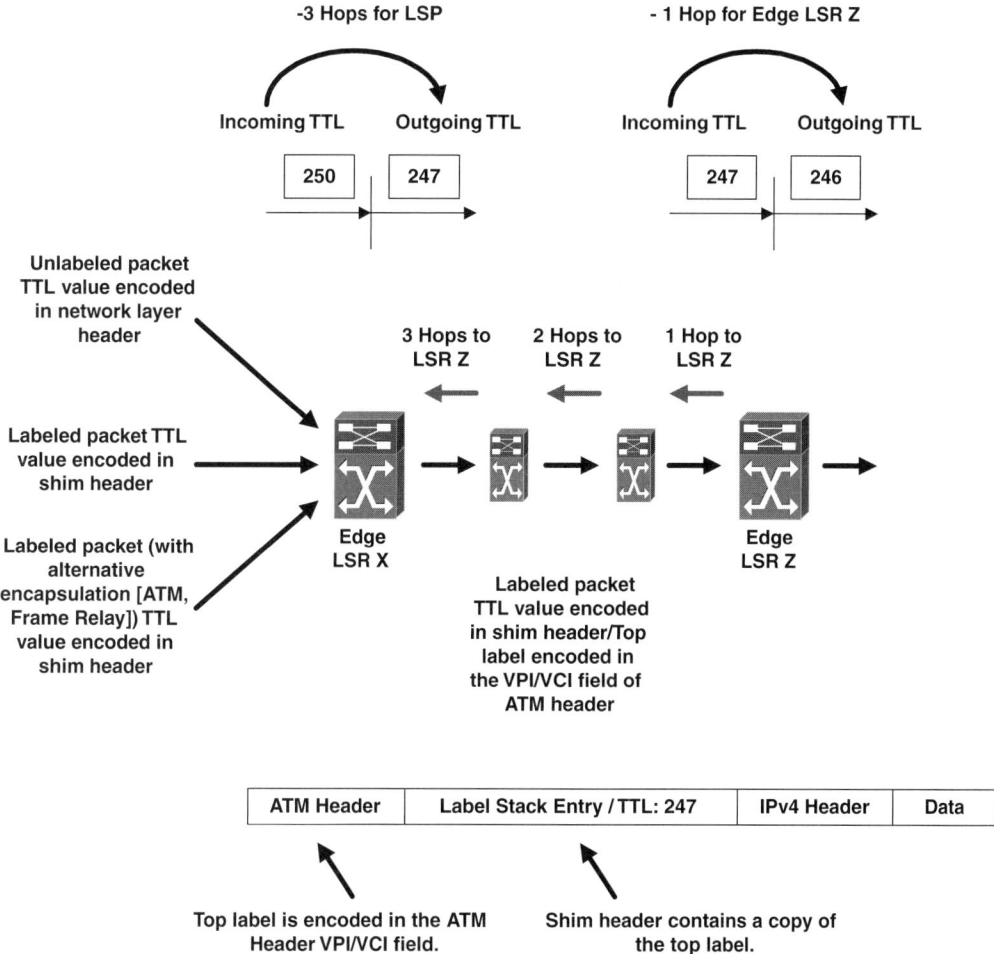

Figure 3-14 Case 3: labeled packet with shim header and alternative encapsulation.

FRAGMENTATION AND PATH MTU DISCOVERY

There may be situations where a packet is too large to be transported over an output link somewhere within the MPLS domain. The reason for this may be either that the unlabeled packet exceeds the maximum transmission unit (MTU) limit of that link or that the unlabeled packet itself is not too large, but with the addition of the MPLS shim header, it exceeds the MTU size of the link. For example, if an unlabeled IP packet has a size of 1500 bytes and the appended label has a size of 4 bytes, the resulting payload for the link encapsulation will be 1504. This size may exceed the limit for certain link types.

Rules for processing labeled packets that are "too large" are specified in [IETF-12]. In particular, [IETF-12] provides rules that ensure that hosts implementing path MTU discovery [IETF-14] and using IPv6 [IETF-15], [IETF-16] are able to generate IP datagrams that do not need fragmentation, even if those datagrams get labeled as they traverse the network. In practice, there are generally no problems with hosts that do not implement path MTU discovery because these hosts send IP packets with a maximum size of 576 bytes. Since most data links can handle an MTU size of at least 1500 bytes, it is not very likely that these packets will get fragmented, even if there are a lot of label stack entries present in the MPLS header. However, some hosts that do not implement path MTU discovery [IETF-14] will generate IP packets containing 1500 bytes as long as the source and destination addresses are in the same subnet. Under this condition, packets will not be fragmented anyway, since these packets will not traverse a router or LSR, but will instead be delivered directly over Layer 2 media such as Ethernet. One other situation to consider is that some hosts will send 1500-byte packets if the source and destination addresses of the packets are in the same classful network number. If these packets traverse an Ethernet segment after they have been labeled and before they get unlabeled again, it is likely that these packets will get fragmented.

[IETF-12] specifies procedures that allow the configuration of a network so that large datagrams from hosts that do not implement path MTU discovery will get fragmented just once, when they are first labeled. These procedures make it possible (assuming suitable configuration) to avoid any need to fragment packets that have already been labeled.

One important concept to note is that of the maximum initially labeled IP datagram size. This concept brings the benefit that if a packet exceeds the maximum MTU size of a data link, it will be fragmented only once, at the ingress LSR of the MPLS domain (see Figure 3–15). Only packets that do not have the DF bit set will get fragmented with this procedure.

To maintain the full functionality of the path MTU discovery procedure, packets with the Don't Fragment (DF) bit set must be treated in a different way (see Figure 3–16).

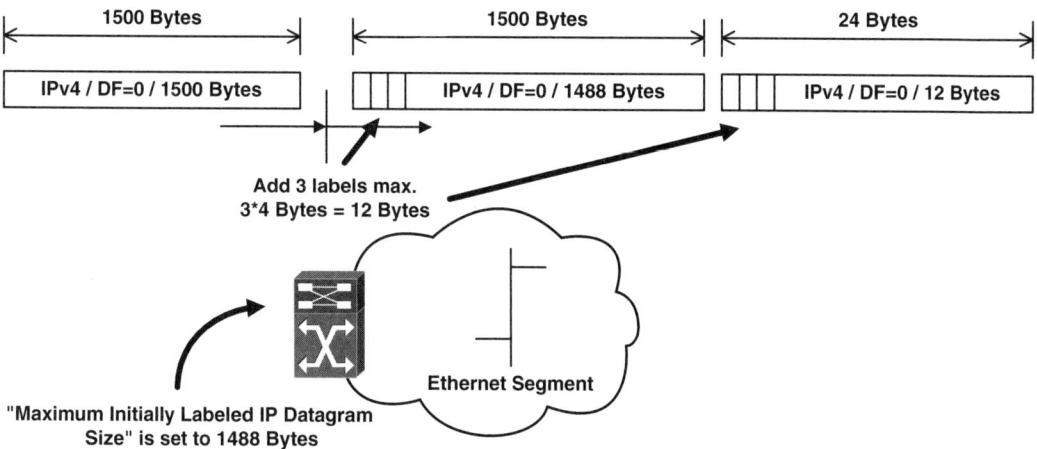

Figure 3–15   Maximum initially labeled IP datagram size; DF bit = 0.

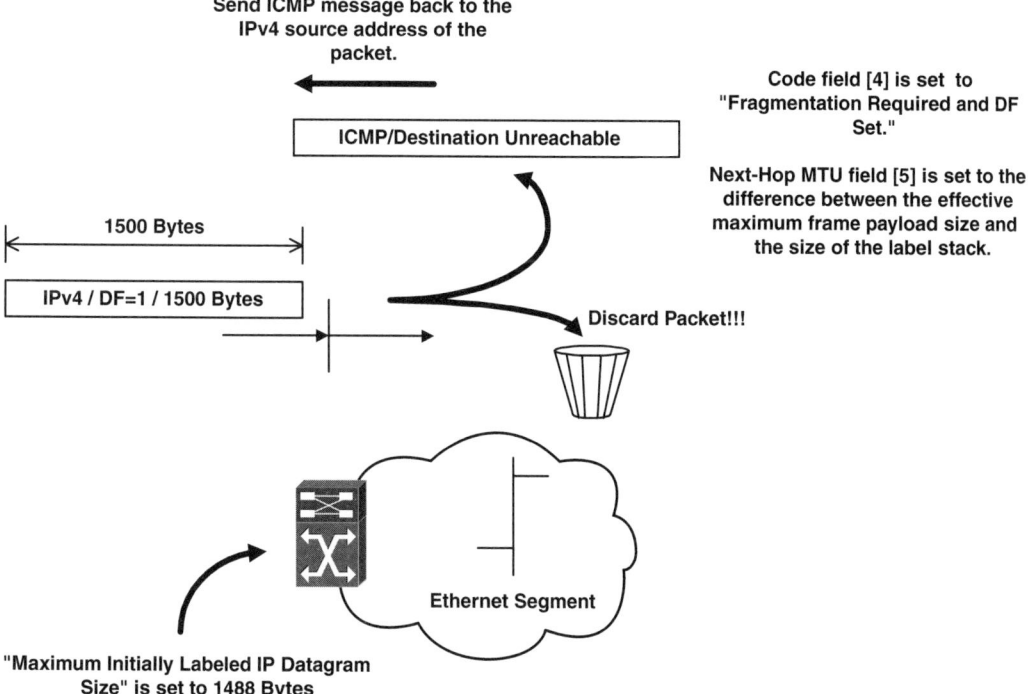

Figure 3–16   Maximum initially labeled IP datagram size; DF bit = 1.

An LSR that supports this feature must perform the following procedure as described in [IETF-12]:

Every LSR that is capable of:
   i. Receiving an unlabeled IP datagram,
   ii. Adding a label stack to the datagram, and
   iii. Forwarding the resulting labeled packet

should support a configuration parameter known as the maximum initially labeled IP datagram size, which can be set to a non-negative value. If this configuration parameter is set to zero, it has no effect. If it is set to a positive value, it is used in the following way:

If:
   i. An unlabeled IP datagram is received, and
   ii. That datagram does not have the DF bit set in its IP header, and
   iii. That datagram needs to be labeled before being forwarded, and
   iv. The size of the datagram (before labeling) exceeds the value of the parameter,

then:
   i. The datagram must be broken into fragments, where each fragment's size is no greater than the value of the parameter, and
   ii. Each fragment must be labeled and then forwarded.

For example, if this configuration parameter is set to a value of 1488, then any unlabeled IP datagram containing more than 1488 bytes will be fragmented before being labeled. Each fragment will be capable of being carried on a 1500-byte data link, without further fragmentation, even if as many as three labels are pushed onto its label stack.

To guarantee that the path MTU discovery procedure will work properly, we have to produce an ICMP/Destination Unreachable message for each packet that exceeds the MTU size and has the DF bit set and send it back to the network layer source address of the packet.

TRANSPORTING LABELED PACKETS OVER PPP

The Point-to-Point Protocol (PPP) [IETF-17] provides a standard method for transporting multiprotocol datagrams over point-to-point links. PPP is composed of three main components:

i. A method for encapsulating multiprotocol datagrams
ii. A Link Control Protocol (LCP) for establishing, configuring, and testing the data link connection
iii. A family of Network Control Protocols (NCPs) for establishing and configuring different network layer protocols.

[IETF-12] describes procedures for how labeled packets can be transported over a PPP link.

To establish communications over a point-to-point link, each end of the PPP link must first send LCP packets to configure and test the data link. After the link has been established and optional facilities have been negotiated as needed by the LCP, PPP must send MPLS Control Protocol packets to enable the transmission of labeled packets. Once the MPLS Control Protocol has reached the Opened state, labeled packets can be sent over the link.

Exactly one labeled packet is encapsulated in the PPP Information field. The PPP Protocol field indicates either type hex 0281 (MPLS unicast) or type hex 0283 (MPLS multicast). The maximum length of a labeled packet transmitted over a PPP link is the same as the maximum length of the Information field of a PPP encapsulated packet.

The two type values can easily be used since they are registered as unicast and multicast packet types for Cisco's tag switching, which migrated into a fully compliant MPLS implementation.

TRANSPORTING LABELED PACKETS OVER LAN MEDIA

The main challenge here is that the MPLS shim header must precede the network layer header, and directly follow any data link headers, including, for example, any 802.1Q headers that may exist. We must also encapsulate one packet into each frame.

The Ethertype value hex 8847 can be used to indicate that a frame is carrying an MPLS unicast packet. The Ethertype value hex 8848 can be used to indicate that a frame is carrying an MPLS multicast packet. These Ethertype values can be used with either Ethernet encapsulation or 802.3 LLC/SNAP encapsulation to carry labeled packets.

[IETF-12] specifies the transport of labeled packets over LAN media.

ALTERNATIVE LABEL ENCAPSULATION TECHNIQUES

One of the most remarkable benefits of MPLS is the integration of the high-performance forwarding and traffic management capabilities of switching technologies such as ATM and Frame Relay and the scalability and flexibility of network layer routing.

Service providers often want to maintain their ATM services because of their migration plans or because ATM features like constant bit rate are quite lucrative. Nevertheless, they also want the benefits of a true peer model for their IP services. MPLS can be implemented in a configuration called "Ships in the Night," which allows legacy ATM services to coexist with MPLS applications within the same network of ATM-LSRs. This functionality is quite important since service providers are looking for differentiating features that they can offer to their customers. IP and ATM integration with MPLS enables many new services and service classes that could simply not be realized with the legacy ATM infrastructure.

OVERLAY VS. LABEL-ENCODED

There is a large demand for the integration of IP and ATM. There are two main implementation possibilities for the integration of these two technologies:

i. Build an overlay model that connects all routers at the edge of the network with PVCs and use generic MPLS encapsulation to encode the labels (see the section in Chapter 2 titled "Overlay Models").

ii. Use ATM VPI/VCI fields for the first one or two labels, and encode the rest of the existing label stack entries with the generic MPLS encapsulation in the payload of the ATM cells.

The first model has the advantage of being relatively easy to implement. It, however, lacks the scalability of a pure ATM network since it also runs into the n^2 problem when the number of connections reaches a certain critical threshold (see the section in Chapter 2 titled "Overlay Models"). Another issue is that the packets have to be examined at each hop through the ATM network because the label information is contained in the encapsulation between Layers 2 and 3. Hence, all the packets in the ATM Adaptation Layer 5 (AAL5) cells have to be extracted, buffered, and processed in a second step. This is a rather CPU-intensive process that results in a severe degradation in performance. There is no way to get the label information out of the Layer 2 ATM header.

The first model is a viable solution if ATM is used as a transport medium on certain links (Figure 3–17). In this configuration, ATM is essentially used as a tunnel through a non-MPLS ATM cloud between two MPLS-capable devices.

The second model possesses the advantage of scalability that comes with a pure ATM network (Figure 3–18). Nevertheless, there are still certain drawbacks such as the lack of a TTL field in the ATM cell header. Further, there is the problem of VC-merge support for ATM-LSRs. These problems are discussed in the next section. This is a possible solution for a service provider that deploys MPLS in its own switching infrastructure, and does not have to tunnel through ATM clouds that are not under its control.

In this model, all links in the ATM network use ATM-MPLS encapsulation. The forwarding decision at each hop is exclusively made based on the top label. The top label is represented by the VPI/VCI fields in the ATM cell header. The next section, "Encapsulating Top Labels with ATM," discusses these procedures in more detail.

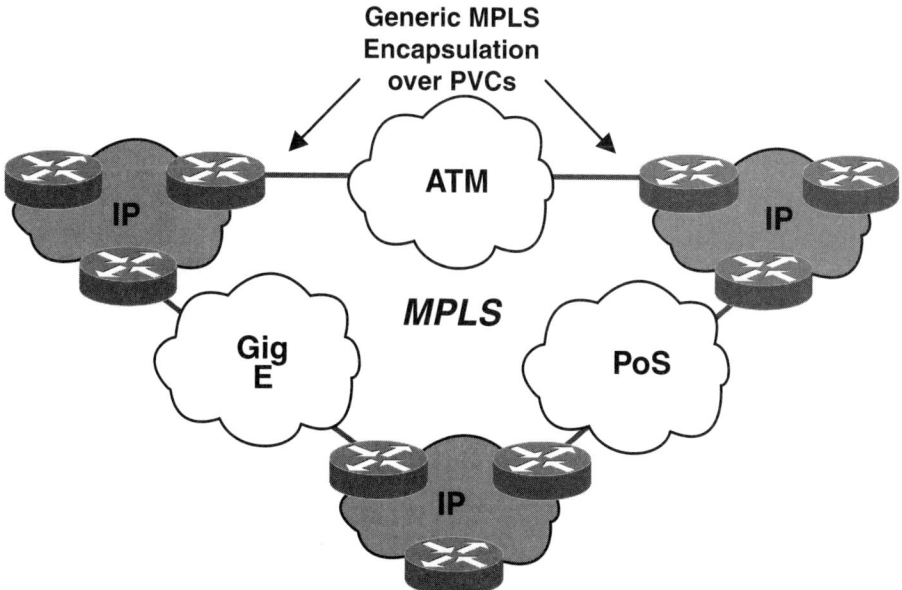

Figure 3–17   Model i: ATM on a point-to-point link with generic MPLS encapsulation.

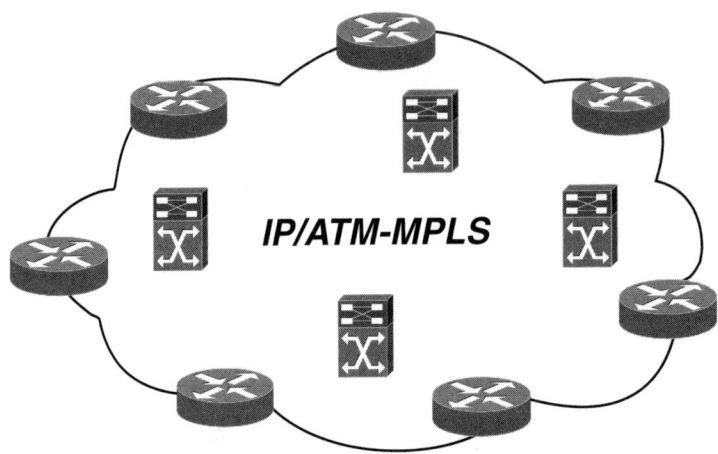

Figure 3-18 Model ii: Pure IP/ATM network cloud with alternative label encapsulation.

ENCAPSULATING TOP LABELS WITH ATM

ATM switches that run routing protocols like OSPF and/or IS-IS, etc., and are capable of forwarding cells that carry label information in their VPI/VCI field are called ATM-label switch routers (ATM-LSRs). The forwarding decision of an ATM-LSR is based on the information learned by Layer 3 routing protocols.

Unlike legacy ATM switches, these devices store, update, and forward Layer 3 topology information to their routing peers. These peers can either be other ATM-LSRs or legacy Layer 3 routing devices with ATM interfaces that are physically attached, or attached through an ATM connection (VP tunnel), to the ATM-LSR.

Note that no ATM addressing or routing like PNNI is involved in this whole process.

There are several characteristics of ATM switches that affect their behavior as ATM-LSRs. Since many ATM switches are built to support legacy ATM features and not especially MPLS features, some restrictions in terms of functionality exist. These restrictions are listed below [IETF-18].

VC-merge is the process by which a switch receives cells on several incoming VCIs and transmits them on a single outgoing VCI without causing the cells of different ATM Adaptation Layer 5 Protocol data units (AAL5 PDUs) to become interleaved.

- The label swapping function is performed on fields (the VCI and/or VPI) in the cell header; this dictates the size and placement of the label(s) in a packet.
- Multipoint-to-point and multipoint-to-multipoint VCs are generally not supported. This means that most switches cannot support VC-merge as defined above.
- There is generally no capability to perform a TTL decrement function as is performed on IP headers in routers.

ATM-LSRs must implement the MPLS control component, which consists of the label allocation, distribution, and maintenance procedures previously outlined. The label binding information is mainly communicated via the Label Distribution Protocol (LDP). There are also other protocols that can be used to communicate label binding information, such as MP-BGP (Multiprotocol Border Gateway Protocol) and others. In most ATM-LSR architectures, it is likely that this information is only relevant to members of the edge LSR domain. For example, this information might be used to carry VPN information from one edge LSR to another edge LSR. An ATM-LSR is called an ATM edge LSR if it has some interfaces that are connected to networking devices that do not use any kind of MPLS encapsulation on their links. These devices are outside the MPLS domain. On the other hand, ATM-LSRs that have interfaces connected only to devices that use MPLS encapsulation are simply called ATM-LSRs. Figure 3–19 illustrates both types.

In cases where label binding information that is not communicated via LDP is relevant to ATM-LSRs, all ATM-LSRs must take part in the protocol process. For example, TE may raise the need to integrate the ATM-LSRs in an RSVP process to support label allocation and distribution based on information from RSVP.

USING THE VPI/VCI FIELD ON DIFFERENT CONNECTION TYPES
The ATM user-to-network interface (UNI)header consists of the fields shown in Figure 3–20 and in the list that follws.

- **GFC (Generic Flow Control)**—This can be used to provide local functions, such as identifying multiple stations that share a single ATM

52   Chapter 3 ▸ MPLS Architecture and Operation

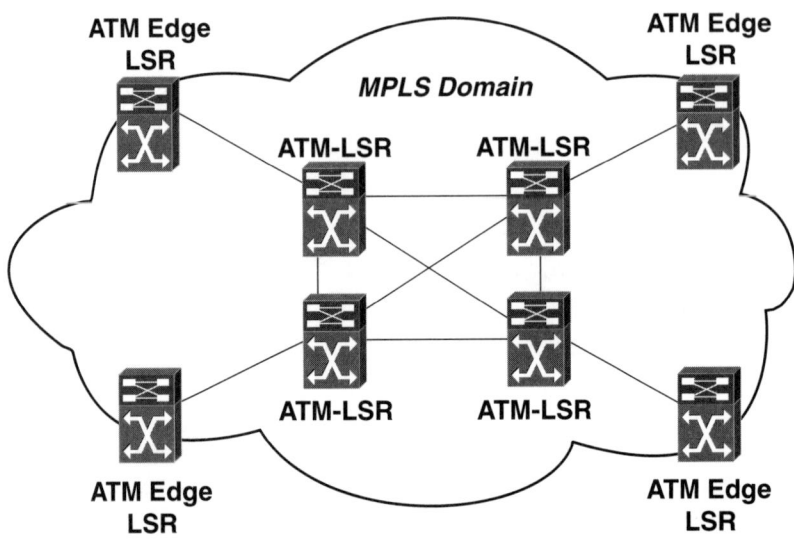

Figure 3–19   ATM edge LSRs and ATM-LSRs.

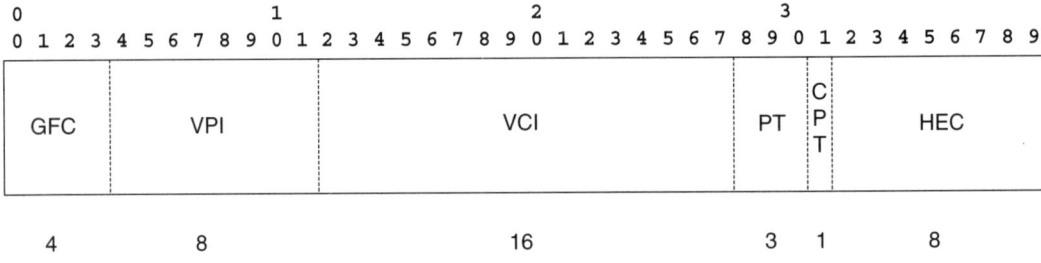

Figure 3–20   ATM UNI header format.

interface. The GFC field is typically not used and is set to a default value.

- **VPI (Virtual Path Identifier)**—This is used in conjunction with the VCI to identify the next destination of a cell as it passes through a series of ATM switches on its way to its ultimate destination.
- **VCI (Virtual Channel Identifier)**—This field is used in conjunction with the VPI to identify the next destination of a cell as it passes through a series of ATM switches on its way to its ultimate destination.
- **PT (Payload Type)**—The first bit indicates whether the cell contains user data or control data. If the cell contains user data, the second bit

indicates congestion, and the third bit indicates whether the cell is the last in a series of cells that represent a single AAL5 frame.
- **CLP (Congestion Loss Priority)**—This bit indicates whether the cell should be discarded if it encounters extreme congestion as it moves through the network.
- **HEC (Header Error Control)**—This is a checksum calculated only on the header itself.

The VPI and VCI fields can carry label information. These fields can be used to encode the labels associated with an FEC, depending on the type of the connection.

Labeled packets are transmitted using null encapsulation as defined in RFC 1483, Section 5.1 [IETF-21].

DIRECT CONNECTION

An ATM interface that is controlled by a label control component is called an LC-ATM interface. If two LC-ATM interfaces are directly connected without passing another ATM switch, MPLS will use both the VPI and VCI fields to encode the label information (see Figure 3–21). The control connection used to negotiate label bindings will carry the LDP and is defined to use VPI or VCI 32.

It is possible to divide the VP/VC space into different partitions, where one partition uses MPLS and another partition uses legacy PVC or SVC connections. For example, the VP range 1–10 may be used for label VCs and 11–255 may be used for legacy PVCs. MPLS will use the VPI fields (1–10) and the VCI fields (0–65536) for label assignments. The available label space is defined as (10 * 65536), which clearly exceeds half a million labels. It is anticipated that this number of labels should be more than sufficient for current and future applications.

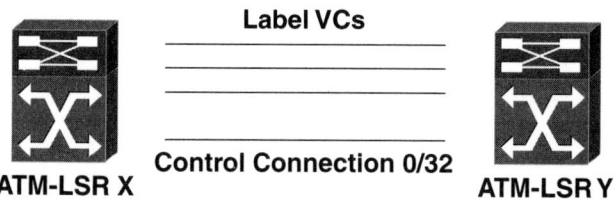

Figure 3–21   ATM-LSRs—direct connection.

CONNECTION VIA A VP TUNNEL

If two LC-ATMs are connected via an ATM cloud, they may use a VP tunnel (see Figure 3–22).

In the example above, the default VCI value of the non-MPLS connection between the LSRs is 32. The VPI is set to whatever is required to make use of the virtual path.

The allowable ranges for VPIs/VCIs are communicated through LDP. If more than one VPI is used for label switching, the allowable range of VCIs may be different for each VPI, and each range may be communicated through LDP.

CONNECTION VIA SVC

Sometimes it may be useful to treat two LSRs as adjacent within the context of some LSP across an LC-ATM interface. This is possible even though the connection between them is made through an ATM cloud via a set of ATM SVCs (see Figure 3–23).

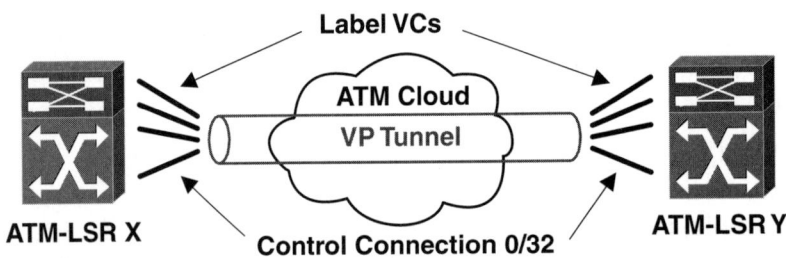

Figure 3–22   ATM-LSRs—VP tunnel connection.

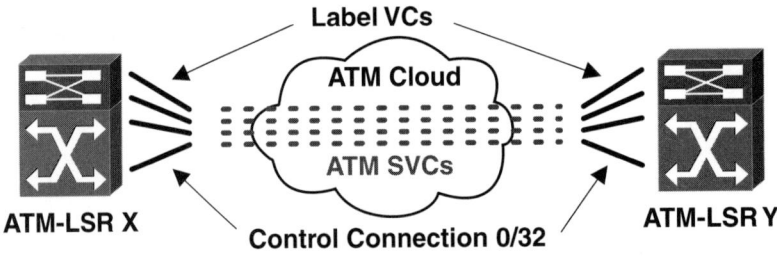

Figure 3–23   ATM-LSRs—SVC connection.

The procedures described in **[IETF-19]** allow a VCID to be assigned to each such VC and specify how LDP can be used to bind a VCID to an FEC. The top label of a received packet would then be inferred (via a one-to-one mapping) from the virtual circuit on which the packet arrived. There would not be a default VPI or VCI value for the non-MPLS connection.

LABEL BINDING PROCEDURES WITH ATM-LSRS
The MPLS architecture specifies that the decision to bind a particular label to a particular FEC must be made by each LSR independently. The downstream LSR subsequently informs the upstream LSR of each binding. Thus, labels are "downstream-assigned," and label bindings are distributed in a "downstream-to-upstream" direction. The method used for distributing the label binding information by ATM-LSRs is called "downstream-on-demand." ATM-LSRs that support the VC-merge functionality may also support another distribution method called "unsolicited downstream."

A detailed discussion of label binding methods can be found in "Labels and Label Distribution Methods."

ENCAPSULATION
Encapsulation of traffic by MPLS ATM-LSRs is only performed by those LSRs that sit on the edge of the ATM and MPLS domains (see Figure 3–24). ATM-LSRs that do not belong to the edge domain do not alter the encapsulation in any way; instead, they only switch cells according to the forwarding information learned by the LDP. The benefit of this is that the forwarding function of ATM cell switching is preserved. Only the control component of the ATM switches must be changed. This is a very important feature of MPLS when considering the importance of supporting MPLS within (or across) existing legacy technologies.

Labeled packets are encapsulated using AAL5 encapsulation and must be transmitted inside the Payload field of the common part convergence sublayer (CPCS) PDU of AAL5. Labeled packets must be transmitted using null encapsulation as described in Section 5.1 of RFC 1483 [IETF-21]. For example, if the original MPLS packet contains a label stack with n entries, the encapsulated PDU must also carry a shim header containing n entries. The actual value of the top label is encoded in the VPI/VCI field. The label value of the top entry in the

56 Chapter 3 ▸ MPLS Architecture and Operation

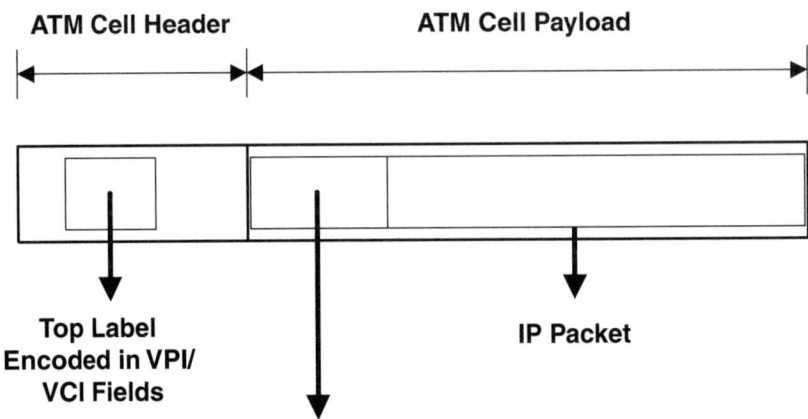

Figure 3-24 ATM label encapsulation.

shim header, which is just a "placeholder" entry, is set to 0 upon transmission and is ignored upon reception. The packet's outgoing TTL, as well as its CoS, are carried in the TTL and CoS fields of the top stack entry in the shim, respectively.

At this stage, the shim header carried in the payload of ATM cells will not be seen by the network unless the ATM cells are reassembled into an MPLS packet. Therefore, the shim header does not impact the existing legacy forwarding function, nor does it influence the forwarding decision in any way. Note that if a packet has a label stack with only one entry, it is required to have a single-entry shim header (four bytes), even though the actual label value is encoded into the VPI/VCI field. This is done to ensure that the packet always has a shim header. If this were not done, there would be no way to determine if additional label stack entries were present in the packet.

KEY CONCEPT!

In an ATM environment, the ATM VPI/VCI fields may be used to carry the top label of the label stack. Additionally, a shim header is always used to encode the rest of the label stack. A shim header will be inserted to carry the information from the TTL and CoS/EXP fields, even if there is only one label present in the label stack.

VC-MERGE

As shown in Figure 3-25, when labeled packets arrive at an ATM-LSR from different sources and belong to the same FEC, it is desirable to have the capability of merging these different incoming labels into one outgoing label in an effort to reduce the number of labels used (i.e., preserve the VPI/VCI space). This also has the effect of simplifying the forwarding tables of ATM-LSRs.

AAL5 is capable of reassembling cells in the same order as they were sent out by the outgoing interface of the last segmentation point. Unlike AAL3/4 with its Message Identifier (MID) field, AAL5 does not have any provision within its cell format for interleaving cells from different AAL5 packets on a single connection. Therefore, all AAL5 packets sent to a particular destination across a particular connection must be received in sequence, that is, without interleaving cells from packets belonging to the same connection. Otherwise, the destination reassembly process would not be able to reconstruct the packets.

Figure 3-26 shows how AAL5 prepares a cell for transmission. First, the MPLS shim header is created and appended to the frame. The convergence sublayer of AAL5 appends variable-length padding bytes as well as an 8-byte trailer to the frame. The pad is long enough to ensure that the resulting protocol data unit (PDU) is divisible by 48 bytes when fragmented into ATM cells. The trailer includes the length of the frame and a 32-bit cyclic redundancy check (CRC) computed across the entire PDU. This allows AAL5 to detect bit errors and lost or out-of-sequence cells at the destination. Next, the segmentation and reassembly function segments the convergence sublayer (CS) PDU into 48-byte blocks. The ATM layer then places each block into the Payload field of an ATM cell. All cells except the last cell contain a bit in the PT (payload type) field that is set to zero to indicate that the cell is not the last cell in a series that in its entirety represents a single frame. For the last cell, the bit in the PT field is set to one.

With this mechanism, it is clear that cells from different streams cannot be commingled without reassembly problems. A way to overcome this problem is to buffer cells until the last cell of a packet is received. The drawback to this approach, however, is that it requires very large buffers as well as much more sophisticated segmentation and reassembly (SAR) Application-Specific Integrated Circuits (ASICs). In RFC 2682 [IETF-22], the impact of VC-merging on cell reassembly buffers is investigated and the results are presented. The document shows that VC-merging incurs a minimal overhead compared to non-

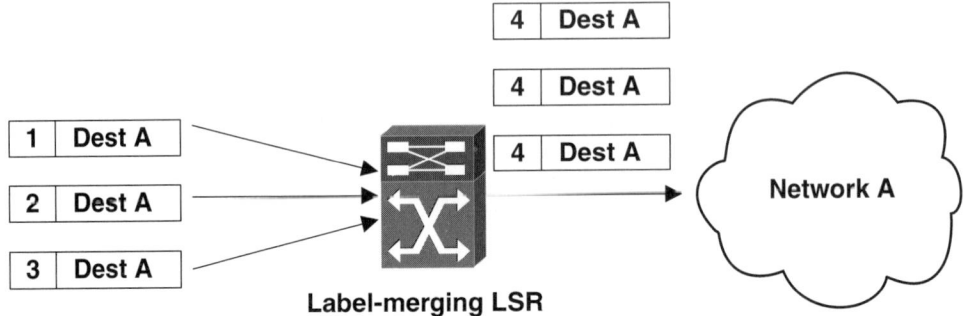

Figure 3–25 Label-merging LSR.

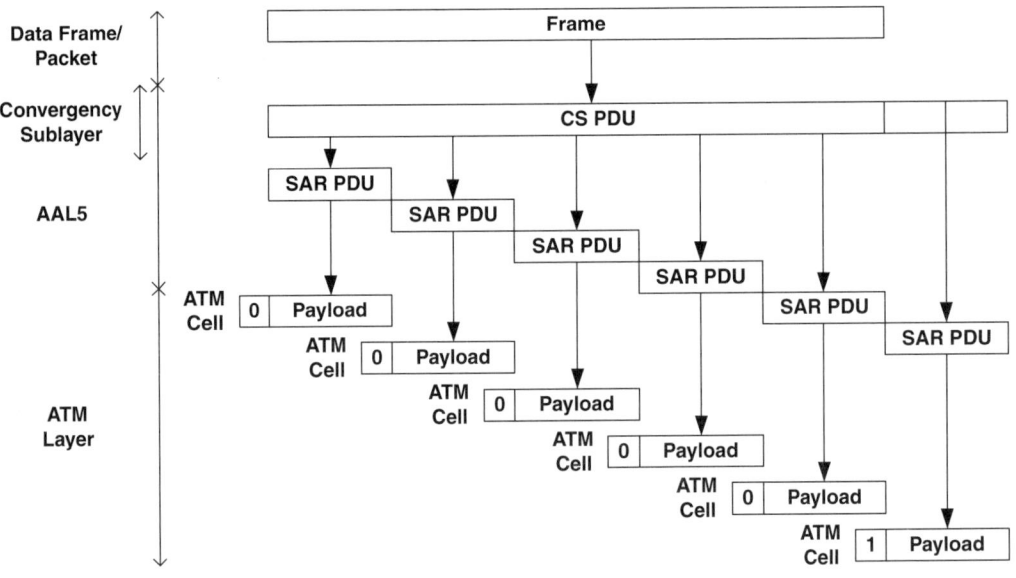

Figure 3–26 AAL5.

VC-merging in terms of additional buffering. Moreover, the overhead decreases as utilization increases, or as traffic becomes more bursty.

MANIPULATING THE TTL FIELD
Only members of the edge ATM-LSR domain can manipulate the TTL field. By contrast, ATM-LSRs in general do not modify the TTL field at all. The TTL field of an unlabeled packet received by an edge LSR is taken from the TTL field of the IP header. If a packet is received by an edge LSR as a labeled

packet, the TTL information is taken from the TTL field of the label stack entry on top of the label stack of the generic MPLS encapsulation.

If a hop count was associated with the label binding, then the outgoing TTL value is set to the difference between the incoming TTL value and the hop count. The result is encoded in the TTL field of the placeholder label stack entry, on top of the label stack. There is no way to encode a TTL value in the ATM header itself. If the result is zero or less than zero, the packet will be discarded and an ICMP message may be returned to the source if possible. If no hop count was associated with the label binding, the outgoing TTL value is set to one less than the incoming TTL value. Again, if the result is zero or less than zero, the packet will be dropped and an ICMP message may be generated (see above).

Labels and Label Distribution Methods

The MPLS architecture describes a label as representing an FEC. The information about which label is bound to which FEC has to be shared between adjacent LSRs. Various procedures can be used to exchange this label binding information between LSRs. The label binding information can be exchanged by a dedicated protocol such as the LDP or by legacy protocols that use additional attributes to "piggyback" the label binding information. This is done, for example, by protocols such as RSVP, MP-BGP, Protocol Independent Multicast (PIM), and others. There are also efforts to standardize new protocols for certain applications of MPLS like CR-LDP for TE. However, we will focus on LDP as a basic method for label distribution/binding for unicast, destination-based traffic, and on legacy protocols with specific extensions that will support MPLS applications like MPLS VPNs (MP-BGP) and TE (RSVP). Defining a specific new protocol set, like CR-LDP and others, for each new application may slow down the introduction of new MPLS applications and may introduce new problems in terms of multivendor interoperability.

LDP—The Label Distribution Protocol

The most prevalently used means of distributing labels in MPLS is with the Label Distribution Protocol (LDP). LDP is a protocol that is run between adjacent LSRs and is used to exchange label-to-FEC mappings between LSRs. Two

LSRs that run LDP and that have an LDP session with each other are called LDP peers. LDP peers may be connected via multiple interfaces, but will always have one single LDP session if these interfaces share the same label space. By exchanging FEC-to-label mappings, they can communicate and propagate information about label assignment. LDP is a bi-directional protocol, so only one LDP session is needed to communicate label information between the two LDP peers.

There are two types of label spaces:

- **Per-interface label space**—Interface-specific incoming labels are used for interfaces that use interface resources for labels. Examples of such interfaces are label-controlled ATM interfaces that use VCIs as labels and Frame Relay interfaces that use DLCIs as labels. The use of a per-interface label space only makes sense when the LDP peers are "directly connected" over an interface and the labels being distributed are only going to be used for traffic sent over that interface.
- **Per-platform label space**—Platform-wide incoming labels are used for interfaces that can share the same labels. This label space is commonly used on non-ATM and non–Frame Relay interfaces.

An LDP identifier is a six-octet quantity used to identify an LSR label space. The first four octets encode an IP address assigned to the LSR, which is typically the base IP address of the LSR. The last two octets identify a specific label space within the LSR.

```
<IP address> : <label space ID>
(e.g., 10.1.1.1:0, 195.0.0.5:2)
```

Figure 3–27 shows an example of multiple interfaces that share the same label space.

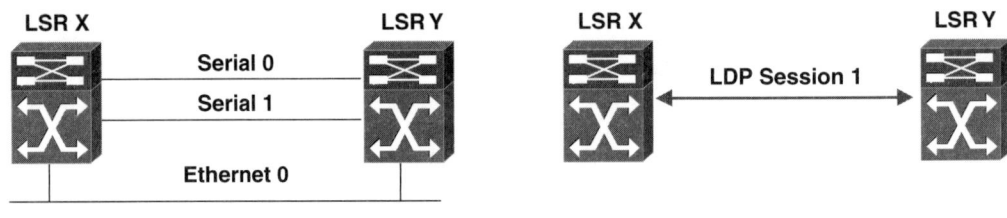

Figure 3–27 LDP sessions—Scenario 1.

Figure 3–28 shows an example where the ATM interface has a different label space from the other interfaces. Thus, there are two simultaneous LDP sessions running between the two LDP peers.

As described in [IETF-23], there are four categories of LDP messages:

i. **Discovery messages**—These are used to announce and maintain the presence of an LSR in a network.
ii. **Session messages**—These are used to establish, maintain, and terminate sessions between LDP peers.
iii. **Advertisement messages**—These are used to create, change, and delete label mappings for FECs.
iv. **Notification messages**—These are used to provide advisory information and signal error information.

LDP OPERATION

The initialization procedure of LDP is handled via a mechanism whereby directly connected LSRs send Hello messages destined to all routers present on a particular subnet. Each Hello message is sent as a UDP packet and is directed to a specific port. Once established, the LDP session between two LSRs runs over a TCP connection to provide reliability during the LDP message exchange phase.

LDP PROTOCOL STRUCTURE

[IETF-23] describes the LDP in the following way:

LDP message exchanges are accomplished by sending LDP PDUs over LDP session TCP connections (TCP port 646), with the exception of Hello messages, which use UDP port 646.

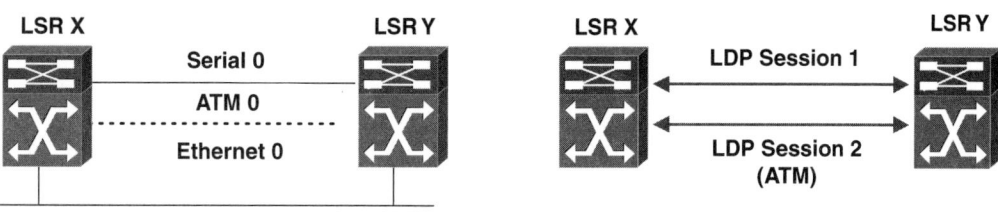

Figure 3–28   LDP sessions—Scenario 2.

Each LDP PDU can carry one or more LDP messages. Note that the messages in an LDP PDU need not be related to one another. For example, a single PDU could carry a message advertising FEC label bindings for several FECs, another message requesting label bindings for several other FECs, and a third Notification message signaling some event.

Each LDP PDU is an LDP header followed by one or more LDP messages as shown in Figure 3–29.

- **Version**—A two-octet unsigned integer containing the version number of the protocol. This version of the specification specifies LDP version 1.
- **PDU Length**—A two-octet integer specifying the total length of this PDU in octets, excluding the Version and PDU Length fields. The maximum allowable PDU Length is negotiable when an LDP session is initialized. Prior to completion of the negotiation, the maximum allowable length is 4096 bytes.

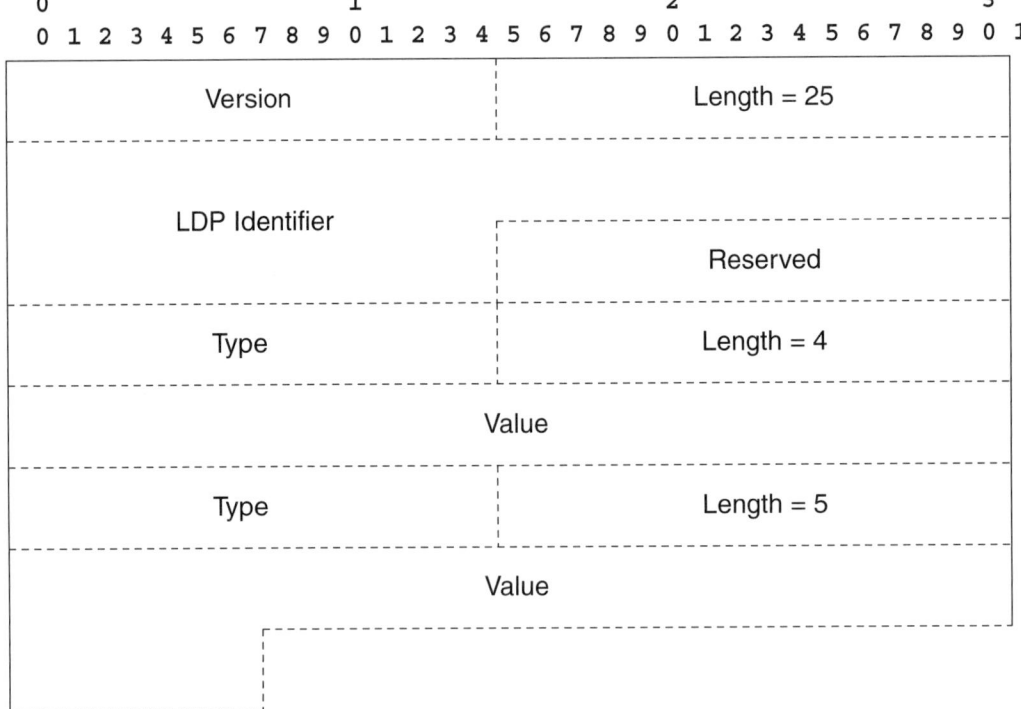

Figure 3–29 LDP header.

- **LDP Identifier**—A six-octet field that uniquely identifies the label space of the sending LSR to which this PDU applies. The first four octets encode an IP address assigned to the LSR. This address should be the router ID, which is also used to identify the LSR in loop detection path vectors. The last two octets identify a label space within the LSR. For a platform-wide label space, these should both be zero.

The following message types are defined in [IETF-23] for LDP:

- Notification message
- Hello message
- Initialization message
- KeepAlive message
- Address message
- Address Withdraw message
- Label Mapping message
- Label Request message
- Label Abort Request message
- Label Withdraw message
- Label Release message

LDP messages use the format illustrated in Figure 3–30:

- **U bit**—Unknown message bit. Upon receipt of an unknown message, if U is clear (=0), a notification is returned to the message originator; if U is set (=1), the unknown message is silently ignored.
- **Message Type**—Identifies the type of a message.
- **Message Length**—Specifies the cumulative length in octets of the Message ID, Mandatory Parameters, and Optional Parameters.
- **Message ID**—A 32-bit value used to identify this message. Used by the sending LSR to facilitate identifying Notification messages that may apply to this message. An LSR sending a Notification message in response to this message should include this Message ID in the Notification message; see the section titled "Notification Message."
- **Mandatory Parameters**—A variable-length set of required message parameters. Some messages have no required parameters.
- **Optional Parameters**—A variable-length set of optional message parameters. Many messages have no optional parameters.

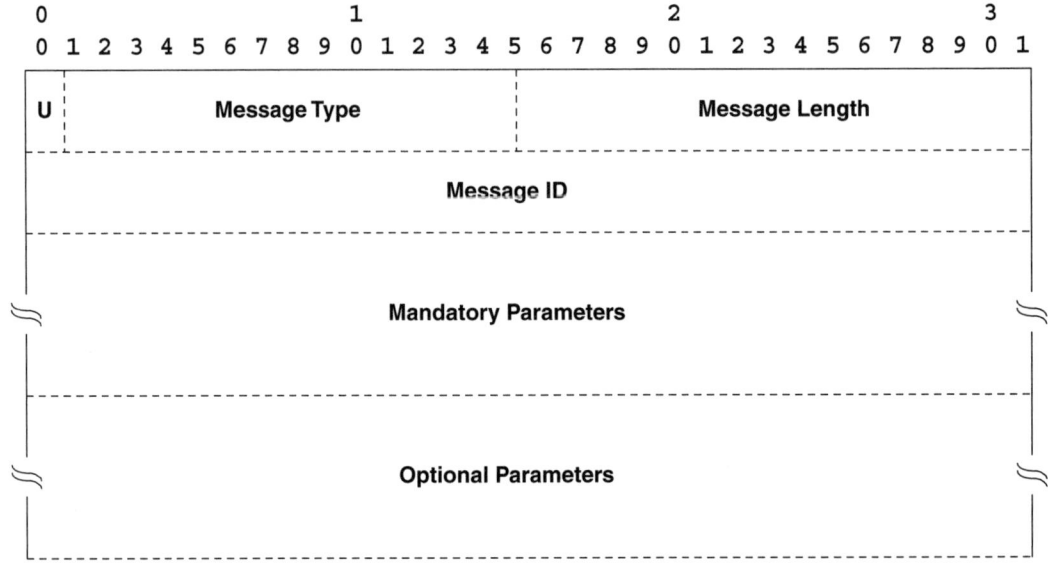

Figure 3–30 LDP message format.

LDP uses the Type/Length/Value (TLV) encoding scheme for almost all parameters carried in LDP messages.

An LDP TLV is encoded as a two-octet field that uses 14 bits to specify a type, 2 bits to specify a behavior when an LSR doesn't recognize the type, followed by a two-octet Length field and a variable-length Value field (see Figure 3–31).

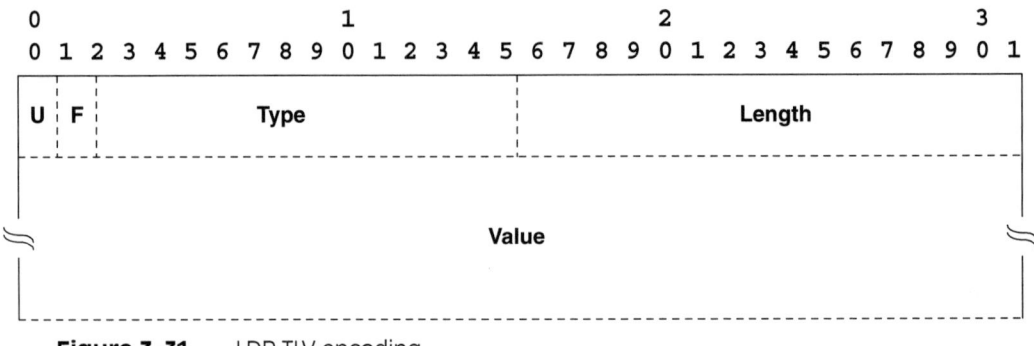

Figure 3–31 LDP TLV encoding.

- **U bit**—Unknown TLV bit. Upon receipt of an unknown TLV, if U is clear (=0), a notification must be returned to the message originator and the entire message must be ignored; if U is set (=1), the unknown TLV is silently ignored and the rest of the message is processed as if the unknown TLV did not exist.
- **F bit**—Forward unknown TLV bit. This bit applies only when the U bit is set and the LDP message containing the unknown TLV is to be forwarded. If F is clear (=0), the unknown TLV is not forwarded with the containing message; if F is set (=1), the unknown TLV is forwarded with the containing message.
- **Type**—Encodes how the Value field is to be interpreted.
- **Length**—Specifies the length of the Value field in octets.
- **Value**—An octet string of Length octets that encodes information to be interpreted as specified by the Type field.

LABEL DISTRIBUTION—DOWNSTREAM VS. DOWNSTREAM-ON-DEMAND

There are two basic mechanisms for assigning labels. If the upstream LSR explicitly asks for a label binding to a certain FEC and the downstream LSR answers with a Label Binding message, this is called downstream-on-demand (Figure 3–32). If the upstream LSR does not ask for a specific label binding and the downstream LSR sends out a Label Binding message, this is called unsolicited downstream, or simply downstream label distribution (Figure 3–33).

If ATM is used as the encapsulation method for the labels, then downstream-on-demand is used for label allocation. FECs, where the upstream LSR uses the downstream LSR as a next hop, will get a label binding. Unsolicited downstream label distribution may be used only if all ATM-LSRs support VC-merge.

In many situations, MPLS with ATM as a link encapsulation method is used in a Ships-in-the-Night configuration, where MPLS shares the same links with legacy ATM connections, like PVCs or SVCs that use a certain predefined VPI/VCI range. This may lead to a smaller label space than on links with generic MPLS encapsulation, where 20 bits can be used to encode label values.

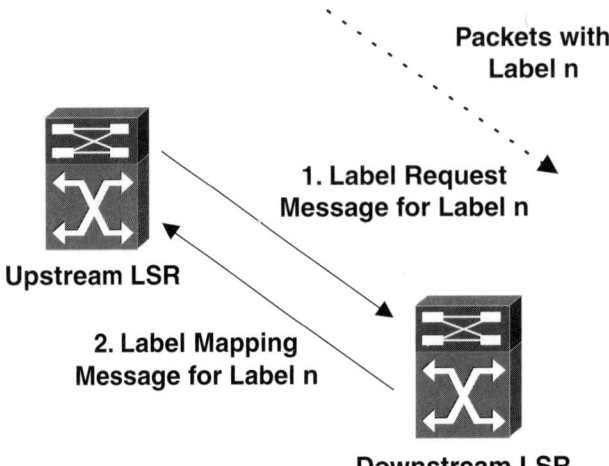

Figure 3-32   Label distribution—downstream-on-demand.

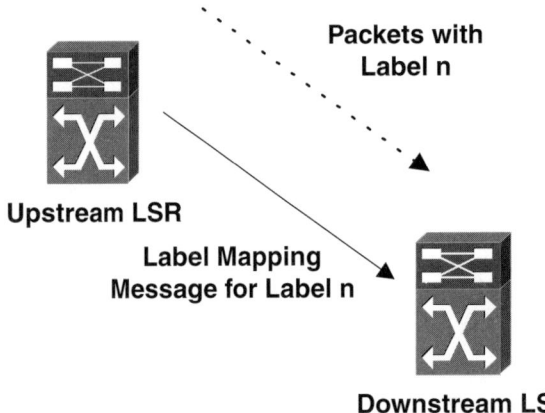

Figure 3-33   Label distribution—unsolicited downstream.

It is expected that both label distribution methods will be implemented in LSRs. The method actually used on a link between two LSRs has to be negotiated by two adjacent LSRs.

In the downstream and downstream-on-demand modes, label binding for outgoing labels is performed by the remote downstream LSR, and binding for incoming label values is performed locally. Conversely, upstream label distribution operates the other way around. That is, the local decision for label binding determines the outgoing label. Label binding for incoming label values is performed by the remote upstream LSR. Another way of distributing the label binding information is to perform the binding at the upstream neighbor (Figure 3–34).

Currently, LDP only concerns itself with the downstream and downstream-on-demand distribution methods just described. There is presently no support for upstream label distribution included in LDP [IETF-23]. Nevertheless, there may be some benefits in upstream label allocation if multicasting is used. Namely, easier label allocation in multiaccess networks is possible if the same label can be kept when a downstream LSR leaves a multicast group. In addition, faster LSP setup is possible under certain conditions (see IETF-25).

ORDERED VS. INDEPENDENT LSP CONTROL

The setup of an LSP can be done in two different ways: either in ordered or in independent control mode. In *independent control mode* (Figure 3–35), every LSR binds a label to an FEC as soon as it has received a label binding request for that particular FEC. Independent control is defined as a situation whereby each LSR will independently bind labels to FECs and distribute them.

Conversely, *ordered control mode* (Figure 3–36) is defined as a non-egress LSR that must wait until it has received a label binding for a particular FEC from its downstream LSR before distributing that label binding further. This is essentially an egress-controlled process. By ordered, it is meant that an LSR will bind a label to an FEC only if it has received a label for that particular FEC. That is, ordered control mode is used when the LSP has to follow a specific path, hence it is used with TE. Ordered control mode is used over ATM interfaces.

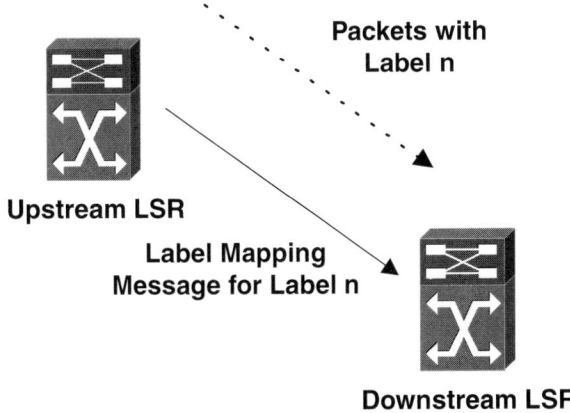

Figure 3–34   Label distribution—upstream.

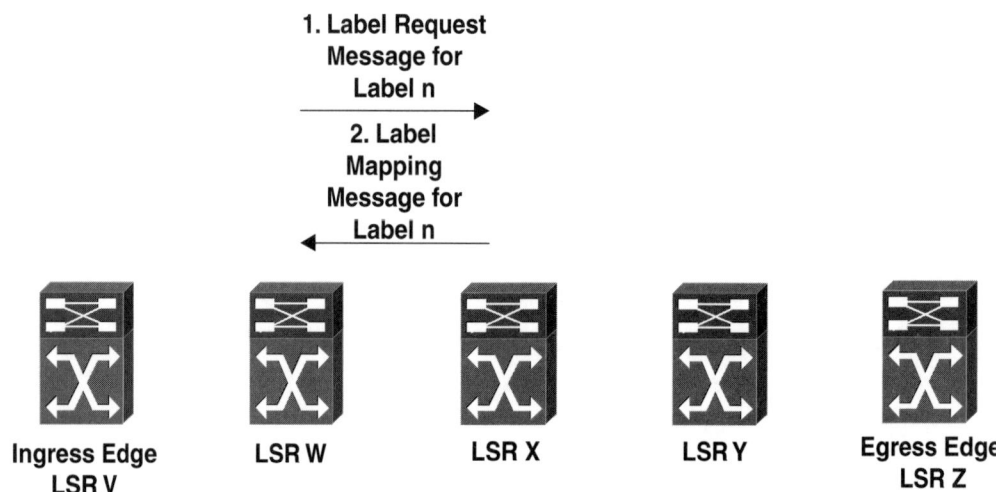

Figure 3–35 LSP setup—independent control.

In Figure 3–35, if LSR W decides to request a label binding from its downstream peer, LSR X will respond immediately with a label value corresponding to the FEC associated with this label without prior notification of its downstream peer, LSR Y. At the same time, another LSR (in our example, LSR Y) could request a label binding from its downstream peer. It would then receive a Label Mapping message with the appropriate label value.

In the scenario depicted in Figure 3–36, LSR W sends a Label Request message to its downstream peer. LSR X will not immediately answer with a Label Mapping message. Instead, it will send a prior Label Request message to its downstream peer. This continues until the egress LSR (LSR Z in the example) is reached. LSR Z will send a Label Mapping message to its upstream peer, LSR Y, and so on, until the Label Mapping message reaches the LSR that initially issued the request. In the example, this process will continue until LSR W is reached.

The mode of operation, either independent or ordered control, affects the overall behavior of the system. While independent control guarantees expedited setup of the LSP, it also imposes the risk of race conditions. For example, if an LSP is set up in different parts of the MPLS network simultaneously, based on different routing information resulting from a route "flap," there is the possibility that routing protocol convergence may influence the behavior and outcome

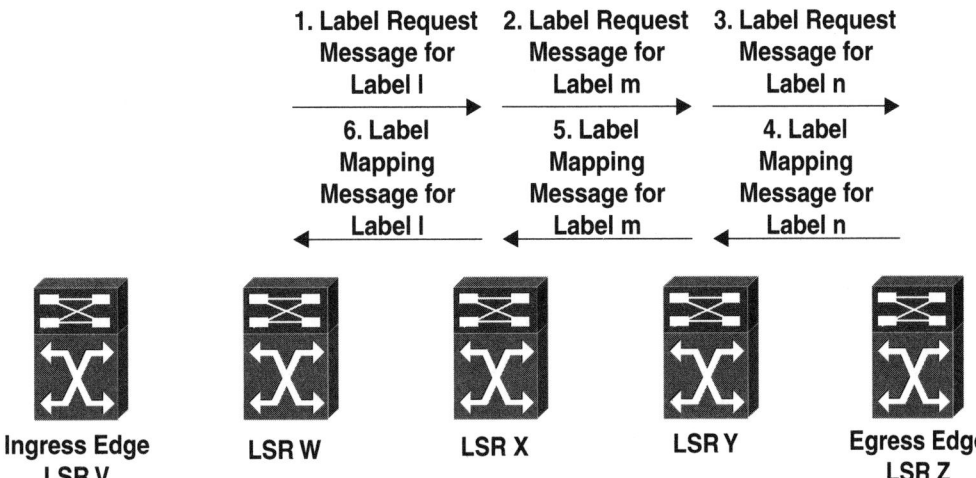

Figure 3–36 LSP setup—ordered control.

of the LSP setup. At the same time, loop prevention based on processing path vectors will not work if labels are bound before the entire path to the egress LSR is known at the time of label binding. In practice, it is a general rule of thumb that independent control mode is used in pure router MPLS networks, while ordered control mode is used for ATM MPLS networks. Ordered control gives us greater stability with the trade-off of greater latency experienced during path setup. Due to higher interdependencies of the LSRs, overall stability is improved and path vector information can be used to avoid loops.

Independent control more closely resembles the model of IP routing with distributed route calculation, while ordered control resembles connection-oriented mechanisms that use signaling protocols to establish connections before actually transferring data traffic.

LOOP DETECTION

The detection of a looping LSP is accomplished by using both the Path Vector field and the Hop Count field. Using the Path Vector field to identify loops during LSP setups gives rise to the possibility of detecting an LSP loop during the first time a Path Setup message is returned to the initiating LSR. The Hop Count field simply uses the Max_Hopcount value, which is typically set to 255, to detect a looping message. As you would expect, the hop count value in the Hop Count field of a message is incremented at each node as it traverses the network. If at any time this value exceeds the value specified by Max_Hopcount, it will be silently dropped. While processing path vectors can prevent the existence of loops completely, it does carry the trade-off of requiring some additional processing power at each LSR, as well as additional time to perform the path vector sanity check. Use of only the hop count value is easier to implement, but has the disadvantage of only restricting looping traffic from consuming too many network resources.

Each LSR appends the Path Vector field with its LSR ID. Thus, each LSR may first scan an incoming message's Path Vector field in an effort to locate its LSR ID. If the LSR finds its LSR ID in the Path Vector entry, it will have detected a loop since the message must have been processed by the LSR once already (Figure 3–37). It will subsequently drop the message. For those familiar with BGP, this method is very similar to how BGP locates routing loops.

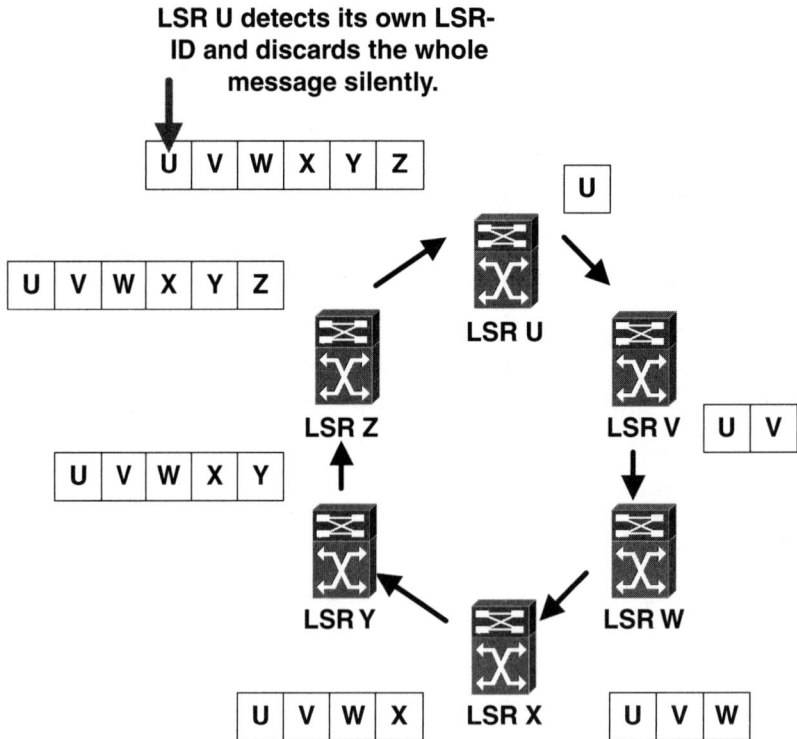

Figure 3–37 Loop detection with path vectors.

LDP EXTENDED DISCOVERY

There may be situations where it would be useful to run an LDP session between two nondirectly connected LSRs. For example, if two peers are physically located in two different ASs and are logically interconnected via an MPLS TE tunnel, this configuration might be desirable. The procedure to set up such an LDP session is called the extended discovery mechanism. To engage in LDP extended discovery, an LSR periodically sends LDP targeted Hellos to a specific IP address. LDP targeted Hellos are sent as UDP packets addressed to a well-known LDP discovery port at a specific address. An LDP targeted Hello sent by an LSR carries the LDP ID for the label space the LSR intends to use and possibly additional optional information.

The decision of when to request or when to advertise a label mapping to a peer is largely a local decision made by an LSR. In general, the LSR simply requests a label mapping from a neighboring LSR when it needs one, and advertises a label mapping to a neighboring LSR when it wants the neighbor to use a label. Correct operation of LDP requires reliable and in-order message delivery. To satisfy these requirements, LDP uses TCP connections between peers to carry Session, Advertisement, and Notification messages. That is, it uses TCP for everything except the UDP-based LDP discovery mechanism.

Label Distribution Protocols for TE

WHY USE MPLS TE?

TE is important because it allows a service provider to reduce the overall cost of operations through the efficient use of bandwidth resources. This is accomplished by preventing a situation that sometimes arises when some parts of a service provider network are over-utilized (congested), while other parts are under-utilized.

TE is a practice that is used by service providers today primarily in Layer 2 infrastructures. Service providers configure Layer 2 circuits, for example, with ATM PVCs that act as conduits for IP traffic. The advantage to this configuration is that since these circuits must be provisioned in the Layer 2 network, the user data does not notice these changes since it is typically only aware of a fully-meshed Layer 3 topology. There is no linkage between Layers 2 and 3 in this configuration other than Layer 3 being aware of some of the underlying interfaces on which Layer 3 interfaces are run. It is, however, desirable for many service providers to have the ability to provision Layer 2 circuits at Layer 3. The advantages to doing this are that it first reduces one layer of complexity (i.e., link state updates, configuration, and management), as well as reduces the amount of equipment required to implement the network. MPLS TE enables ISPs to take advantage of this capability.

Dynamic adaptation is still required. It is needed for MPLS TE to be capable of offering the same level of resilience that Layer 2 technologies offer today. This can be achieved with features like fast re-route and the possibility of calculating and presignaling the backup routes that can quickly take over for unoperational tunnels.

To achieve this goal, an approach similar to the IntServ (integrated services) model was chosen. A traffic trunk can be imagined as a flow from some ingress point to some egress point. Service provider networks today might implement this as a path that begins at some ingress PoP (point of presence), continues through the backbone network, and terminates at some egress PoP. Such an example is shown in Figure 3–38.

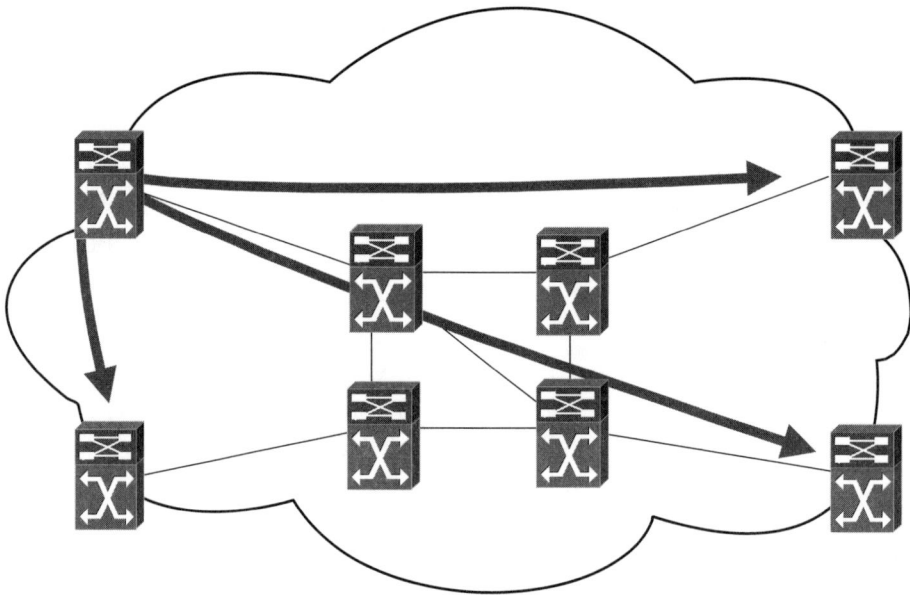

Figure 3–38 Traffic trunks in an MPLS network.

DISTRIBUTING LABELS WITH RSVP

INTRODUCTION TO RSVP

The Resource Reservation Protocol (RSVP) is defined in RFC 2205 [IETF-27]. It was designed to support an integrated services Internet [IETF-28]. RSVP is typically used by a host to specify the quality of service (QoS) from the network for application data streams or flows. RSVP can also be used by routers to deliver QoS requests for trunk connections between nodes. When successful, RSVP requests result in resources being reserved in each node along the data path. Although an application may act as a receiver and a sender at the same time, an RSVP request message may only attempt to allocate resources for unidirectional flows. RSVP does not transport application data; instead, it acts as a control protocol that relies on IPv4 or IPv6 to transmit its messages. To this end, RSVP does not provide routing capability, but again relies on existing (or future) unicast or multicast routing protocols to determine where packets can be forwarded.

To efficiently accommodate large groups, dynamic group membership, and heterogeneous receiver requirements, RSVP places the burden of responsibility on receivers to request a specific QoS for a desired flow. Once instigated, an RSVP request (Path message) from a receiver host application is passed from hop to hop along the data path. At each hop, each router's RSVP process examines the request, makes the appropriate resource reservation, and then forwards it on to the next hop. If the network node grants the reservation, it will keep track of this information in what is referred to as a "soft state" for the reservation. This state information is referred to as "soft" because it must be periodically refreshed or it will expire and be removed. This is actually one of the benefits of RSVP over other resource reservation protocols or schemes, since it allows RSVP to automatically deallocate resources if they are no longer being used. For example, if a route flap breaks the connectivity of a session, the resources for the session will eventually be reclaimed by all nodes as soon as they do not have the soft state refreshed. Sessions are refreshed through the periodic reception of RSVP Refresh messages that are sent at some interval by the source of the flow. When a packet reaches the desired end of the flow, the packet is returned along the reverse path as an RSVP Path Reservation message. If the packet successfully returns to the sender, the sender may then begin using the flow.

RSVP defines a session to be a data flow with a particular destination and transport layer protocol between one or more sources and one or more endpoints. An RSVP session is defined by the three-tuple: (destination address, protocol identifier, destination port). The destination address denotes the IP destination address of the destination of the flow. This address may be a unicast or multicast address. The protocol identifier specifies the IP protocol identifier. Finally, the destination port parameter is used to specify a generalized destination port. This optional value may specify some further demultiplexing point in the transport or application protocol layer. The destination port can define a UDP/TCP destination port field, an equivalent field in another transport protocol, or some other application-specific information [IETF-31].

The traffic control components of RSVP are outlined in Figure 3–39. These components typically consist of the packet classifier, admission control, the packet scheduler, and/or some other link layer-dependent mechanisms that guarantee that packets with higher priority will be sent along the link/interface first. The packet classifier determines the service class for each packet. The admission control module checks if sufficient resources are available on that particular link to satisfy an RSVP request for a certain service class. The control plane of RSVP consists of the application requesting QoS parameters from the RSVP module. The RSVP module that handles these requests passes them to all other necessary components and to other devices. The policy control module is responsible for verifying that the application requesting resources has the appropriate rights to request a certain service class. If this policy check fails, RSVP will return an error message to the application module.

AUGMENTING RSVP WITH MPLS FEATURES (MPLS-RSVP)
Several different protocol objects have been defined to extend basic RSVP to make it suitable as a signaling protocol for the establishment of LSPs in an MPLS network. Using RSVP to signal LSPs in the network results in the capability to have these LSPs automatically re-routed away from bottlenecks, link failures, or congestion. Furthermore, these extensions allow LSPs to support soft re-routing, preemption, and even loop detection. Fortunately, many of the components that are required to enable this functionality are present in basic RSVP. Only a few new components had to be added [IETF-29]. The application for this set of extensions to RSVP is MPLS TE. The augmented RSVP protocol is called MPLS-RSVP.

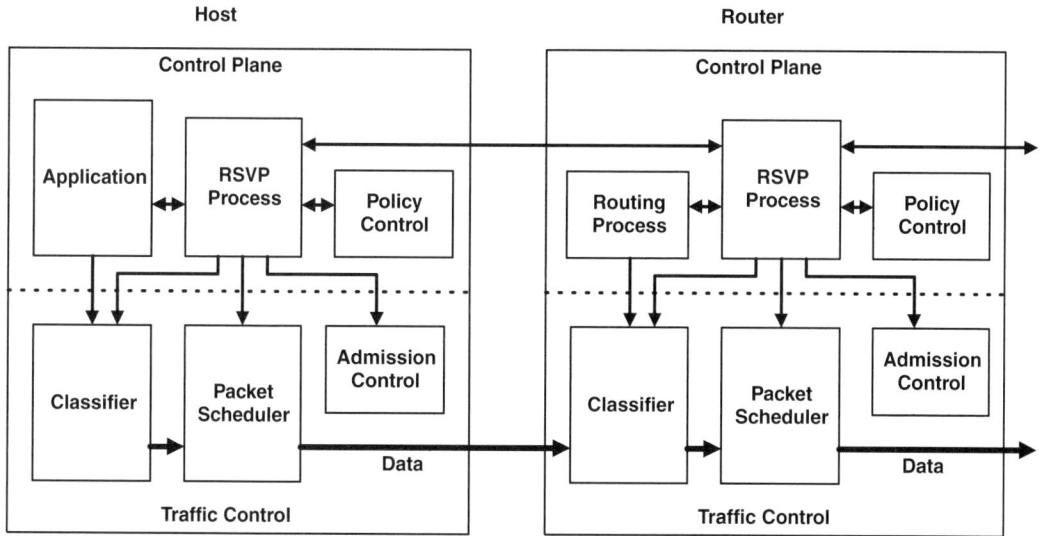

Figure 3–39 RSVP in hosts and routers [REF_WW].

MPLS-RSVP provides the following additional features to RSVP [IETF-30]:

- Downstream-on-demand label distribution
- Instantiation of explicit LSPs
- Allocation of network resources (e.g., bandwidth) to explicit LSPs
- Re-routing of established LSP tunnels in a smooth fashion using the concept of make-before-break
- Tracking of the actual route traversed by an LSP tunnel
- Diagnostics on LSP tunnels
- The concept of nodal abstraction
- Preemption options that are controlled administratively

If a router or switch implements both MPLS and MPLS-RSVP, it has the capability to associate labels with flows (i.e., RSVP sessions). In this situation, each RSVP session represents an FEC. As discussed in the earlier section titled "Simplicity of Operation," an FEC cannot only represent a destination address, but also additional parameters such as service. All packets belonging to the same FEC share the same set of attributes. These include destination address, source address, service class, and/or the path through the MPLS domain. At the ingress of the MPLS network, a label value is mapped to a set of packets (i.e., traffic flow) that is bound to an FEC. When traffic is mapped onto an LSP in this way, we call the resulting LSP an LSP tunnel. When labels are associated with traffic flows, it becomes possible for a router to identify the appropriate reservation state for a packet based on the packet's label value.

The signaling protocol model for RSVP-TE uses downstream-on-demand label distribution. A request to bind labels to a specific LSP tunnel is initiated by an ingress LSR through the RSVP Path message. Labels are allocated downstream and distributed (propagated upstream) by means of the RSVP Resv message. That is, each hop along the flow path learns of the new label upon receiving the RSVP Session/Resv messages. To achieve this, the RSVP Path message was augmented to carry a LABEL_REQUEST object, and the RSVP Resv message was extended with a special LABEL object. Label stacks are also supported by this mechanism [IETF-29].

The operator may specify the path taken by an RSVP-TE flow in several different ways: explicitly or loosely; he/she may calculate these paths manually via an offline calculation; or, he/she may allow the router to automatically calculate the path of the LSR. In any of these cases, the node where the LSP originates is responsible for assigning traffic to the LSP tunnel, and is therefore responsible for signaling LSP using RSVP-TE. In the simplest form, the operator specifies the destination only (the source is implicitly specified). This is a loosely routed path, and is what is typically used. The path taken by the LSP will be the shortest path as calculated by the constraint-based routing algorithm. Loose routes may be specified as additional hops along the path that are desired or are to be avoided. In the extreme case, the entire desired path of the LSP could be specified. This is referred to as an explicit path. When specified, an explicit path must be followed entirely. That is, routers along the path are not allowed to "fill in" any missing pieces of the path, as is possible with loose routing. This allows the operator the ability to completely engineer the path(s) taken by LSPs in the network.

The EXPLICIT_ROUTE object in MPLS-RSVP is used when an explicitly routed LSP is desired. The EXPLICIT_ROUTE object encapsulates a concatenation of hops, which constitutes the explicitly routed path. One additional way to identify the path of an LSP is to define a set of abstract nodes in the network path. An abstract node is a group of nodes whose internal topology is opaque to the ingress node of the LSP. Using this concept of abstraction, an explicitly routed LSP could be specified as a sequence of IP prefixes or a sequence of ASs.

The main advantage of using RSVP to establish LSP tunnels is that it allows operators to allocate resources such as bandwidth along the path of the LSP. If that bandwidth or other constraint is not available, or cannot be met, the LSP tunnel is not established. Bandwidth can also be allocated to an LSP tunnel using standard RSVP reservations and IntServ service classes. Although not mandatory, the reservation of service classes may be useful in situations where TE is deployed. It is also possible to define explicitly routed paths that can carry best-effort traffic without any bandwidth reservations.

SUMMARY OF RSVP ATTRIBUTES

The following list is an enumeration of the attributes of RSVP as defined in RFC 2205 [IETF-27]:

- RSVP makes resource reservations for both unicast and multicast applications, adapting dynamically to changing group membership as well as to changing routes.
- RSVP is a simplex protocol; that is, it makes reservations for unidirectional data flows only.
- RSVP is receiver-oriented. For example, the receiver of a data flow initiates and maintains the resource reservation used for that flow.
- RSVP maintains a "soft" state in routers and hosts, providing graceful support for dynamic membership changes and automatic adaptation to routing changes.
- RSVP is not a routing protocol, but depends on present and future routing protocols.
- RSVP transports and maintains traffic control and policy control parameters that are opaque to RSVP.
- RSVP provides several reservation models, or styles, to fit a variety of applications.
- RSVP provides transparent operation through routers that do not support it.
- RSVP supports both IPv4 and IPv6.

EXTENSIONS TO LDP (CR-LDP)

A while ago, it was determined that the basic functionality of LDP might not be sufficient for some applications of MPLS such as TE or MPLS VPNs. Thus, extensions to LDP were introduced in the form of Constraint-based Routing–

Label Distribution Protocol (CR-LDP) [IETF-26]. CR-LDP introduces some new TLVs that were designed to enable TE functionality in MPLS networks. QoS parameters have also been added to LDP to support different service classes in traffic-engineered paths. CR-LDP introduces a mechanism that supports the creation of end-to-end, constraint-based, and routed LSPs. As with RSVP, resources are reserved at each hop along the path of an LSP. The LSPs are automatically initiated by an ingress LSR, whereas RSVP-TE tunnels must be initiated by the operator.

The CR-LDP specification [IETF-26] introduces procedures that provide support for:

- **Strict and loose explicit routing**—A constraint-based route is a series of explicitly routed hops in a Label Request message. Each explicitly routed hop represents a node or group of nodes that is traversed by the LSP in the order listed in the TLV.
- **Specification of traffic parameters**—The traffic characteristics of a path are described in the Traffic Parameters TLV in terms of peak rate, committed rate, and service granularity. The peak and committed rates describe the bandwidth constraints of a path, while the service granularity can be used to specify a constraint on the delay variation that the CR-LDP MPLS domain may introduce to a path's traffic.
- **Route pinning**—A CR-LSP may be set up using route pinning if it is undesirable to change the path used by an LSP even when a better next hop becomes available at some LSR along the loosely routed portion of the LSP.
- **CR-LSP preemption through setup/holding priorities**—CR-LDP signals the resources required by a path on each hop of the route. If a route with sufficient resources cannot be found, existing paths may be rerouted to reallocate resources to the new path. This is the process of path preemption. Setup and holding priorities are used to rank existing paths (holding priority) and the new path (setup priority) to determine if the new path can preempt an existing path.
- **Resource class**—The network operator may classify network resources in various ways. These classes are also known as colors or administrative groups. When a CR-LSP is being established, it's necessary to indicate which resource classes the CR-LSP can draw from.

- **LSPID**—An LSPID is a unique identifier for a CR-LSP within an MPLS network.

CR-LDP [IETF-26] defines the following new TLVs:
- Explicit Route TLV
- Explicit Route Hop TLV
- Traffic Parameters TLV
- Preemption TLV
- LSPID TLV
- Route Pinning TLV
- Resource Class TLV
- CR-LSP FEC TLV

In this chapter, we focused our discussion on the operation and architecture of MPLS. This will be the foundation for subsequent chapters, where we will drill into VPNs, the predominant application for MPLS networks.

Although much of the complexity of MPLS is hidden under many layers of abstraction and an easy, configurable command-line interface, it is still important to have a good understanding of the technology when it comes to network planning and troubleshooting.

The next chapter will describe the nature of VPNs in general and MPLS VPNs in detail.

4

Introduction to Virtual Private Networks

NOTE

VPN: A Definition

In a very general way, Virtual Private Networks (VPNs) are defined as customer connectivity deployed on a shared infrastructure with the same policies as a private network. This shared infrastructure can leverage a service provider's IP, Frame Relay, or ATM backbone and may or may not utilize the public Internet.

It's All about Connectivity ...

Some years ago, this discussion might have begun with a survey of why network connectivity is important for a company, as well as why access to the Internet, both for the company's own employees as well as for its customers and its suppliers, is so important. We want to point out that these questions have already been decided in favor of a networked economy, where employees share information among themselves in milliseconds via an intranet and customers and suppliers share information with the company via the Internet or an extranet. Only companies that fully understand these principles will be a part of the e-commerce economy, which is not limited only to companies that directly deal with new technologies. Every company, no matter what kind of business they are involved in, will have to compete in a highly competitive landscape, where their competitors draw significant advantages from the use of communication technologies that are built on networking infrastructure. Every company that wants to share information with its customers and among its employees will have to deploy network connectivity between its different sites. The fact that the real capital of a company is in the knowledge of its employees and the fact that it is crucial for employees to have access to the collective knowledge of other employees make the decision to deploy network connectivity between employees and computer systems crucial for success. There are those who would say that all of this technology is unnecessary for a successful business because, after all, Rockefeller made his millions in a time without mobile phones. Although that is true, no one else at that time had a cellular phone either. Things would have been different if Rockefeller had been the only one *without* a cell phone when other businesses had them. Not having your business networked today is analogous to not having a cell phone in a time when everyone has them.

Many corporations today have already deployed intranets, with a large proportion of those providing connectivity to the Internet. When a company decides to deploy a corporate network, it only asks for network connectivity between some or all of its different sites. In general, it does not specify (or care) which technology is used to implement the network infrastructure. Instead, companies care about having connectivity. The aim is to enable communication among different computer systems and/or employees. These employees or systems may be located at different sites, they may be mobile employees, or those who work remotely, who wish to access the company's network resources via network access points.

The networks that connect different sites of a company are called private networks. These networks are referred to as such because they transport traffic that is exclusive to the company that owns these different sites. This was originally accomplished via private, point-to-point circuits that were leased from public carriers. However, in the early 1980s, corporations began to move toward the use of circuits that ran over a shared public network. This was originally an X.25 network. Two of the most remarkable advantages over pure leased-line networks were the link reliability and improved bit error rate. We could also see the first efforts to transport private data over data service provider networks. Additionally, the advantage of statistical multiplexing of data packets outpaced the static assignment of time slots of Time Division Multiplexing (TDM) technologies by far. While TDM always uses up the available bandwidth on a line, statistical multiplexing gave service providers the possibility to assign statistical access to the shared transport medium. Statistical multiplexing was the first big step toward a shared infrastructure for private networks.

The X.25 protocol caught on and soon became the most widely deployed circuit technology until the early 1990s, when Frame Relay came onto the scene. It was at this time that the need for the reliability mechanisms provided by X.25 at the data link layer waned due to the much-improved reliability of the underlying transmission infrastructure used for transport networks. Prior to this time, X.25's retransmission mechanisms were heavily relied upon. However, with the improvement of the Layer 2 network, this additional overhead was unnecessary, and only degraded performance. Thus, a faster data link protocol called Frame Relay began to gain acceptance and quickly took over all leased circuits sold for corporate connectivity purposes. Frame Relay additionally provided the possibility of using increased line speeds over X.25 that had a maximum of 19.2 Kbit/s at the time. Frame Relay also offered trafficshaping mechanisms referred to as backward explicit congestion notification (BECN) and forward explicit congestion notification (FECN). These features led to the implementation of a committed information rate (CIR). These mechanisms made Frame Relay the access protocol of choice for most private network connections. Finally, the ability to define permanent virtual connections (PVCs) with data link connection identifiers (DLCIs) gave network administrators the flexibility to set up connections with a moderate number of connection endpoints in a very easy way. Frame Relay was, however, not the Nirvana of circuit services.

While the demand for bandwidth, additional features, and services was still growing, the standards bodies, namely the International Technical Union—Telecommunication (ITU-T) and ATM Forum, worked on a new standard for circuit services. This new standard was called Asynchronous Transfer Mode (ATM). ATM was supposed to solve most of the problems encountered by Frame Relay. ATM uses the concept of fixed-size cells instead of the variable-length packets used by all other technologies of the time. ATM additionally defines a variety of different service types that facilitate the differentiated treatment of traffic in an effort to transport different kinds of services (voice, data, and video) over the same network.

The reality was that the deployment of this new technology showed that these features and services were rarely accessible to the end-user because the corresponding customer premise equipment was never cost-effective. Deployment of ATM also proved to be quite cumbersome due to the many different parameters and layers that needed to be configured for even the simplest of configurations to operate. Finally, the so-called killer application for ATM never materialized. It was thought that desktop video over ATM would be this application, but it did not yet exist. Thus, the high costs involved in deploying an ATM infrastructure for end-users were not justified, and consequently, the adoption of ATM technology waned. The use of ATM as a backbone technology for Frame Relay and Circuit Emulation Services (CES) for service providers has led to a moderate demand for the technology, but has not produced the breakthrough that was once promised by proponents of the technology. Although there are a number of limitations involved in ATM networking, it has to be mentioned that ATM was the only high-speed Wide Area Network (WAN) transport technology that was available for quite some time. ATM was available long before the introduction of Packet over SONET (POS), Gigabit Ethernet (GigE), or different implementations of Optical IP.

The third wave of the network revolution was initiated by a protocol, or better, a whole suite of protocols, that very few people would have given a chance when it was first deployed. This protocol was the Internet Protocol (IP) suite. The rise of the Internet changed the fundamental business communication focus from internal office-to-office to global interaction with both customers as well as other businesses. This shift in thinking began when it was clear that networking could and would change the way we live, work, and play. One important observation to make during all of this change is that it did not occur because of the IP itself; rather, it arose because of the way we are using these technologies. The real drivers behind networking technologies are the applications that create the value and opportunity for their users. E-commerce, private communication, new entertainment possibilities, and access to information are what were and are the driving forces behind the explosive acceptance of the Internet.

These were the drivers that forced IP into nearly every computer system, beginning with PCs, and later into mainframes and devices like mobile phones, personal digital assistants (PDAs), and TV set-top boxes.

The ubiquity of the IP protocol suite made it the protocol of choice for every kind of end-to-end communication. The use of IP is not limited to the pure transport of data traffic, but instead it supports applications like voice, video, and email. It should be clear then that if a company desires connectivity, what it needs is IP connectivity—not because of an ideological point of view, but because of very practical reasons such as the deployment of real services, including interactive learning, packet voice services, electronic commerce, multimedia applications (including videotelephones and videoconferencing), Web hosting (external Web sites), application hosting (intranet/extranet content hosting), and future IP applications that we have not yet envisioned.

Service providers have traditionally offered pure Layer 2 data transport services. This type of service forces service providers to compete only in terms of bandwidth, points of presence, service levels, and pricing. There is no efficient way to offer additional value-added services to customers when offering pure Layer 2 services. This may be a suitable business model when the market for circuit services is growing heavily and there is much greater demand for those services than providers can deploy. However, when the first saturation of the market is reached, it will be difficult to compete without further differentiation among service providers. The opportunity to allow customers to take responsibility for key parts of their networks gives service providers one such opportunity for service differentiation and customization. Companies are also embracing the needs of their customers, suppliers, and partners by deploying extranets. An extranet is an intranet that encompasses multiple businesses. With extranets, companies can reduce business process costs by facilitating supply-chain automation, electronic data interchange (EDI), and other forms of network commerce. A requirement of being able to provide such applications and services is an IP network infrastructure as well as an IP awareness by applications that will utilize this network.

It should now be clear that IP and VPNs, which are constructed from and which provide IP services, are not only a technological or efficiency issue for a service provider; instead, they play a major role in the economic future of service providers. IP VPNs allow service providers to stay competitive and keep their businesses growing.

A Taxonomy of VPNs

There are several technologies available that enable a service provider to offer VPN services. There are ways to build VPNs with Layer 2 networks such as ATM and Frame Relay. These techniques have been used during the last couple of years. They are well understood and are widely deployed in the field today.

Another way of building VPNs is to use Layer 3 networks. A very common approach is to use generic route encapsulation (GRE) for this purpose. GRE encapsulates an IP packet into another IP packet. The service provider can then build "tunnels" between customer sites to provide private services over a public infrastructure, which gives the customer the impression that they have private point-to-point services. This is accomplished by encapsulating and optionally encrypting customer packets before they travel between sites. These tunnels can be considered normal interfaces on the routers at each customer site, and have the advantage of transporting traffic in a manner that does not require any special handling within the service provider's network. The simplicity of this solution might seem to be appealing for service providers; however, GRE lacks scalability in large VPN implementations for several reasons.

Hub-and-Spoke vs. Fully-Meshed

There are two ways to connect customer sites in a VPN. The first method is the so-called "hub-and-spoke" topology. This topology connects all sites (the spokes) to a central site (the hub). The example depicted in Figure 4-1 illustrates this. The obvious feature of this model of interconnection is that all traffic between remote sites must be routed through the central site. This architecture is useful when the majority of the traffic goes to the central site. If traffic patterns show that all sites communicate frequently with each other, this model becomes less attractive than the fully-meshed model. The obvious drawback in this topology is the problem of connectivity if the hub goes down, or if any of the connections to the hub are lost. To solve this problem, a second backup hub is frequently connected to add an element of redundancy.

If traffic patterns indicate that the majority of sites communicate directly with each other, the fully-meshed topology depicted in Figure 4-2 is the better

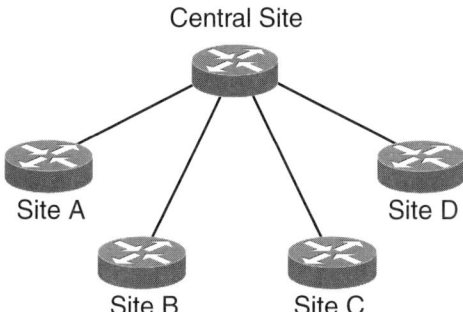

Figure 4–1 Hub-and-spoke topology.

choice. In this topology, all sites are at most only a single hop away from each other. That is, every site is directly connected with all other sites. This topology is optimized for peer-to-peer traffic between all sites.

If we now consider the number of GRE tunnels that would be necessary to connect all sites in the fully-meshed topology, it should be clear that this number grows with a square factor. When compared to the linear growth of tunnels in hub-and-spoke configurations, this is unappealing in large network deployments due to the fact that the provisioning expenditure for such a service becomes prohibitively high when the number of sites grows (see also the section in Chapter 2 titled "Scalability").

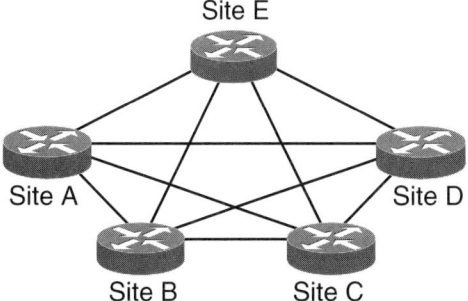

Figure 4–2 Fully-meshed topology.

IPSec

A similar approach is to use IP Security Protocol (IPSec) tunnels to build VPNs. The benefit of using IPSec is clearly the security aspect of this solution. All data that is transported over the service provider network is encrypted. IPSec and generic route encapsulation (GRE) can also be used together. While the limitation of GRE in fully-meshed topologies is the provisioning expenditure, the additional limitation with IPSec is the processing power requirements of the site routers. One other limitation of using IPSec is that the encryption/decryption function is very processor-intensive. This is prohibitive on low-end routers, and therefore limits its deployment.

Other VPN Technologies

Other protocols that allow service providers to offer VPN services are L2TP, L2F, and PPTP. Each of these protocols possesses very similar functionality. L2F and PPTP are the predecessors of L2TP, which is standardized by the IETF. The protocols relay PPP sessions and forward them to an aggregation device called an L2TP network server (LNS). A typical application of this model is the use of L2TP with dial-up or ADSL services to build VPNs. Both access technologies use Point-to-Point Protocol (PPP) as the Layer 2 protocol. The limitation is clearly the use of PPP as the Layer 2 protocol. Other Layer 2 technologies are simply not applicable to be used for VPNs with L2TP, L2F, or PPTP. A very common combination is the use of L2TP and MPLS. L2TP is used to put dial-up or ADSL users in a certain VPN (see also Chapter 7).

MPLS VPN

Service providers can use MPLS as a VPN technology. MPLS has the benefit of being very scalable due to its distributed architecture and flexibility. This scalability is further enhanced by its independence of Layer 2 technologies. MPLS also offers a variety of additional services such as traffic engineering (TE) and Quality of Service (QoS), which may be used in conjunction with the VPN service.

Feature Matrix

Table 4–1 illustrates which type of VPN technology is best-suited for which application:

Table 4–1 Different VPN Technologies at a Glance

	ATM/FRAME RELAY	GRE	IPSEC	L2TP, L2F	MPLS
Topology	Hub-and-spoke, fully-meshed	Hub-and-spoke, fully-meshed	Hub-and-spoke, fully-meshed	Hub-and-spoke	Hub-and-spoke, fully-meshed
Scalability — Configuration Management	Limited in fully-meshed configuration	Limited in fully-meshed configuration	Limited in fully-meshed configuration	No architecture limitations—configuration information can be stored in centralized servers.	Not limited
Scalability — Processing Requirements	No limitations on Layer 2. Overlay model for Layer 3 has limitations (described in "Overlay Model—Layer 2 VPNs").	Performance can be degraded because of different switch mode in the router when routing GRE traffic.	Limited in fully-meshed configuration. Number of concurrent IPSec sessions and IPSec throughput per router limited.	No architecture limitations	Not limited because of distributed architecture.
Security	High security	No security features; can be combined with IPSec for traffic encryption.	High security	Uses authentication algorithm; can be combined with IPSec for traffic encryption.	High security similar to ATM and Frame Relay; can also be combined with IPSec.

Table 4–1 Different VPN Technologies at a Glance *(Continued)*

	ATM/FRAME RELAY	GRE	IPSEC	L2TP, L2F	MPLS
Static — Dynamic	Static (PVCs) and dynamic (SVCs)	Static	Static	Dynamic	Static and dynamic
Quality of Service	ATM Forum service classes (CBR, ABR, VBR, UBR); Frame Relay uses CIR	IP QoS (type of service, IP precedence, or DiffServ code point)	IP QoS (type of service, IP precedence, or DiffServ code point)	IP QoS (type of service, IP precedence, or DiffServ code point) only per-tunnel configurable; no per-user QoS possible	MPLS EXP bits or multi-VC in ATM
Access Technology Dependent	Limited to ATM and Frame Relay access	Not limited to any particular access technology	Not limited to any particular access technology	Depends on PPP access technology	Not limited to any particular access technology
Management	Managed by Layer 2 NMS; no information on Layer 3 (IP) available	Customized configuration management	Configuration management available	Managed from AAA server (e.g., with Radius)	Provisioning management available

Overlay Model—Layer 2 VPNs

One way a service provider can build VPNs is to use a connection-oriented data link protocol to run network protocols "on top" of these logical links. This is the case with ATM and Frame Relay.

In Figure 4–3, each customer is connected to the service provider network with one or more virtual circuits. These virtual circuits are switched inside the service provider network to build paths to the other sites of the customer network. The customer will build routing adjacencies between its routers located at the various sites and run a routing protocol "on top" of these pipes. The routing topology is invisible to the service provider in this case, since the service provider only switches Layer 2 traffic through the pre-established virtual circuits.

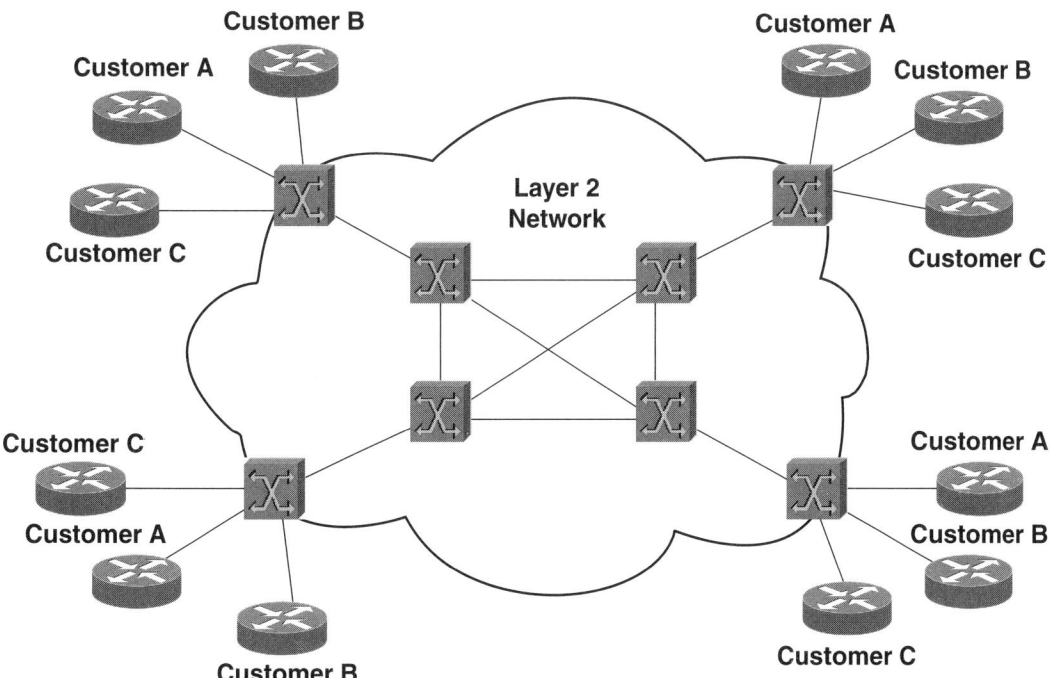

Figure 4-3 Layer 2 VPN architecture—overview 1.

In Figure 4–4, IP intelligence is only present at the customer's router; the service provider network devices will not participate in any Layer 3 routing process. Layer 2 VPNs are used in many different applications. For example, the aggregation of dial-in traffic in VPNs is accomplished with L2TP, a Layer 2 VPN service. The connection of several sites in a hub-and-spoke style is often implemented with ATM or Frame Relay, which are Layer 2 VPN services. It should be said that many services could be implemented with Layer 2 VPNs. Only in scenarios where a large number of sites in a fully-meshed connection style are required will MPLS VPN be more scalable. Another advantage of using MPLS VPNs in this situation is the inherent convergence of Layer 2 and Layer 3 networks. The advantage of this convergence is simply that where service providers need an ATM, a Frame Relay, and an IP network, they can now offer the same VPN services over a single MPLS network.

In Figure 4–5, every router at the customer site has to maintain a connection to all of its routing peers to maintain optimal routing between all sites. This

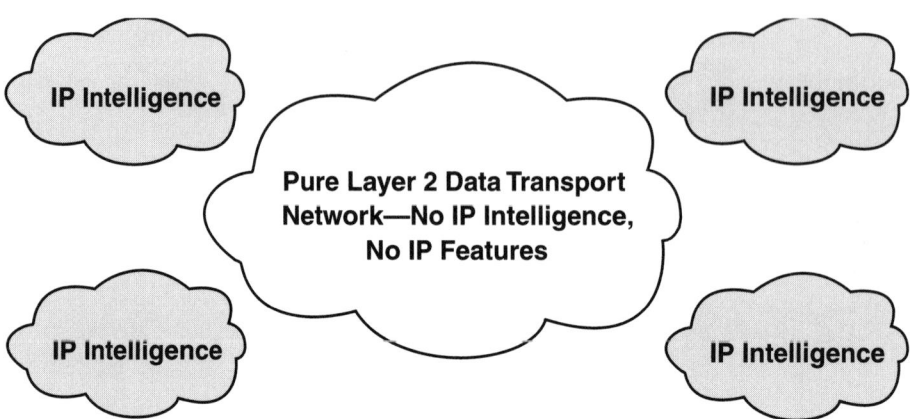

Figure 4-4 Layer 2 VPN architecture—overview 2.

model may be suitable for a moderate number of interconnected sites, but it has scalability problems from a routing perspective when the number of sites reaches a certain critical threshold. There is no exact limit when this critical level is reached, but one can say that either the number of routing peers or the administrative overhead of setting up all these new connections by the service provider may influence the maximum number of edge nodes.

In terms of scalability problems, this networking model has the property that each additional site will increase the number of connections by (n-1)/2, where n is the total number of connected sites. The number of endpoints in this model is twice as high as the number of PVCs between all attached routers at the edge of the network. The increase of the number of PVC endpoints vs the number of nodes is shown in Figure 4-6. The administrative costs to maintain such a topology is directly proportional to the number of attached sites as follows:

```
N = (n*(n-1))
```

One possible way to abate this problem is to build a partially-meshed system. The drawback of this approach is that one or more additional hops will have to be introduced, and the loss of certain connections in this network will result in a total loss of connectivity for some users. That may be suitable for certain applications, depending on either the additional latency introduced by the new hop(s) or the average time lost due to the loss of connectivity. In fact, the fully-meshed system can be dismantled insofar as to make it approximate the connections of a hub-and-spoke model. This, of course, will approximate the performance and

Overlay Model—Layer 2 VPNs 93

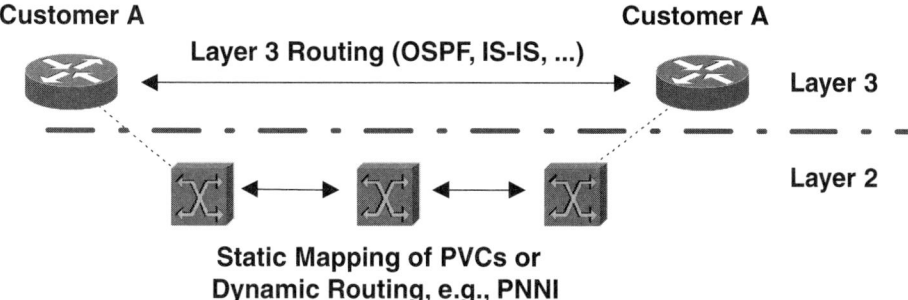

Figure 4-5 Layer 2 VPN architecture—routing.

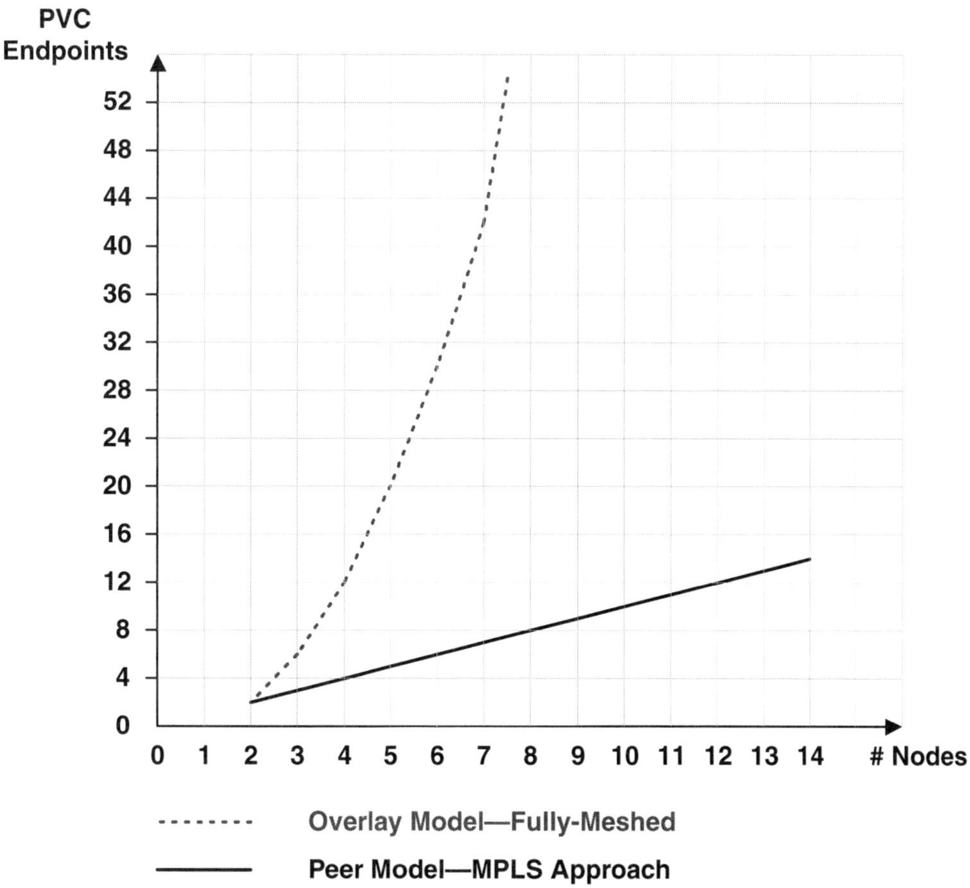

Figure 4-6 Scalability problem in a fully-meshed network—number of PVC endpoints vs. number of nodes.

fault-handling characteristics of the hub-and-spoke model discussed earlier. The important point to note here is that reducing the level of connectivity will have the potential of developing a situation where there are a small number of connections, thereby providing few avenues for the recovery of connections in the event that the hubs are disabled.

Another problem related to the routing architecture of Layer 2 VPNs is the possible overload of the customer routers due to routing updates as mentioned in [DAVIE-1]. Under a worst-case condition, these routing updates may overload the routers and the actual data throughput may become unsatisfactory. This situation may occur if a link in the core of the service provider network that transports a significant number of connections of a customer routing domain fails. If this happens, on the order of N routers would start sending out link state advertisements (LSAs) to their n-1 routing peers. This would give us a total of n^2 routing updates. All of the n-1 routing peers would respond and reflood this information to n-1 neighbors, which would result in a total of n^3 routing. If we argue that the size of each routing update is also an order of n due to having to carry n-1 neighbors, we can then say that the total amount of information that is exchanged during a link failure in the core of a service provider network may be as high as n^4. Although this calculation represents a worst-case scenario, this still reflects a potential problem that could bring a fully-meshed network to its knees [DAVIE-1].

If we now consider the QoS over a service provider network, we will discover that a problem of mapping network layer service classes to Layer 2 service classes exists (see Figure 4–7). In short, a mapping between the network layer service classes and the Layer 2 service classes at the border of the service provider network must exist. This will allow a service provider to provide consistent QoS at both ends of a connection.

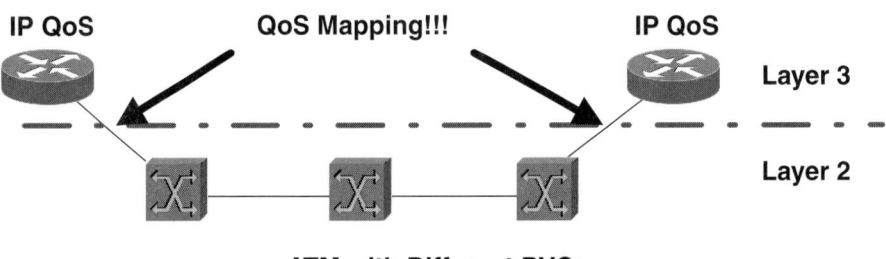

Figure 4-7 Mapping of service classes on Layer 2.

Each networking model or technology has its own ways to implement QoS features. Some models use the integrated services approach [IETF-28] to request certain traffic parameters from networking devices. Other networking models employ the differentiated services (DiffServ) architecture [IETF-2]. This model requires the use of certain codes in the header of each packet to obtain a certain treatment within the network in terms of queuing and packet prioritization. Whichever QoS model is implemented in a network, the problem of mapping the QoS features from the network layer, the IP protocol, to the underlying data link technology exists. The problem is to find an adequate way to map these QoS features to the adjacent layer. A solution would be to use a signaling protocol like RSVP that acts as a protocol-independent signaling protocol. Although this model has been discussed for RSVP over ATM in [IETF-1], it seems unlikely to be implemented in the short term because it lacks scalability in very large networks. The traffic patterns of today's Internet consist mainly of very short-lived flows. The other concern is that the number of these short-lived flows would be requested from host-to-host flow pairs and would overwhelm the processing power of the routers/switches in the core of the network. Therefore, the mapping of QoS features must be performed at the Open Systems Interconnection (OSI) layer boundaries. Another problem is to integrate IP multicasting with different WAN technologies.

The Peer Model—Layer 3 VPNs

The limitations of the overlay model combined with the possibility of providing virtually all existing and future services over one common network drove the demand for an alternative to Layer 2 VPNs. The primary requirement of a Layer 3 VPN is to provide a customer with a Layer- 3 network that resembles a privately installed one. This network must provide transport layer functionality to support services such as voice, video, and data over this common Layer 3 infrastructure. The common network should also be implemented with the same policies as a private network in terms of security and access (i.e., firewalls).

One such VPN architecture that facilitates the aforementioned requirements is called the "peer model" (see Figure 4–8). In this configuration, the customer equipment maintains a routing adjacency with the service provider edge routers. This is called "the peer model."

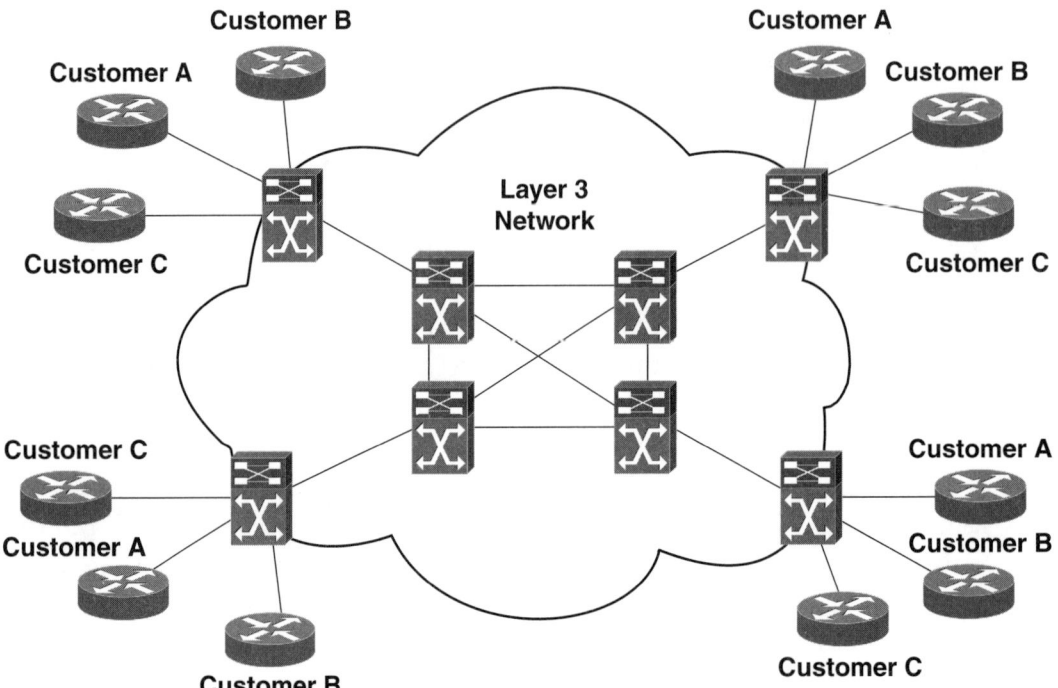

Figure 4-8 Layer 3 IP VPN architecture—overview 1.

All customer routers are connected to the service provider network and have only one routing neighbor (see Figure 4–9). This is in contrast to the overlay model, where every customer router has to maintain a logical connection to all its routing peers.

The customer router and service provider router must run an IGP or BGP routing protocol such as OSPF, IS-IS, BGP, etc., to exchange routing information between them (see Figure 4–10). The number of routing neighbors as well as the number of routing updates are drastically reduced with this approach. The possibility to reduce the number of routing peers from n(n-1) in the overlay model to one or two routing peers gives us a much higher level of scalability. Only two connections are required in the case of a redundant connection to the service provider's edge node. The possibility to scale the number of customer sites up to many thousands and beyond is an attractive feature of this architecture.

Figure 4-9 Layer 2 VPN architecture—overview 2.

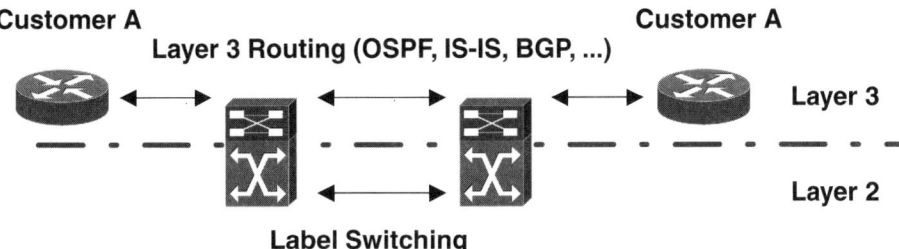

Figure 4-10 Layer 3 VPN architecture—routing.

If we recall the QoS mapping problems that were discussed in the overlay model, we should notice that these issues are not present in this model (see Figure 4-11). This is because devices in the true peer model are IP-aware and can adjust their input and output queues depending on the requested service class. For example, the devices in the service provider network can recognize a Voice over IP stream as an application with the highest demand on latency without any QoS mappings at the edge of the IP carrier network. A further advantage to this approach is that both the integrated services and the DiffServ models can be leveraged to guarantee a service class to the customers' data streams.

Imagine a situation where a company with sites in various countries wanted to multicast its quarterly financial results over its intranet in an effort to update all employees. The employees are physically located across the globe at numerous, physically disparate locations. If this company employed a service provider that offered Layer 2 services, the customer's video server would have to serve up mul-

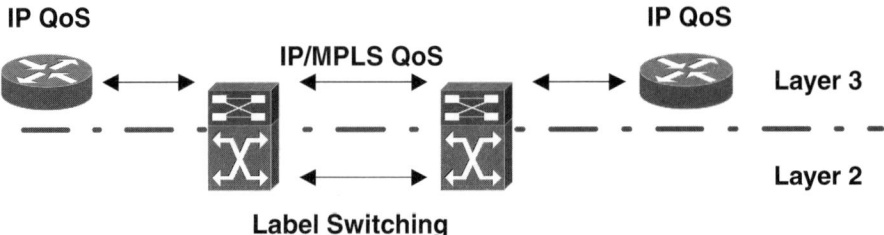

Figure 4-11 Layer 3 VPN architecture—QoS.

tiple streams, one stream to every location via different PVCs. The video streams could be multicasted to every client only at the edges of the customer's IP network because the service provider's Layer 2 network is unaware of any Layer 3 services that are being transported through its PVCs, and therefore cannot know that the customer's traffic would be better distributed using a Layer 3 multicast scheme. The benefit of using a multicast application would be diminished because the video server has to play out more than one video stream. However, by using a Layer 3 VPN network in this case, it is possible to handle the multicast information inside the service provider network (see Figure 4-12). This results in the customer's video server only having to serve up a single multicast video stream for all connected sites. This is possible because the Layer 3 network is aware of the customer's multicast group [IETF-25], and thus can more efficiently forward the traffic.

This chapter pointed out some of the specific problems involved with setting up VPNs. There are different ways to implement VPNs, either Layer 2- or Layer 3-based, and we discussed the pros and cons of both approaches. Our conclusion is that if we want to build VPNs that scale up to a couple of hundred or thousands of sites, we must move to a Layer 3-based peer model approach.

The next chapter focuses on the components of such Layer 3 peer model VPNs that are built with MPLS as a foundation.

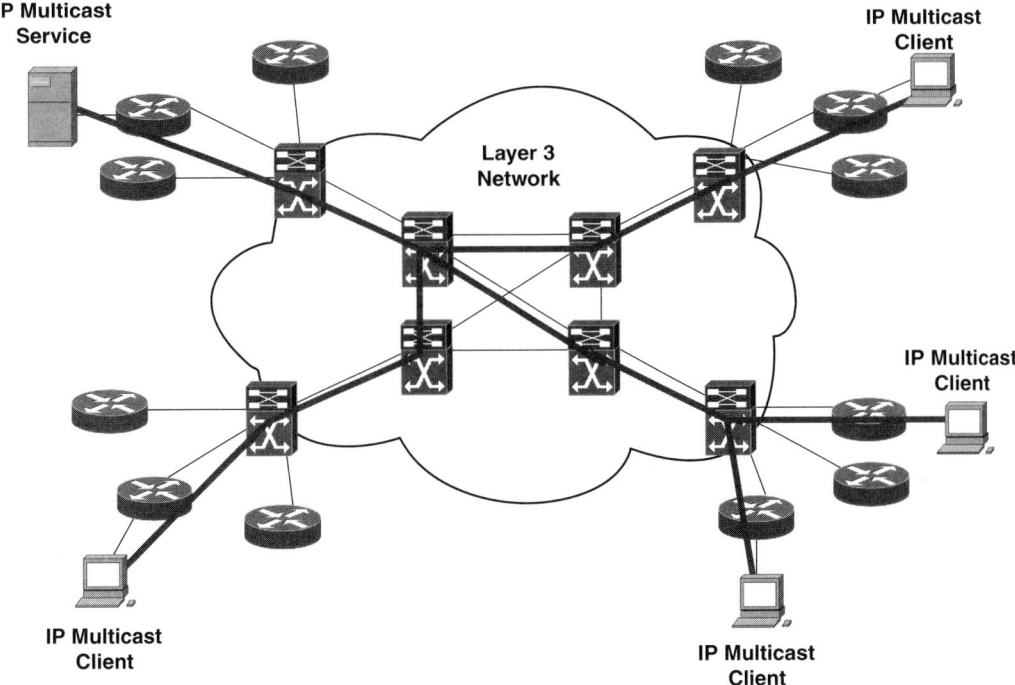

Figure 4-12 Layer 3 VPN architecture—IP multicasting.

5

Components of MPLS VPNs

Introduction to the Border Gateway Protocol (BGP-4)

The Internet is a collection of many independently managed networks that are divided into autonomous systems (ASs). An AS is a group of networks that shares the same routing policies. In most cases, the networks in an AS are under the same administrative authority (i.e., the IP address ranges of the networks belong to the same Internet service provider, or (ISP). Each AS has an autonomous system number (ASN). An ASN is a 16-bit field that is assigned by the Internet Assigned Numbers Association (IANA). There are also the following regional registries: Réseaux IP Européens (RIPE), American Registry for Internet Numbers (ARIN), and Asia Pacific Network Information Center (APNIC).

As the Internet grew, so did the demand for a very scalable protocol that could handle a large number of networks/prefixes and ASs. The ability to handle the exchange of reachability information for tens of thousands of Internet Provider (IP) prefixes between AS borders was a basic requirement of this new protocol. Another requirement was the ability to deploy very flexible routing policies between different ASs. This is crucial since there is no single authority that defines the routing policies of the Internet. The ability to deploy routing policies allows administrators to define the traffic trajectories through and between ASs. This is important because traffic will ultimately follow the path that has been laid out by the routing protocols.

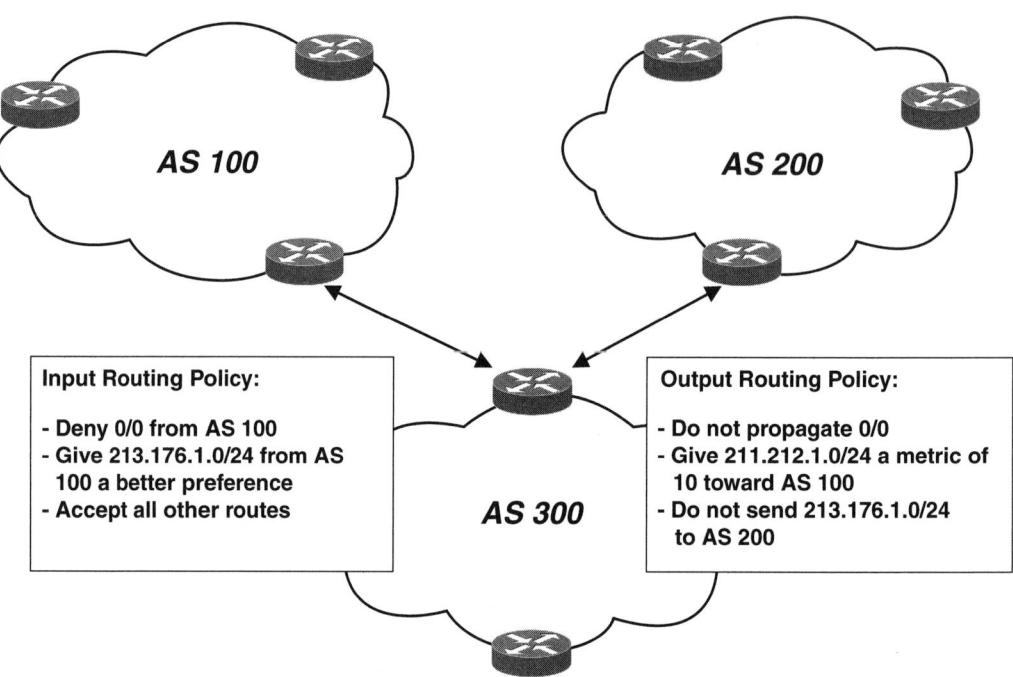

Figure 5–1 BGP-4 routing policies between ASs.

The information exchanged between an AS border router via BGP-4 not only consists of the pure IP prefix reachability information, but also contains additional, route-specific information called path attributes. These attributes contain information about the AS path of the route. The AS path is defined as a path vector and is constructed by every router along the path of a routing update. Every router will add its own ASN to the path vector. This information is sufficient to construct a graph of AS connectivity from which routing loops may be pruned. Other attributes that are included are the local preference attribute and community attributes. These are used in the route filtering and route decision processes to enforce routing policies. The example shown in Figure 5-1 shows BGP-4 routing policies implemented between ASs. Also, see the section in Chapter 16 titled "Route Distribution" for a detailed description of the BGP-4 attributes used with BGP/MPLS VPNs.

BGP-4 does not compute topology maps nor does it run any version of the Dykstra shortest-path algorithm; instead, it uses a decision engine to choose the best route based on the route path attributes as shown in Figure 5–2.

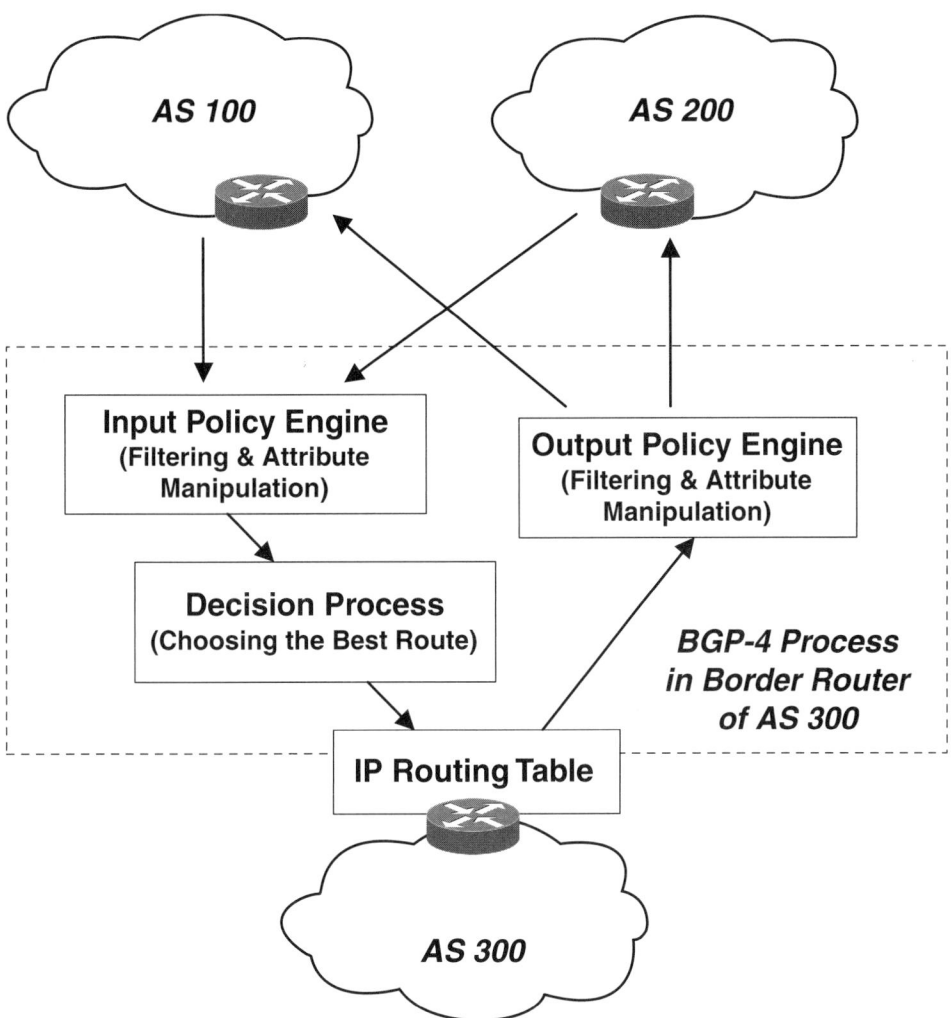

Figure 5–2 BGP-4 decision process.

BGP-4 also provides a set of mechanisms for supporting classless interdomain routing. These mechanisms include support for advertising an IP prefix as a classless entity by eliminating the concept of network class (e.g., network A, B, C, and D). The predecessors of BGP-4 were called BGP-1, 2, 3 and EGP. These have been obsoleted by BGP-4, which is today the protocol of choice when routing information has to be exchanged between ASs within the Internet. BGP-4 is described and standardized in RFC 1771 [IETF-31].

Although BGP is designed for use between ASs to provide an interdomain loop-free topology, BGP can be used to connect border routers that are running external BGP sessions to other ASs. Connections between BGP speakers of different ASs are referred to as "external" links. BGP connections between BGP speakers within the same AS are referred to as "internal" links. Similarly, a peer in a different AS is referred to as an external peer, while a peer in the same AS may be described as an internal peer. When BGP is established between internal peers, it is referred to as internal BGP, or iBG, in comparison to external BGP, or eBGP, which runs between external peers (see Figure 5–3).

Both during neighbor session establishment and initial message exchange negotiation, BGP peers compare their ASNs in an effort to determine if they are part of the same AS. If they find that they are in the same AS, the BGP peers will begin an iBGP session. This session differs from a normal BGP session mainly in the manner in which the peers process routing updates coming from other peers. Additionally the sessions differ in the way different BGP attributes are carried on external versus internal links [HALA-1].

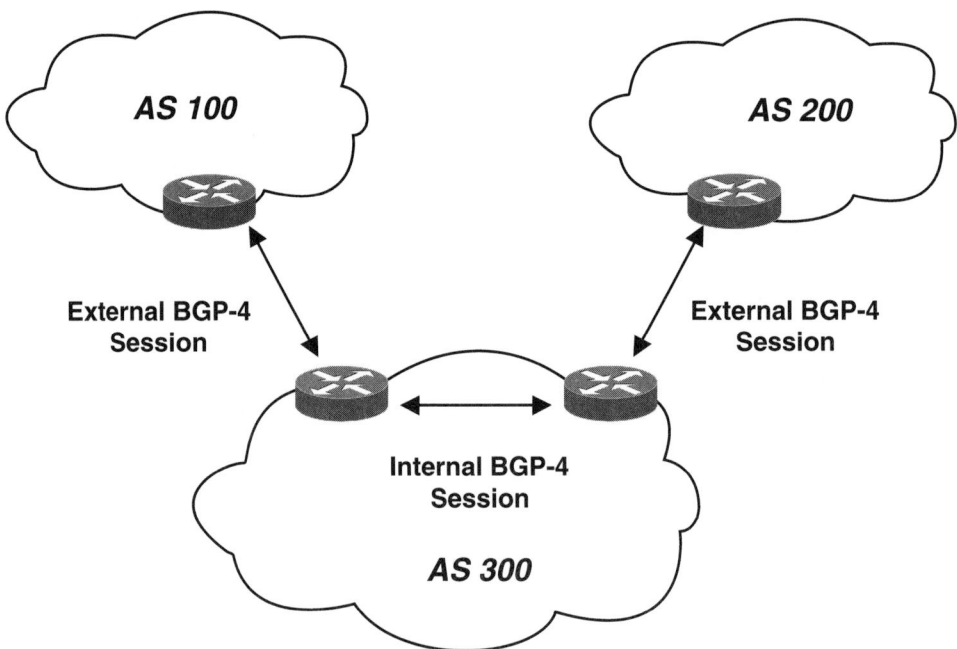

Figure 5–3 Internal vs. external BGP sessions.

Why Use Multiprotocol BGP-4 for MPLS VPNs?

MPLS VPNs are seen as one of the major applications for MPLS. MPLS VPNs provide a highly scalable technology for service providers that want to offer Layer 3 VPN services to their customers. Many service providers that offer MPLS VPNs to customers want to have hundreds or even thousands of sites for any given VPN, as well as at least a few thousand routes for each VPN network. The protocol that exchanges routing information in this configuration must be extremely scalable and proven. BGP-4 is definitely a proven protocol. It is also widely accepted and understood in the industry. Fortunately, it is also very well-suited to carrying additional information in its routing updates, which in this case, is required in the MPLS VPN architecture.

Extensions were made to BGP-4 to enable it to carry information about IP prefixes from customer VPNs as well as label information for MPLS (see Figure 5–4). These extensions are defined in RFC 2858 "Multiprotocol Extensions for BGP-4" [IETF-33] and in "Carrying Label Information in BGP-4" [IETF-32]. RFC 2858 defines how BGP-4 can be used to carry network layer reachability information from protocols other than IPv4, for example, IPv6 or IPX. The second document defines how label information is carried by BGP-4. The exact mechanisms of how customer routes are transported over an MPLS network and how labels are associated with customer VPNs will be explained in detail in the next chapter.

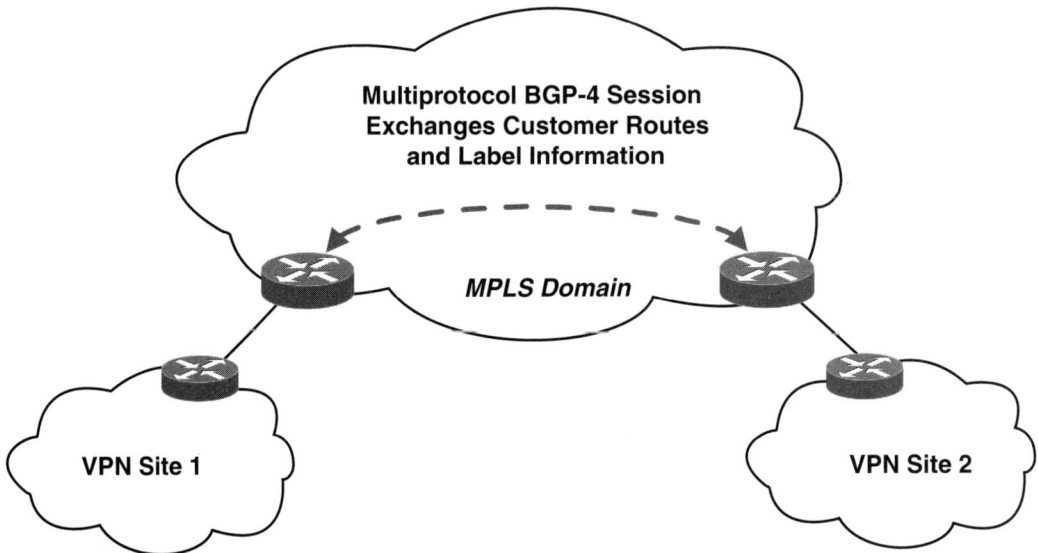

Figure 5–4 Multiprotocol BGP-4 and MPLS.

6
Details of MPLS VPNs

Many contributions concerned with Virtual Private Network (VPN) architectures have been submitted to the International Engineering Task Force (IETF) and other standards bodies. Various vendors have worked out drafts of how VPNs can be implemented over a Multiprotocol Label Switching (MPLS) infrastructure. We will focus on the approaches that have proposed to use Border Gateway Protocol (BGP) or extensions to BGP as the underlying routing protocol. The decision to focus on these implementations over others was influenced mainly by the personal experience of the authors and the early availability of a real BGP/MPLS VPN implementation. We are aware of other implementations that have been proposed by different vendors, but we feel that many of these approaches are or will be less successful than BGP/MPLS VPNs. Thus, we will focus our discussion on BGP/MPLS VPNs.

Definition of BGP/MPLS VPNs

In the BGP/MPLS VPN model [IETF-4], it is assumed that different customer sites are attached to a backbone network. This backbone network is assumed to be under the authority of one or more service providers. Within the context of BGP/MPLS VPNs, the term VPN is NOT defined as a pure matter by which a permanent virtual connection (PVC) at some site is attached to any other site; instead, the VPN is defined as a common subset of sites conforming to a certain subset of policies. In the example shown in Figure 6–1, six different

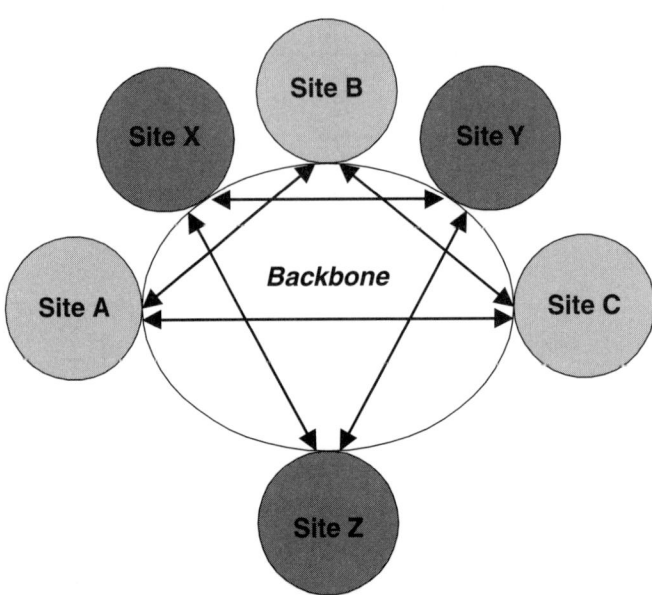

Figure 6–1 BGP/MPLS VPN sites and backbone network.

sites are attached to a service provider backbone network. Assume that sites A, B, and C belong to one company and sites X, Y, and Z belong to another company. Sites A, B, and C may share IP connectivity among each other because they are part of the same subset of policies; hence, they are in the same VPN (VPN ABC). Sites X, Y, and Z are part of a different VPN, XYZ, which is built on a common set of policies and also shares a common set of policies.

It is important to note that the policies among sites A, B, and C are disjointed from those among sites X, Y, and Z since both groups represent different private companies. This relationship is depicted in Figure 6–2.

If a new set of policies is introduced that defines that site A and site Z may share Internet Protocol (IP) connectivity, the following scenario arises (see Figure 6–3).

Once the new policy is applied, site A has IP connectivity with site Z. This is depicted in Figure 6–4. Note that in this example, site A still cannot share connectivity with sites X and Y. They are still separated because they are not in a subset of the same policies; that is, they are not members of the same VPN. Two sites may only have IP connectivity across the backbone network if there is at least one VPN that contains them both! There may be situations where all sites that are in a VPN belong to one single company. In these cases, the VPN may be called an intranet. VPNs ABC and XYZ in our example are two such exam-

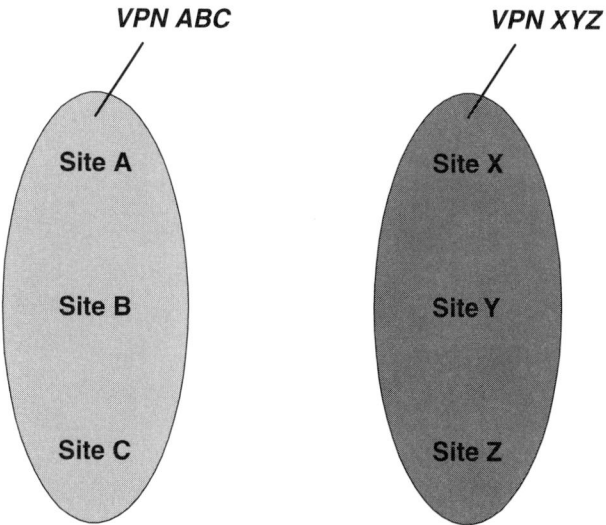

Figure 6–2 BGP/MPLS VPN sites and VPNs.

ples. If the sites in a VPN belong to more than one company, like VPN AZ in our example, this is referred to as an extranet VPN.

Terminology

To simplify the discussion about the various elements in the BGP/MPLS VPN architecture shown in Figure 6–5, a naming convention must be introduced which clearly denotes the roles of particular network elements.

- **Provider network (P network)**—The backbone under the control of a service provider.
- **Provider (core) router (P router)**—This type of router has no knowledge of VPNs.
- **Provider edge router (PE router)**—A part of the P network that interfaces to CE routers.
- **PE-CE link**—The connection between the PE and CE can be built with any type of data link. This may be ATM, Frame Relay, Ethernet, PPP, GRE tunnels, and others.
- **Customer edge router (CE router)**—A part of the C network that interfaces to a PE router. In most cases, this device will be a router, although there may be situations where this device can be a switch or

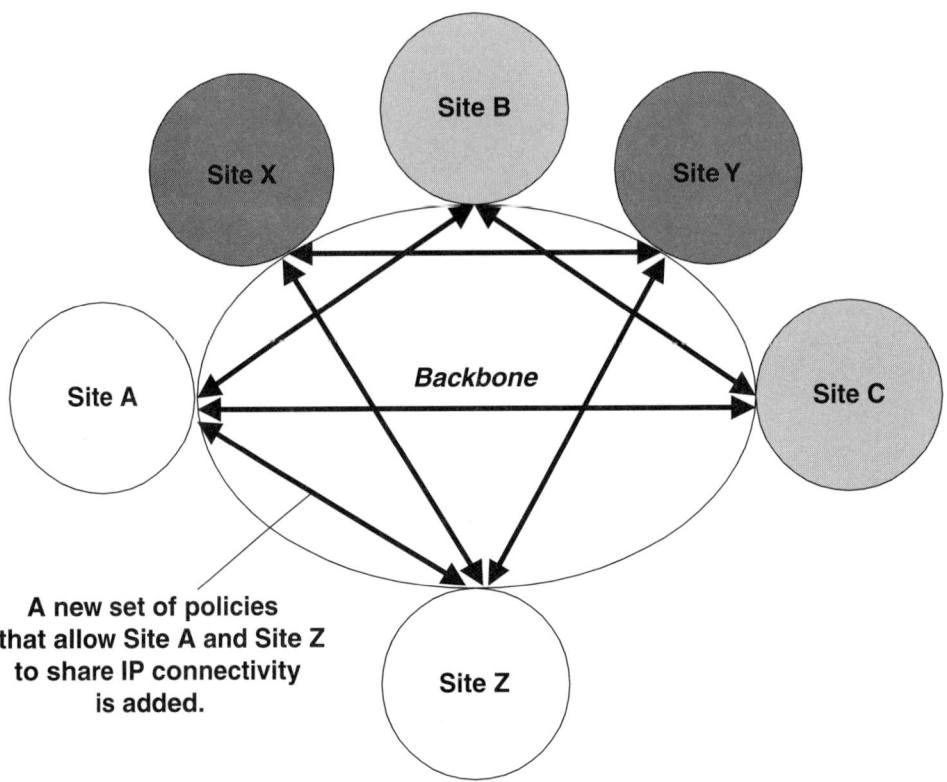

Figure 6-3 A new subset of policies is added.

even a workstation (see the section titled "Virtual Sites"). If the CE device is a router, it is a routing peer of the PE router. However, in this case, it is not a routing peer of any other CE router.

- **Site**—A set of (sub)networks that are part of the C network, but which are co-located. A site is connected to the VPN backbone through one or more PE-CE links. There may be situations where the site consists of a collection of different networks that belong to different VPNs. This site is called a virtual site and the different logical connections from the CE router into the PE router can be VLANS (virtual LANs), Frame Relay, or ATM links with "subinterfaces" (see Figure 6–6). Another possibility for a virtual site is a workstation that is directly connected to the PE router and is part of different VPNs (see Figure 6–7). If this is the case, the workstation must either possess more network interfaces to connect to the PE or use VLANs to differentiate between packets from different VPNs.

Terminology   111

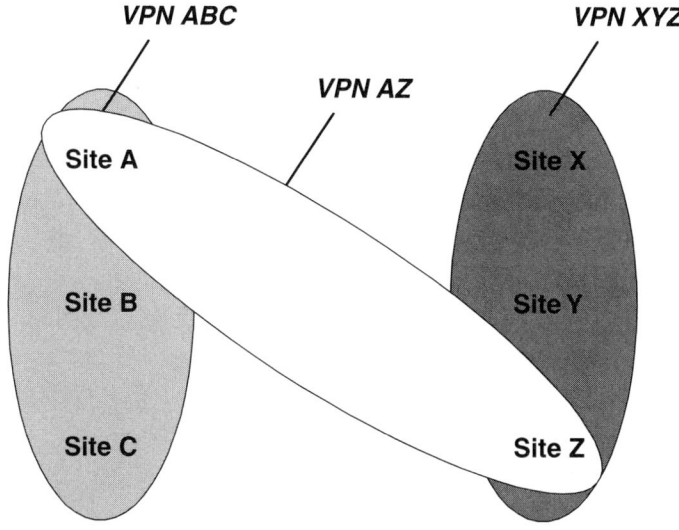

Figure 6–4   A third VPN is created.

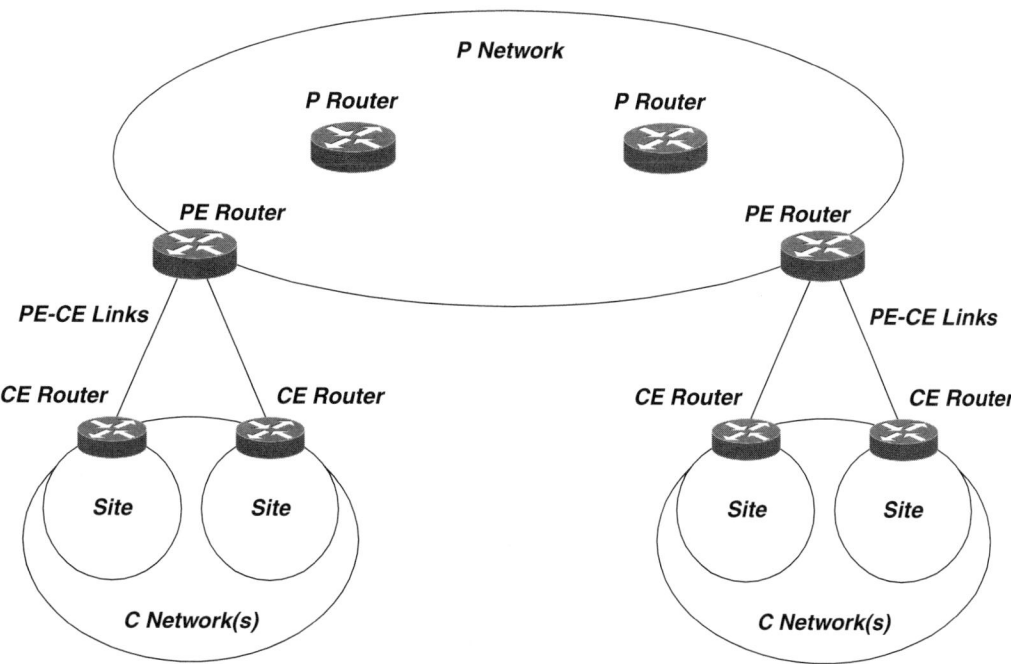

Figure 6–5   BGP/MPLS VPN terminology.

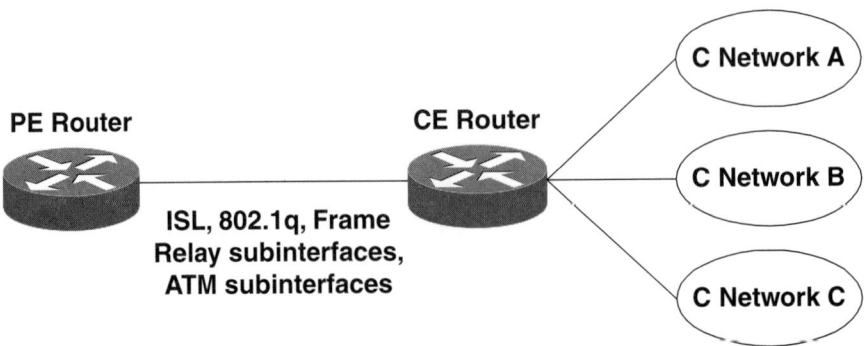

Figure 6-6 Virtual site—multiple VPNs behind a single CE.

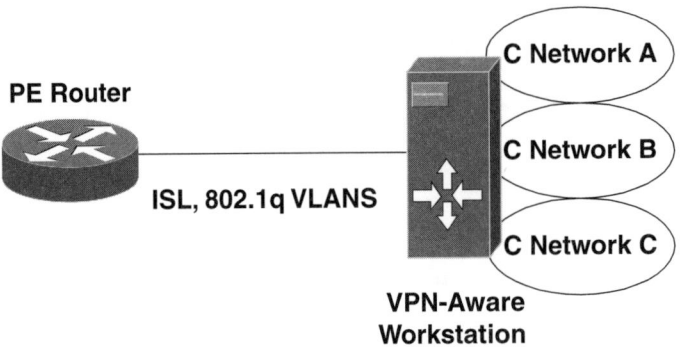

Figure 6-7 Virtual site—VPN-aware workstation.

- **VPN Routing and Forwarding table (VRF)**—A key concept in the BGP/MPLS VPN architecture is an element called the VPN Routing and Forwarding table (see Figure 6-8). The VRF can be considered a separate routing and forwarding table in the PE routers. A VRF is private and is accessible only by the interfaces that are "in" the corresponding VPN. Every site attached to the PE router must be linked into one VRF. All of the routing information for the VPN is reflected in the VRF. All packets that travel through that site will be routed and forwarded based only on information found in its correspnding VRF. The process for how a route is injected in a certain VRF will be explained in the section titled "Route Distribution." The VRF associated with a certain site, for instance, site A, is populated only with routes that lead to other sites that have at least one VPN in common with site A.
- **Customer network (C network)**—A network under customer control.

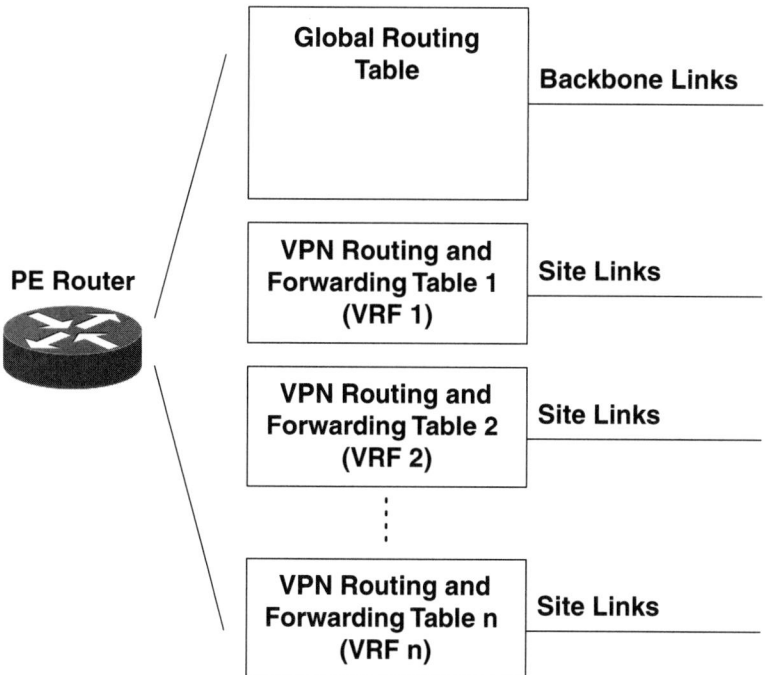

Figure 6–8 A VRF.

KEY CONCEPT!

Sites that share IP connectivity must be in the same VPN.

One key benefit to BGP/MPLS VPNs is the ability to have overlapping IP address spaces between two or more VPNs. This is possible since they will never share the same routing table (i.e., the same VRF). This allows members of one VPN to use private addressing schemes in their customer networks and exchange their private routes over the service provider backbone without interfering with other customers who use exactly the same private address space in their C networks (see Figure 6-9). This also allows service providers to allocate so-called illegal addresses to these VPNs, since these addresses are not used for external connectivity. In cases where they are, some sort of network address translation (NAT) is required.

Routes that are not part of a VPN are injected into the global routing table. The global routing table is the "normal" routing table that is present in legacy

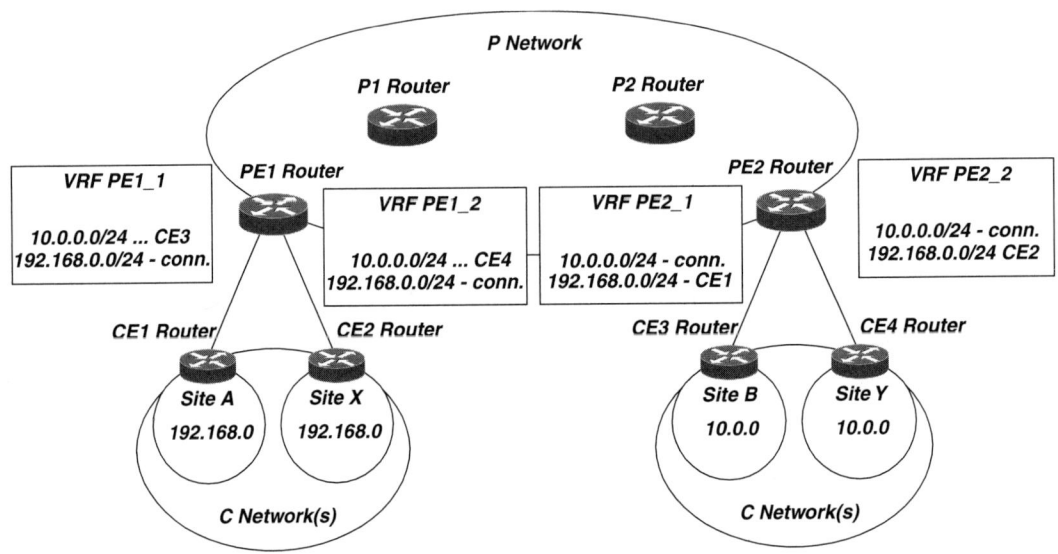

Figure 6-9 Private addresses inside C networks.

IPv4 routers such as the P routers. For example, routes learned via the Interior Gateway Protocol (IGP) of the service provider backbone are injected into the global routing table.

The complete Internet routing table is not stored in any VRF table. The Internet routing table, if present at all, is part of the global routing table of the PE routers. This is done primarily due to its size. The Internet routing table currently consists of over 100,000 routes. There are mainly three possibilities for how routing to the Internet can be configured in the PE routers. The first way is to put a default route in the VRF that refers to a single Internet exit point. This may be a firewall or an Internet gateway that is located either in the customer site or in the service provider backbone network. The second implementation method is to pass a packet that has not matched any entry in the VRF to the global routing table. The policy would be to then attempt to forward these packets based on the Internet routing table. Another approach is to maintain two logical PE-CE links, where one of the links is part of the VPN and heads into a VRF, and the other link is a legacy Internet uplink that is connected to the global routing table of the PE router. The advantage of this approach is that the CE site may announce and receive routes to and from the Internet, without any intervention on the part of the service provider. The last approach is likely to be implemented at larger central sites, where firewalls are also co-located.

KEY CONCEPT!

Due to the nature of Virtual Routing and Forwarding (VRF), it is impossible for packets of one VPN to be forwarded to another VPN because there will be no route in the VRF to a site in another VPN. This mechanism guarantees a high level of security in this architecture.

We have seen that the BGP/MPLS VPN architecture specifies elements called VRFs that hold VPN and site-specific routing information. We still have not discussed the way in which the routes, which are contained in the VRFs, are distributed among the PE routers, nor have we discussed how the different routes are sorted depending on a specific VPN. We need to investigate how routes are exchanged between PE and CE routers. We will see how these mechanisms work and why they are scalable in large-scale environments in the following chapter.

Route Distribution

Multiprotocol BGP (MP-BGP) is a protocol that is used to distribute VPN routes among PE routers. Before we discuss how routes are distributed among PEs, we must first investigate how BGP/MPLS VPNs facilitate the uniqueness of customer routes. We have mentioned that customer routes are independent and that they are isolated from other VPNs. We previously mentioned that customer routes are separate from service provider backbone routes. We also stated that it is possible for more than one VPN to, for example, use a private 10.0.0.0 network and spread reachability information across the service provider backbone to its different sites. The only way to accomplish this is to guarantee that these routes can be distinguished from each other. BGP/MPLS VPNs achieve this by adding a unique identifier to the IPv4 address. The identifier is called a route distinguisher (RD) and it is added by the PE. The resulting address family is called VPN-IPv4.

RDs and the VPN-IPv4 Address Family

The aim of BGP/MPLS VPNs is to have a distinct address space for each VPN. Customer routes must be treated in different ways depending on the VPN they belong to. The BGP multiprotocol extensions [IETF-33] allow BGP to carry routes from multiple "address families." The notion of the "VPN-IPv4 address family" is introduced in [IETF-4]. A VPN-IPv4 address is a 12-byte quantity, beginning with an 8-byte RD and ending with a 4-byte IPv4 address (see Figure 6–10). If two VPNs use the same IPv4 address prefix, the PEs translate these into unique VPN-IPv4 address prefixes. This ensures that if the same address is used in two different VPNs, it is possible to install two completely different routes to the same address, one for each VPN [IETF-4].

An RD consists of a 2-byte Type field, an Administrator field, and an Assigned Number field. The value of the Type field determines the lengths of the other two fields, as well as the semantics of the Administrator field. The Administrator field identifies an assigned number authority, and the Assigned Number field contains a number that has been assigned by the identified authority for a particular purpose [IETF-4]. These two variants have been defined to allow network administrators to choose a unique RD based on either the ASN or a public IP address. Nevertheless, the semantics do not influence the behavior of BGP in any way. When BGP compares two such address prefixes, it ignores the structure entirely.

The RD consists of an 8-byte field. Together with the four bytes of an IPv4 address, it builds the VPN-IPv4 address family. The RD is encoded as follows and is defined in [IETF-4]:

- Type field: 2 bytes
- Value field: 6 bytes

The interpretation of the Value field depends on the value of the Type field. At the present time, two values of the Type field are defined: 0 and 1. When the Type field is 0, the Value field consists of two subfields (see Figure 6–11):

- Administrator subfield: 2 bytes
- Assigned Number subfield: 4 bytes

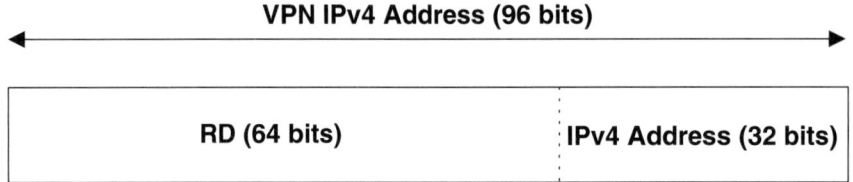

Figure 6–10 VPN-IPv4 address.

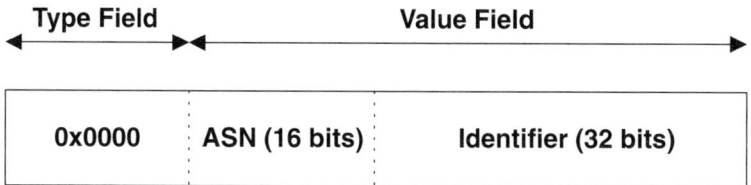

Figure 6-11 RD Type=0.

The Administrator subfield must contain an ASN. If this ASN is from the public ASN space, it must have been assigned by the Internet Assigned Numbers Association (IANA) (use of ASN values from the private ASN space is strongly discouraged). The Assigned Number subfield contains a number from a numbering space that is administered by the enterprise to which the ASN has been assigned by the IANA. When the Type field equals 1, the Value field consists of two subfields (see Figure 6–12):

- Administrator subfield: 4 bytes
- Assigned Number subfield: 2 bytes

The Administrator subfield must contain an IP address. If this IP address has been assigned by the IANA to a particular enterprise, the Assigned Number subfield contains a number from a numbering space that is administered by the enterprise to which the IP address has been assigned (use of addresses from the private IP address space is strongly discouraged) [IETF-4].

KEY CONCEPT!

The RD is only used to make IPv4 addresses unique. There is NO direct relation between the RD field and a VPN or the origin of the route. The RD is configured at the VRF on PE routers. Although not required, it is common practice to configure a common RD in all VRFs that together comprise a VPN. This approach is used to follow a scalable RD numbering scheme and not because of any architectural reasons!

So far, we have seen how the RD is defined and how it is appended to IPv4 addresses. We now want to have a look at the actual process of how routes are distributed and how policies can be defined so that VPNs can be built.

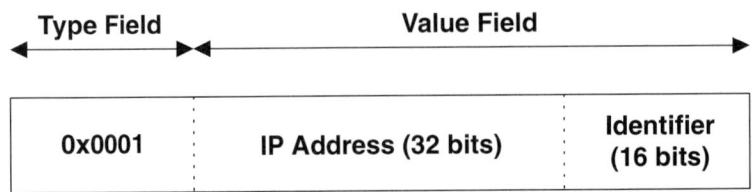

Figure 6-12 RD Type=1.

Route Targets (RTs)

Each VRF can assign one or more route targets (RTs) to a customer route that is distributed via MP-BGP to other PEs. Each VRF can be configured to accept only routes with certain RTs. This mechanism is the foundation for VPN functionality. The model for the exportation and importation of RTs resembles the buy/sell approach of the stock market. PEs "sell" routing update messages and only PEs that have interest in routes with certain route target attributes will "buy" these routing updates and install them in their routing tables (if they pass the BGP decision process).

RTs are transported in the Extended Communities path attribute of BGP Update messages. The Extended Communities path attribute is defined in "BGP Extended Communities Attribute" [IETF-5]. The Extended Communities attribute uses Type Code 16. The Extended Communities attribute is an optional, transitive BGP attribute. The attribute consists of a set of "extended communities." Each extended community is coded as an 8-octet value. All routes with the Extended Communities attribute belong to the communities listed in the attribute. Each extended community is 8 bytes long. Similar to the encoding of the RD, the 8 bytes are divided into a Type field (2 bytes) and a Value field (6 bytes). There are two possible ways to encode the Value field, which depend on the value of the high-order byte of the Type field. The two variants are:

  i. **Type field: 0x00**

  Value field:

  2 bytes: ASN

  4 bytes: Assigned Number subfield (This field contains a number assigned by the organization to which the ASN has been assigned by the IANA.)

ii. **Type field: 0x01**

Value field:

4 bytes: IPv4 address assigned by IANA

2 bytes: Assigned Number subfield (This field contains a number assigned by the organization to which the IPv4 address has been assigned by the IANA.)

Two extended communities are defined: the RT community is used to build VPNs in the BGP/MPLS VPN architecture; the route origin community is used to define a set of one or more routers that inject a set of routes (that carry this community) into BGP.

The RT community uses Type fields of 0x0002 or 0x0102, respectively.

The route origin community uses Type fields of 0x0003 or 0x0103, respectively. For a more detailed view of the different BGP path attributes, have a look at the section titled "Route Distribution among PEs."

Each VRF has a configured route import/export policy. VPN-IPv4 routing updates that are distributed to other PEs are marked with one or more export RT attributes. VPN-IPv4 routes that are received by other PE routers are checked if their route target attribute matches the import RT of the VRF. Only if there is at least one RT attribute that is both an import RT and an RT carried in the routing update is the route eligible to be installed. Whether it really is installed depends on the BGP decision process. This flexible mechanism allows for the construction of different VPN topologies such as any-to-any (fully-meshed) and hub-and-spoke.

PE1 (SEE FIGURE 6–13):

1. An IPv4 routing update is sent from the CE to the PE router.
2. The route is installed in the appropriate VRF.
3. The VRF-specific RD is appended to the IPv4 address and a VPN-IPv4 address is created from this route. The export RT#Donna: Will the figure be in color? is added as an attribute to the MP-BGP routing update, and the routing update is sent out to all MP-iBGP (internal BGP) peers or to a route reflector.

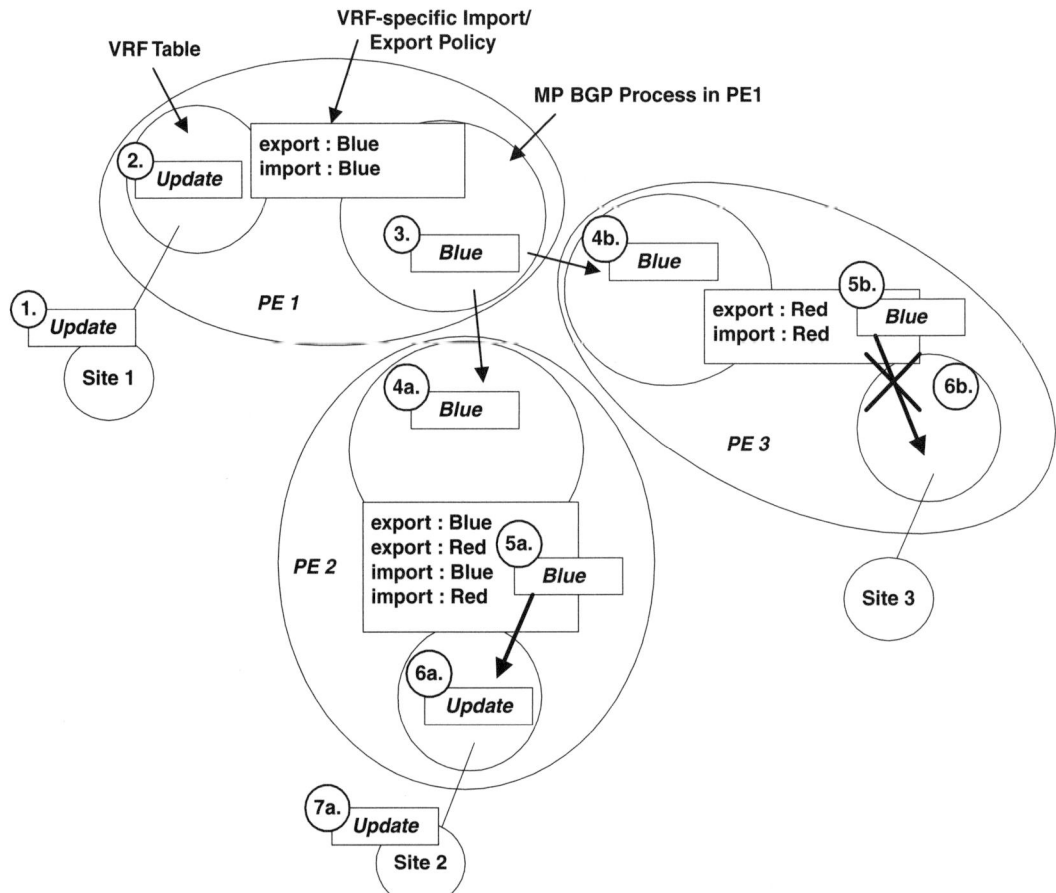

Figure 6-13 Building VPNs with RTs.

PE2:
- **4a.** The MP-iBGP process in PE2 receives the VPN IPv4 routing update.
- **5a.** The VPN-IPv4 routing update is checked against the configured import RTs of the appropriate VRF in PE2. The RT carried in the routing update (Blue) matches the configured RT (Blue), is translated into an IPv4 address, and gets installed in the VRF table.
- **6a.** The routing process between PE2 and Site 2 sends the routing update to CE2.
- **7a.** The route gets installed in customer router CE2. Site 2 now has an installed route to Site 1.

PE3:

4b. The MP-BGP process in PE3 receives the VPN-IPv4 routing update.

5a. The VPN-IPv4 routing update is checked against the configured import RTs of the appropriate VRF in PE3. The RT carried in the routing update (Blue) does not match the configured RT (Red).

6a. The route will not get installed in the VRF table and it will not be propagated to the customer router. Site 3 has no route to Site 1; they are not part of the same VPN.

The resulting VPN topology is shown in Figure 6–14 and in Tables 6–1, 6–2, and 6–3.

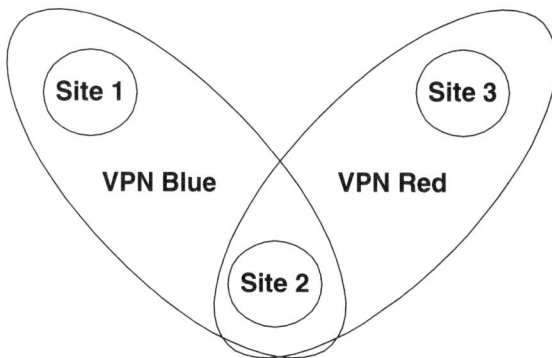

Figure 6–14 VPN topology.

Table 6–1 Site Connectivity Matrix

Site	1	2	3
1	c	c	n
2	c	c	c
3	n	c	c

c ... connected
n ... not connected

Table 6-2 Site—VPN Connectivity Matrix

	VPN Blue	VPN Red
Site 1	c	n
Site 2	c	c
Site 3	n	c

c ... connected
n ... not connected

Table 6-3 VRF RT Configuration Matrix

VRF	RT Blue	RT Red
1	imp/exp	n
2	imp/exp	imp/exp
3	n	imp/exp

imp/exp ... import/export route targets configured in appropriate VRF
n ... route targets not configured

Route Distribution among PE Routers

There are different methods available for distributing VPN-IPv4 routes among PE routers. It is also possible to specify an entirely new protocol or set of protocols to perform this function. It has been discussed in an IETF working group to use extensions to CR-LDP to build VPN topologies, but there is a strong tendency in the industry to build on a well-understood and proven protocol like BGP. Thus, MP-BGP (Multiprotocol Border Gateway Protocol) was chosen as the distribution method for VPN-IPv4 routes [IETF-4].

In a very basic scenario, all PE routers are located in a single AS, are configured as fully-meshed, and are running internal Border Gateway Protocol (iBGP) sessions among each other as shown in Figure 6–15.

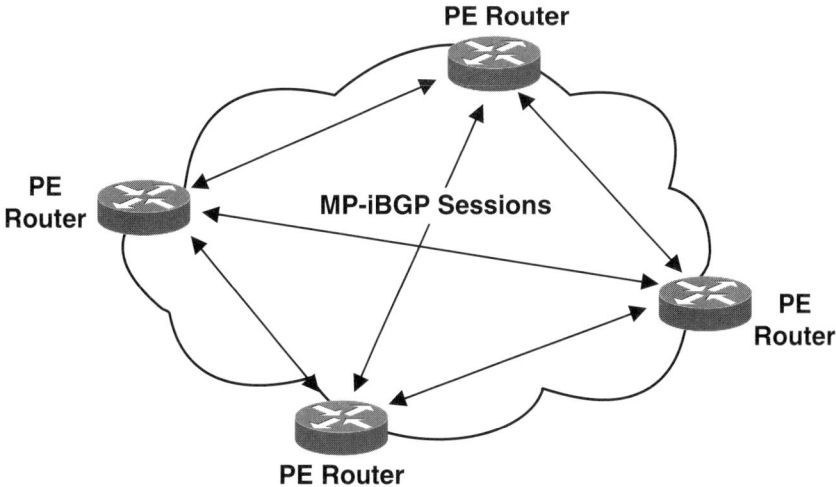

Figure 6–15 BGP session among PE routers.

When a PE router distributes a VPN-IPv4 route via BGP, it uses its own address as the "BGP next hop." This address is encoded as a VPN-IPv4 address with an RD of 0 because multiprotocol extensions to BGP [IETF-33] require the next-hop address to be in the same address family as the network layer reachability information (NLRI). It also assigns and distributes an MPLS label. PE routers distribute labeled VPN-IPv4 routes instead VPN-IPv4 routes.

When the PE processes a received packet that has this label at the top of the stack, the PE will pop the stack and send the packet directly to the site to which the route leads. This will usually mean that it just sends the packet to the CE router from which it learned the route. The label may also determine the data link encapsulation. In most cases, a label assigned by a PE will cause the packet to be sent directly to a CE, and the PE that receives the labeled packet will not look up the packet's destination address in any VRF. However, it is also possible for the PE to assign a label that implicitly identifies a particular VRF. In this case, the PE receiving the packet with that label would look up the packet's destination address in the associated VRF. This allows the route distributed and labeled by BGP to be an aggregate of several routes that appear in the VRF. This can be very useful if the VRF contains a large number of host routes (e.g., as in dial-in) or if the VRF has an associated LAN interface (where there is a different outgoing Layer 2 header for each system on the LAN, but a route is not distributed for each such system) [IETF-4].

Since all PEs are in the same AS, all labeled VPN-IPv4 routes are exchanged via MP-iBGP between PE routers. To support the VPN-IPv4 address family in the NLRI field of the BGP Update message, it was proposed to use the multiprotocol extensions for BGP as defined in RFC 2283, "Multiprotocol Extensions for BGP-4" [IETF-33]. The way in which labels are carried in the NLRI field is specified in "Carrying Label Information in BGP-4" [IETF-32].

Two BGP speakers must agree that they are both capable of processing VPN-IPv4 addresses. This is done during an initial BGP capability negotiation. The ability to handle these additional multiprotocol extensions is signaled by setting the AFI (address family identifier) to 1 and setting the SAFI (subsequent address family identifier) to 128.

BGP uses the concept of Routing Update messages to construct a loop-free picture of the Internet. A legacy BGP Update message consists of the following fields:

- Unreachable Routes
- Path Attributes
- Network Layer Reachability Information (NLRI)

The first field contains routes that are unreachable and should be withdrawn by the receiving BGP peer. The Path Attributes field carries information that prevents loops and enforces local and global routing policies in addition to advertised routes. The NLRI field carries IPv4 prefixes of routes being advertised. The format of the BGP Update message is shown in Figure 6–16.

To enable BGP to support network layer protocols other than IPv4, "Multiprotocol Extensions to BGP-4" [IETF-33] have been defined. To provide backward compatibility as well as a way to simplify the introduction of the multiprotocol capability into BGP-4, two new attributes, Multiprotocol Reachable NLRI (MP_REACH_NLRI) and Multiprotocol Unreachable NLRI (MP_ UNREACH_NLRI), have been defined. The first (MP_REACH_NLRI) is used to carry the set of reachable destinations together with the next-hop information to be used for forwarding to these destinations. The second (MP_UNREACH_NLRI) is used to carry the set of unreachable destinations. Both of these attributes are optional and nontransitive. This way, a BGP speaker that does not support the multiprotocol capability will ignore the additional information carried by these attributes and will not pass the information to other BGP speakers.

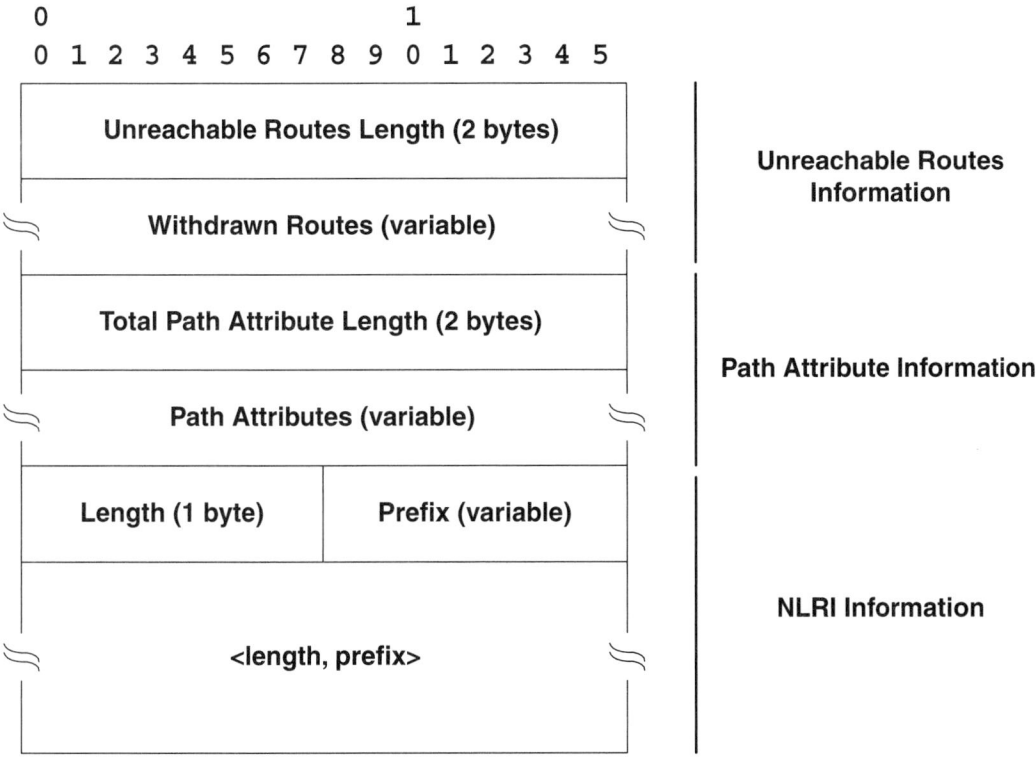

Figure 6-16 BGP Update message format.

The Path Attributes field is identified by type codes. The following list presents an overview of the BGP Path Attributes field. This list also notes where the new multiprotocol Path Attributes field fits in.

- Type Code 1: ORIGIN (well-known, mandatory)
- Type Code 2: AS_PATH (well-known, mandatory)
- Type Code 3: NEXT_HOP (well-known, mandatory)
- Type Code 4: MULTI_EXIT_DISC (optional, nontransitive)
- Type Code 5: LOCAL_PREF (well-known, discretionary)
- Type Code 6: ATOMIC_AGGREGATE (well-known, discretionary)
- Type Code 7: AGGREGATOR (optional, transitive)
- Type Code 8: COMMUNITY (optional, transitive)
- Type Code 9: ORIGINATOR_ID (optional, nontransitive, Cisco-defined)

- Type Code 10: CLUSTER_LIST (optional, nontransitive, Cisco-defined)
- Type Code 11: DESTINATION_PREFERENCE (optional, nontransitive, MCI-defined)
- Type Code 12: ADVERTISER (optional, nontransitive, Nortel-defined)
- Type Code 13: RCID_PATH (optional, nontransitive, Nortel-defined)
- Type Code 14: MP_REACH_NLRI (optional, nontransitive, RFC 2283-defined)
- Type Code 15: MP_UNREACH_NLRI (optional, nontransitive, RFC 2283-defined)
- Type Code 16: EXTENDED_COMMUNITIES (optional, transitive, Cisco-defined)
- Type Code 255: Reserved

Different attributes have different levels of significance. For example, some attributes are mandatory, while others are optional.

- **Well-known, mandatory**—These attributes must exist in every BGP implementation. If such an attribute is missing in a BGP Update message, a Notification Error message will be generated to inform the sender about the missing attribute.
- **Well-known, discretionary**—This group of attributes may or may not be sent by different BGP implementations, but every implementation has to recognize these attributes.
- **Optional, transitive**—If a BGP implementation receives an optional attribute and does not recognize it, it will look to see if the transitive flag is set or not. If set, the attribute is transitive and the attribute should be passed on to other BGP peers.
- **Optional, nontransitive**—If a BGP implementation receives an optional attribute, does not recognize it, and the transitive flag is NOT set, the attribute is nontransitive and should not be passed on to other BGP peers.

Type Code 14 and Type Code 15 are used to carry the Multiprotocol Reachable and Multiprotocol Unreachable attributes, while Type Code 16 is used to carry the Extended Communities attribute. The Extended Communities attribute contains the RT community and route origin community; the latter was discussed in a previous section, "Route Targets (RTs)."

Let's have a look at MP_REACH_NLRI in more detail. A Path Attribute field is a three-tuple of the following form: <attribute type, attribute length, attribute value>. MP_REACH_NLRI is defined as follows (see Figure 6–17):

The Attribute Value field contains the following information elements:

- **AFI (2 octets)**—This field carries the identity of the network layer protocol associated with the network address that follows. Presently defined values for this field are specified in RFC 1700 [IETF-24]. This field is set to 1 for IP.
- **SAFI (1 octet)**—This field provides additional information about the type of the NLRI carried in the attribute. This field is set to 128 for MPLS-labeled VPN-IPv4 addresses.
- **Length of next-hop network address (1 octet)**—The length of the next-hop network address field measured in octets.
- **Network address of next hop (variable; RD = 0 + IPv4 address)**
- **Number of SNPAs (1 octet)**—A 1-octet field that contains the number of distinct SNPAs (subnetwork points of attachment) to be listed in the following fields. The value 0 may be used to indicate that no SNPAs are listed in this attribute.
- **Length of 1 to nth SNPA (1 octet)**
- **1 to nth SNPA (variable)**

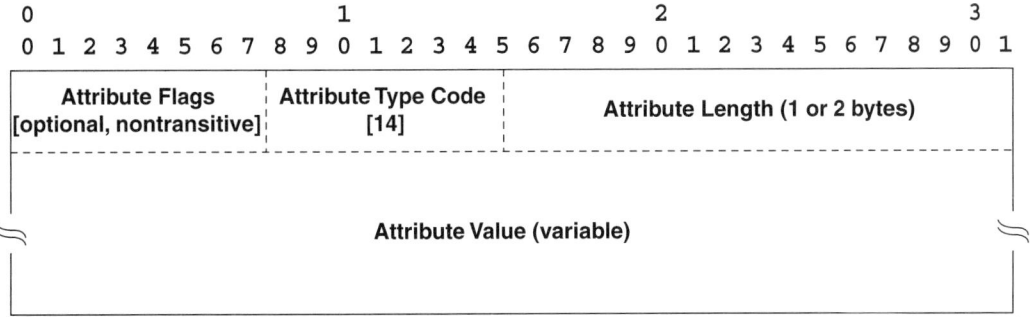

Figure 6–17 MP_REACH_NLRI path attribute.

- **NLRI (variable)**—A variable-length field that lists the NLRI for the feasible routes being advertised in this attribute. This field contains the labeled MPLS VPN-IPv4 addresses.

To carry MPLS-specific information in the multiprotocol attributes, the exact format of the NLRI field must be specified. This has been done in "Carrying Label Information in BGP-4 " [IETF-32]. The format of an NLRI field containing label information is shown in Figure 6–18.

The NLRI is encoded as one or more triples of the following form: (label, length, prefix) as shown in Figure 6–19.

- **Label**—The Label field carries one or more labels that correspond to the stack of labels [IETF-12]. Each label is encoded as three octets, where the high-order bit contains "Bottom of Stack" (as defined in [IETF-12]). The following high-order three bits must be zero. The remaining 20 bits contain the label value.
- **Length**—The Length field indicates the length of the address prefix plus the label(s).
- **Prefix**—The Prefix field contains address prefixes followed by enough trailing bits to make the end of the field fall on an octet boundary. The Prefix field contains VPN-IPv4 addresses. The label(s) specified for a particular route must be assigned by the LSR, which is identified by the value of the next-hop attribute of the route. They must also be associated with its address prefix.

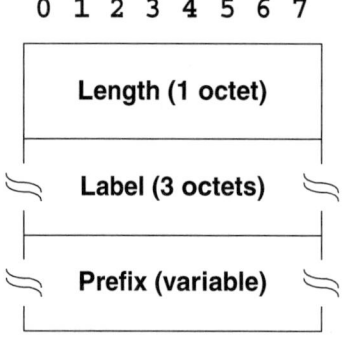

Figure 6–18   MP-BGP-4 NLRI encoding.

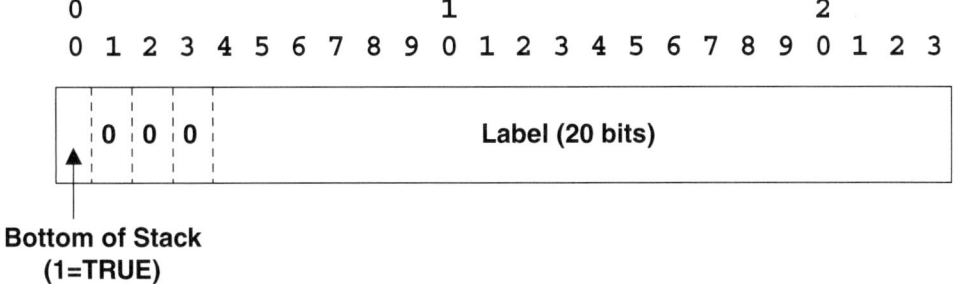

Figure 6–19 Encoding the label values in the NLRI field.

Route Exchange between PE and CE Routers

While the BGP/MPLS VPN architecture proposes only one distribution method between PE routers inside the provider MPLS backbone, it does provide us a full choice of routing protocols between provider edge (PE) and customer edge (CE) routers. Thus, the decision of which protocol to employ is influenced by the needs of the customer as well as the technical requirements. For example, a customer may require the use of a particular protocol because the administrators are familiar with it, or it may already be in use in the existing network. The decision which protocol should be used could also be influenced by the capabilities of the customer's premise equipment (CPE) used at the customer site. If the customer is using routers with less processing power or routers that are incapable of running certain more sophisticated routing protocols such as BGP, it may be desirable to have a choice between some protocols.

The following protocols are defined (see Figure 6–20):

- Static Routes
- RIPv2
- OSPF
- eBGP

Static Routes may only be useful if the number of routes is rather small, and if the C network has only one link, the PE-CE link, to reach the outside world. This is referred to as a stub VPN.

Unlike its predecessor RIP, RIPv2 also carries subnet information in the routing updates. This is primarily why RIPv2 was chosen over RIP. RIPv2 is very easy to handle by customer network administrators and may be useful if the

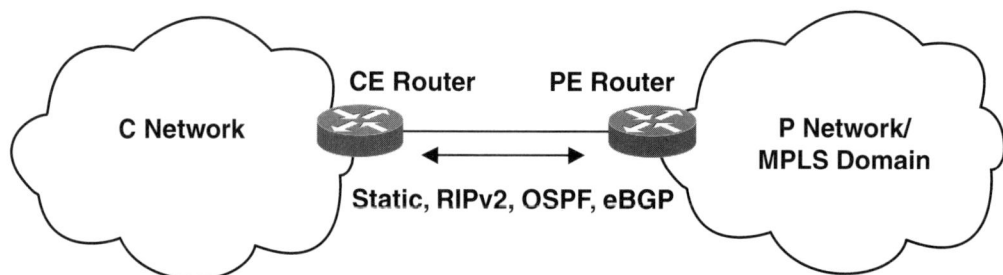

Figure 6–20 PE/CE protocols.

number of routes inside the VPN is small and stable. RIPv2 has rather long convergence times and may be a good choice for small sites without any Wide Area Network (WAN) connections going to other, more remote subsites inside the VPN.

OSPF may be an appropriate choice if the customer currently uses OSPF as a routing protocol between sites, and changing the routing protocol would impose significant configuration work. Care has to be taken with regard to the number of VPNs connected with OSPF to the PE router. PE routers run one OSPF instance per VRF. This may consume significant processing resources in the PE router if the number of different VRFs exceeds a certain amount, which is related to the PE hardware platform. Depending on the implementation, there may also be a limit on the concurrent instances of a routing process per PE router. This should also be taken into account.

There are different ways to implement OSPF as a PE-CE protocol and to guarantee seamless integration of the OSPF architecture within the BGP/MPLS VPN architecture. The main issue is to map the OSPF LSAs into MP-iBGP attributes and to transport these LSAs transparently across the BGP/MPLS backbone to other PEs. The goal is to let the provider backbone behave as if it was in area 0. There are two ways to implement this architecture:

  i. Let each PE-CE link be an area 0 (see Figure 6–21).
  ii. Let the MPLS backbone itself behave like an area 0 and attach customer areas directly to PEs (see Figure 6–22).

In case i (Figure 6–21), the Open Shortest Path First Protocol (OSPF) PE-CE link behaves as if it was an area 0 link (i.e., in the backbone area). The CE router acts as an area border router (ABR) for the customer areas, and the PE router acts as an ABR for the MPLS-VPN backbone. The PE and CE form an

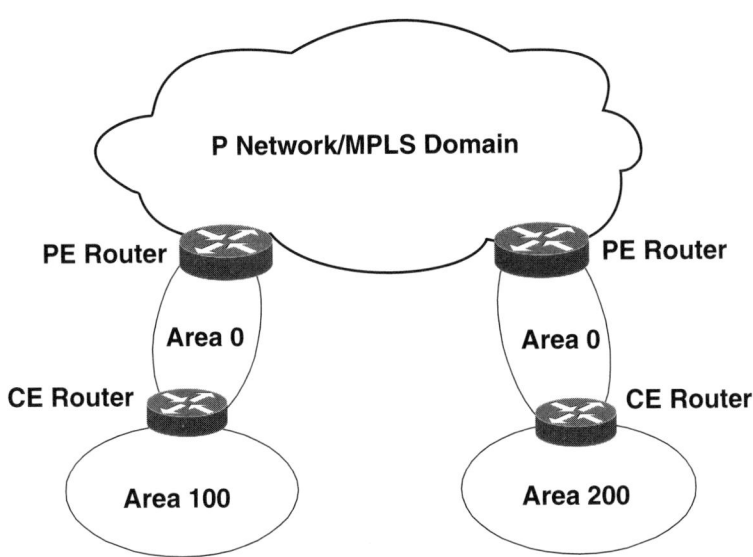

Figure 6-21 OSPF between PE and CE routers (case i).

adjacency and exchange LSAs. The CE router will propagate summary link state advertisements (LSAs) for routes from the site area to the PE. The PE will propagate summary LSAs from the MPLS-VPN backbone to the CE. The PE will propagate summary LSAs to the MPLS-VPN backbone only if another PE has not already injected these routes. This is checked by inspecting a certain bit, called the "down bit." This bit is placed in the summary LSA and marks whether the route has already been propagated by another PE from the MPLS-VPN backbone to the site areas. This mechanism is one measure by which the protocol prevents routing loops.

In case ii (Figure 6-22), the PEs are directly attached to the site area. The PE and CE form an adjacency and exchange LSAs. The PE acts as an ABR for the site area. The PE generates summary LSAs for routes from the MPLS-VPN backbone to the site area. The same mechanism using the "down bit," like in case i, is used to prevent routing loops.

In both cases, MP-iBGP has to use special attributes to carry OSPF-specific information (actually LSA information) across the backbone and pass it to all other PEs that are connected to sites within a certain OSPF domain. This information is carried in Extended Community attributes within BGP Update messages.

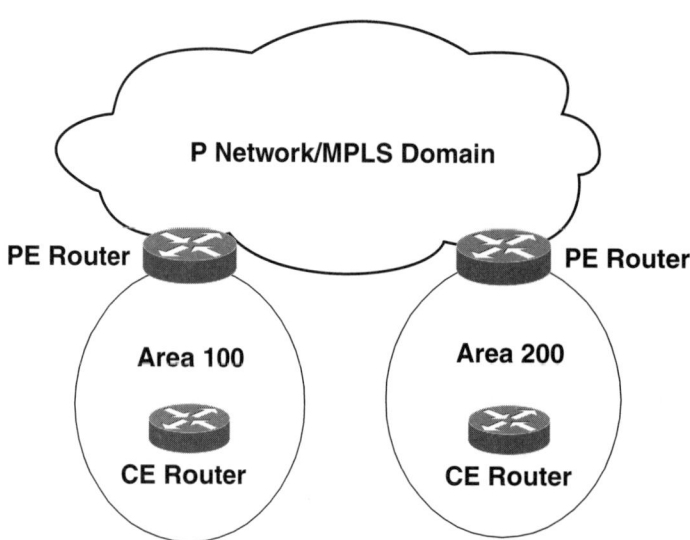

Figure 6–22 OSPF between PE and CE routers (case ii).

From a purely technical perspective, eBGP is the best choice as a routing protocol between the PE and CE routers. BGP is designed to maintain sessions with peers in multiple ASs and is therefore best suited for this task. In addition, the possibility to pass attributes from the CE router to the PE router and vice versa may be desirable under certain conditions or for future applications. The drawbacks of using eBGP are definitely the larger requirements placed on the CE devices. Another reason why one would prefer other protocols to eBGP might be the lack of knowledge at the customer site. However, if the service provider is offering a managed CPE service, eBGP should be the protocol of choice.

Topologies

There are two ways of configuring inter-service provider network site routing. In many cases, it will be desirable to allow optimal inter-VPN routing for all sites. The benefit of this is very efficient traffic forwarding. The best path from a metric perspective will be chosen to forward the client data. On the other hand, it might be desirable to force all traffic to a central site, where security checks and/or address translation, etc. can be performed. The hub-and-spoke routing configuration may be chosen if the customer has such a type of centralized infrastructure (e.g., firewall, network address translation [NAT], etc.).

VPN Sites with Optimal Inter-VPN Routing

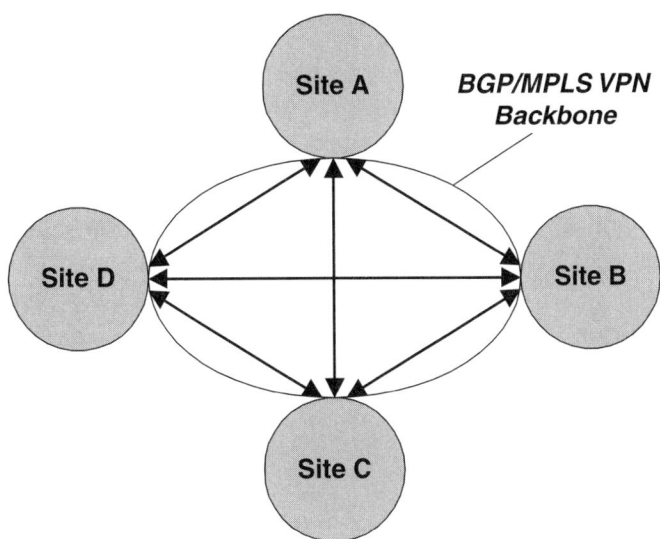

Figure 6–23 Optimal inter-VPN routing.

In Figure 6–23, sites A, B, C, and D are connected via CE and PE routers to the BGP/MPLS VPN network. If a client located in site C wanted to send traffic to site D, it would find a route in the appropriate VRF of the PE router that site C is attached to that points directly to site D. If the CE router at site C did not have any access restrictions configured for site D, all traffic would be routed to site D.

VPN Sites with Hub-and-Spoke Routing

In Figure 6–24 above, sites A, B, C, and D are connected via CE and PE routers to the BGP/MPLS VPN network in a hub-and-spoke configuration. The route distribution on the PEs is configured in such a way as to allow sites B, C, and D to only communicate via site A. In Figure 6–24, site A is the hub and acts as the central site for B, C, and D. If a client located in site C wanted to send traffic to a client located in site D, all traffic would go to site A first, and then it would be routed to site D. The benefit of this scenario is that it is relatively easy to maintain the access restrictions between sites. It might also be desirable to perform NAT functions between sites or before clients access the Internet. Hub-and-spoke routing allows such features to be configured.

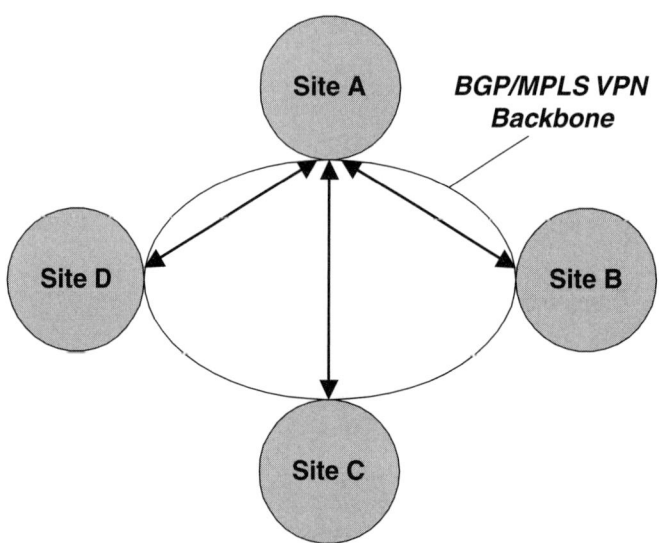

Figure 6–24 nter-VPN hub-and-spoke routing.

The configuration for hub-and-spoke routing is done in the following way:

All hub sites are configured with two different RTs: one is called "HUB," the other is called "SPOKE;" both represent two different RTs in their generic format (e.g., ASN : assigned number or IPv4 address : assigned number [see "Route Targets (RTs)"]).

The RT "HUB" is configured as an export RT, while the RT "SPOKE" is configured as an import RT. This means that each PE at a hub site will import only routes that carry an RT "SPOKE" in their BGP attributes, and will export their routes with the RT "HUB."

Two VRFs are configured at the PE connected to the central site: one is called HUB_VRF; the other is called, appropriately, SPOKE_VRF. HUB_VRF has only an import RT statement configured; in other words, it will install every route that carries the HUB RT.

The CE_HUB is connected to the central PE VRF_HUB, either with a logical or a physical link (e.g., LL, Ethernet, FR PVC, etc.). The routing protocol between PE and CE_HUB will now propagate the routing information from VRF_HUB to the routing table of CE_HUB. This PE-CE protocol might be eBGP or RIPv2.

CE_HUB and CE_SPOKE will exchange routing information with an IGP, and CE_SPOKE will learn the routes to all other sites from CE_HUB. Again,

CE_SPOKE will advertise the routes learned from CE_HUB to the VRF_SPOKE in the PE to which it is connected (see Figure 6–25). The PE-CE protocol in this case is also eBGP, OSPF, or RIPv2. Now, the PE VRF_SPOKE has learned all routes to the other sites via CE_SPOKE, which is the next hop for all other sites.

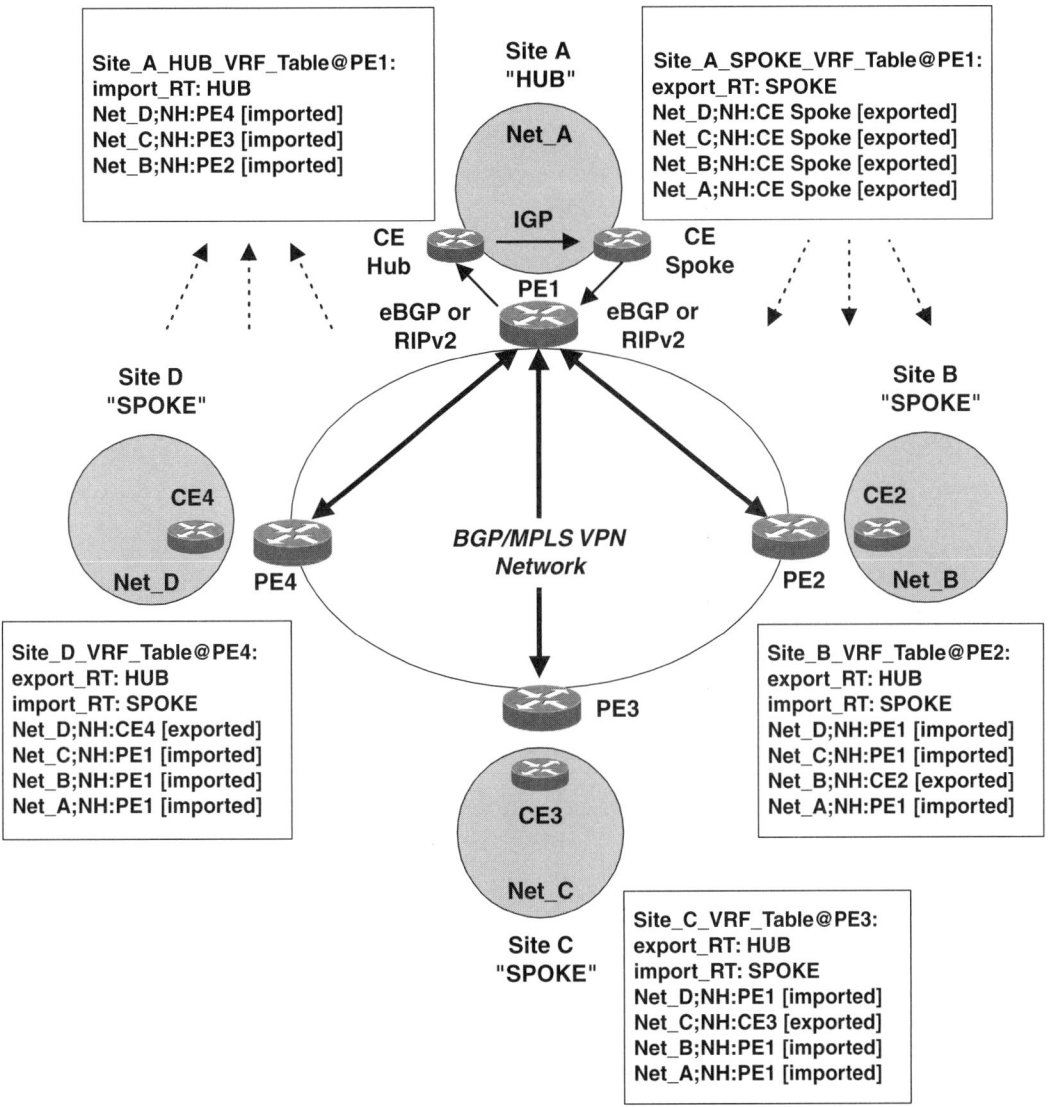

Figure 6–25 Hub-and-spoke VRF tables.

If a packet now travels from site C to site D, it will first go to the PE connected to the central site, then it will be sent to CE_SPOKE. Between CE_SPOKE and CE_HUB, security checks or any kind of central network services may be applied to the packet. The packet will then leave the central site via CE_HUB and the central PE again, down to its final destination, site D (see Figure 6–26).

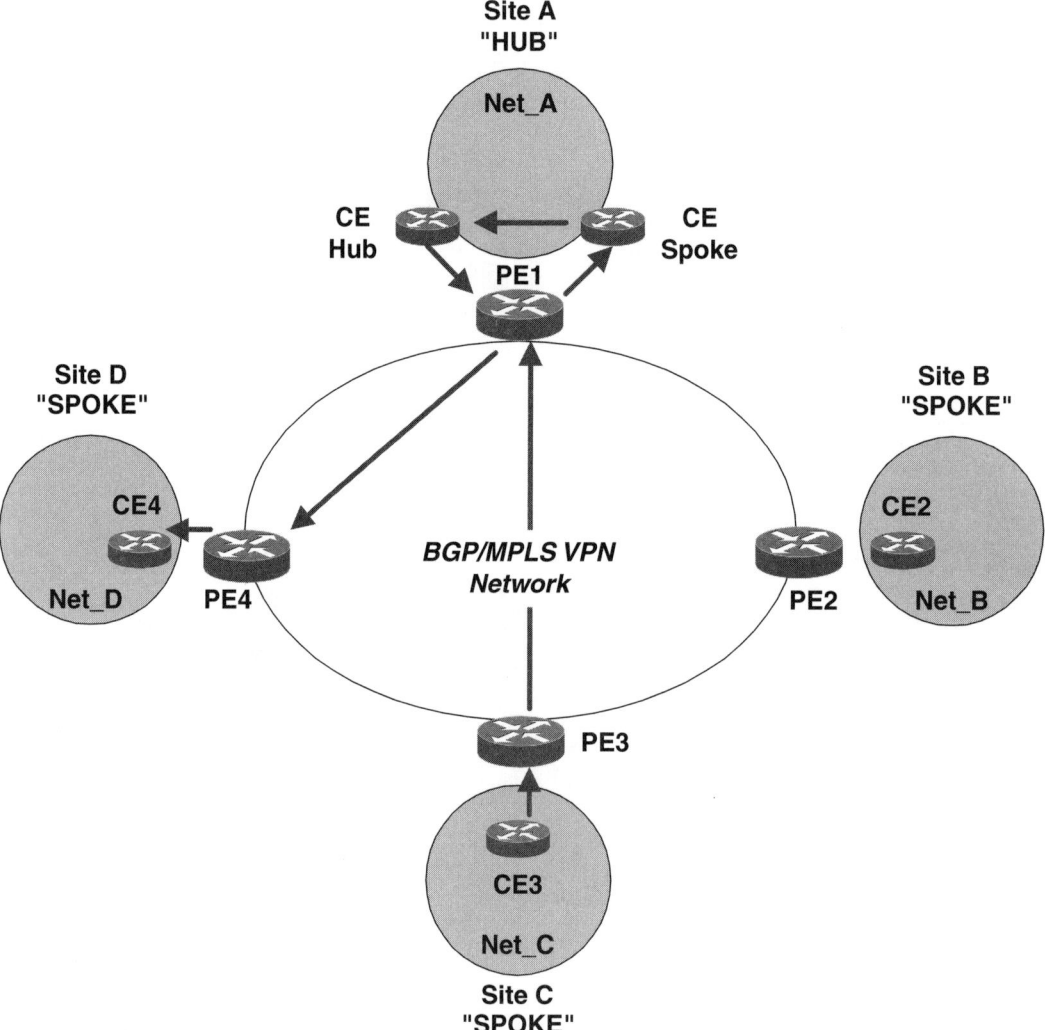

Figure 6–26 Hub-and-spoke traffic flow.

Internet Routing

Depending on the client's needs and technical constraints, there are two different ways to connect VPN sites to the Internet. In the first case, the customer has one or more sites where Internet connectivity is installed, and the service provider BGP/MPLS network is only used for site-to-site VPN connectivity. In the second case, the service provider provides Internet access as well as site-to-site VPN connectivity.

INTERNET ACCESS AT CUSTOMER SITE

This type of Internet connectivity has nothing special to do with BGP/MPLS VPNs; rather, it operates the same way it does in a legacy-routed environment. In essence, one or more customer sites has Internet connectivity. An injection of all Internet routes by the MP-iBGP process into all VRFs should be avoided. The result would be an enormous allocation of resources in the PE routers due to having to store n times the Internet routing table. To work around this problem, the customer should inject default routes from its Internet gateway routers into the site via IGP. These default routes will then be propagated via MP-iBGP to all other sites, where they will again be injected by IGP.

In Figure 6–27, the customer has two Internet gateways and border routers installed at site A. They are connected to two different ISPs. Both gateways hold full Internet routing tables and exchange routing information between each other with an iBGP session. Every gateway can determine the best route to the destination network in the Internet, either via ISP A or via ISP B. Both inject their loopback addresses as the default gateway for all other routers at this site and in all other sites. Depending on the metrics, the router ID, and whether or not both paths have the same metrics, the routers in the sites in the example will send packets destined for the Internet to either gateway 1 or gateway 2. The advantage of this configuration is that even if one gateway goes down, the other gateway can still transport Internet traffic and is still reachable from all routers.

INTERNET ACCESS HANDLED BY SERVICE PROVIDER

In the case where the VPN service provider also provides Internet access, the following possibilities exist:

> i. The VRF has a default route in the global routing table of the PE (e.g., an Internet gateway of the service provider).

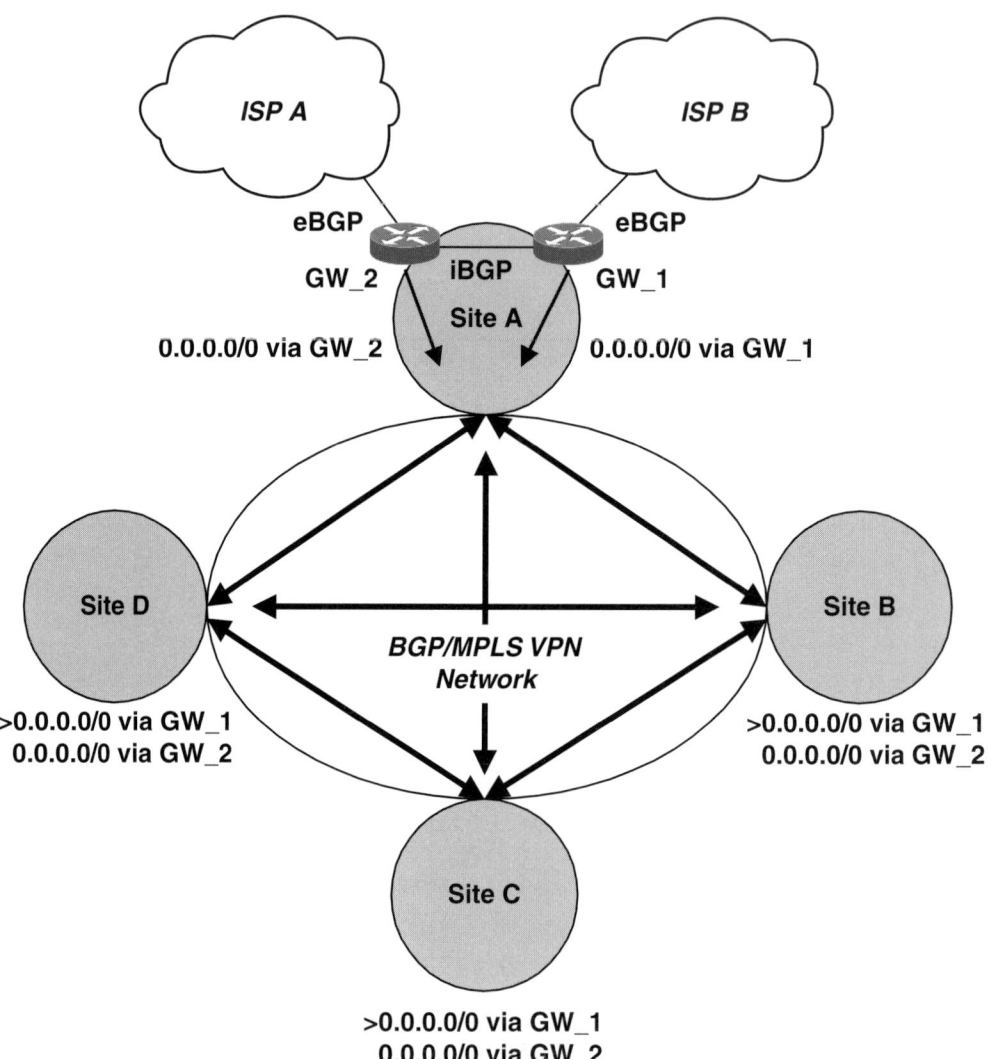

Figure 6-27 Internet connectivity at the customer site.

ii. The CE and PE routers are connected via two logical or physical links. One link handles the VPN routes and VPN connectivity; the other link handles the Internet routes and transports the Internet traffic.

In the first case (i), which is depicted in Figure 6-28, the Internet gateway is part of the service provider network and is not part of a VPN. The VRF at PE_D holds a default entry that says all packets that have no match in the VRF table should be sent to the Internet gateway router, which can be found in the global routing table outside the VRF. The PE has to have another entry that points to Net_D inside the VRF for packets traveling back from the Internet. This configuration is static because all reachable public networks inside the customer sites have to be statically configured at the PE level by the service provider.

In the second case (ii), shown in Figure 6–29, the customer wants to announce and receive routes to and from the Internet. In this example, the customer has connections with two different subinterfaces to the PE router. One connection carries the VPN traffic and is assigned to a certain VRF in the PE, and the other link is assigned to the global routing table of the PE router. The BGP session between the customer peer and service provider peer will run over the link connected to the global routing table. The CE router has to decide where to route the traffic, to the VPN (sub)interface on the PE or to the global (sub)interface on the PE. This must not be confused with the Carrier's Carrier (CsC) architecture, where PEs and CEs distribute labels. This is not the case here. The Internet traffic is routed in a legacy way over the global PE-CE link.

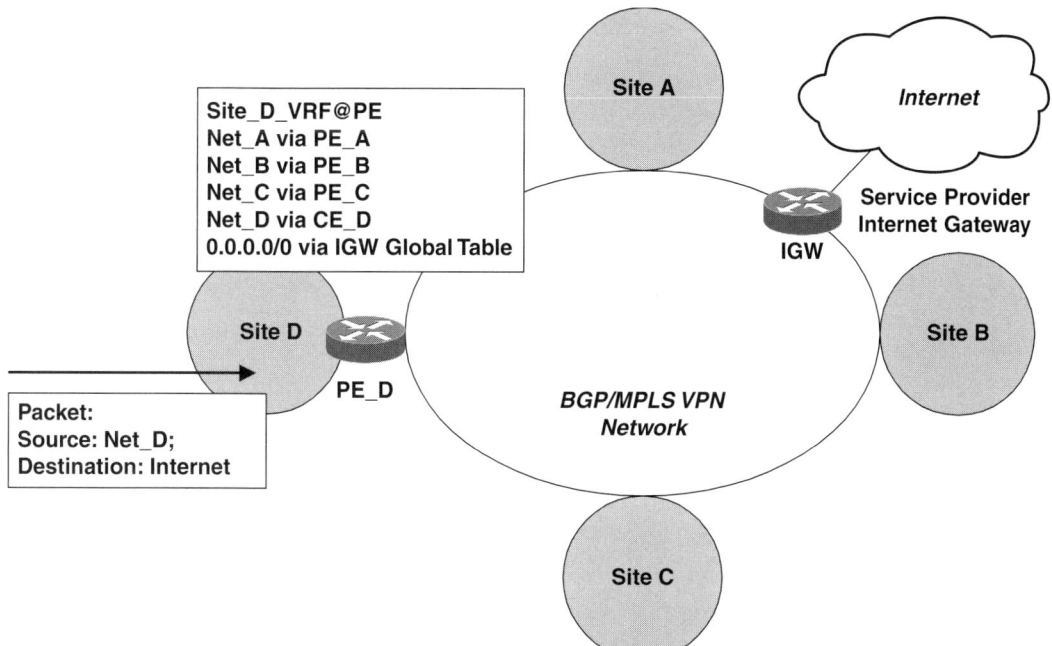

Figure 6–28 Internet connectivity from the service provider—global default route.

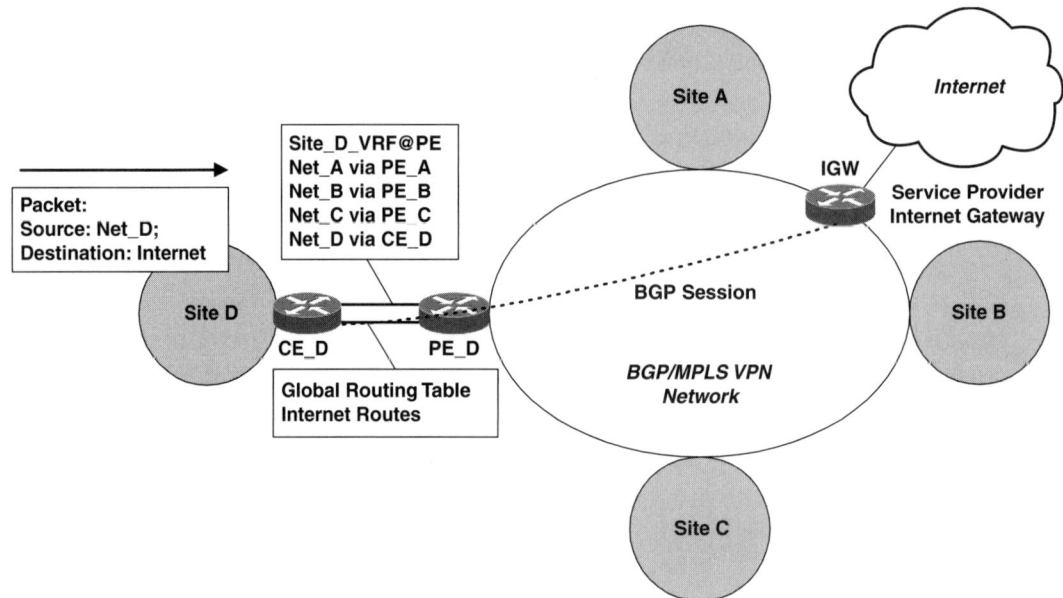

Figure 6-29 Internet connectivity from the service provider—two PE-CE links.

This scenario is suitable for larger customers who want to advertise their own networks directly to the Internet. It is also suitable for small service providers with only one site that holds the full Internet routing table and all other sites having a default route to the main site. This scenario is not suitable when the service provider has an inter-site BGP session to other sites, where the Internet routing table is exchanged. The latter example would be suitable for CsC.

NETWORK ADDRESS TRANSLATION (NAT)

One of the major challenges of deploying large networks is the limited address space of IPv4. Two solutions are available to handle this problem. One entails using the private address ranges as defined in RFC 1918 [IETF-7]. The addresses are not routed via the Internet and can be used without registration. The other method is NAT.

When we examine the networks of mobile operators, we see that the number of mobile devices such as cell phones and PDAs is expected to grow in the range of hundreds of millions in the next years. These service types are in most cases General Packet Radio Service (GPRS) or Universal Mobile Telecommunication System (UMTS), which are expected to be "always on." Most Internet users today use dial services, and they use addresses only for the duration of time they are connected to the access servers. Once disconnected, their address is returned to a pool of addresses. This will change dramatically during the beginning of this first decade of the millennium. The tendency is clearly toward services that are always on. Such services require static IP addresses regardless of the interaction from the user since they are always connected. Private address ranges are an appropriate solution to handle intra-corporate traffic, while NAT must be used to access the Internet from hosts within private address ranges.

Two strategies can be chosen by network designers and administrators to handle the deployment of the NAT function in their networks. This function can be deployed at either the PE level or at the central site. If the service provider wishes to offer application services that can be accessed from every VPN, it is useful to perform address translation at the PE-VRF level, when the packet is received at the PE. If the central site is a VPN, routes are announced via BGP/MPLS VPN route distribution methods to the other sites so that every VPN site may reach the central site. However, VPNs are not allowed to exchange routing information with each other.

Avoiding a second level of address translation is optimal; public addresses may be used for this purpose (see Figure 6–30).

Another scenario entails the use of address translation to reach the Internet from hosts in private address ranges (e.g., service provider consumer customers). This is only applicable if all hosts have different IP addresses, unlike the example above (see Figure 6–31).

Scalability

Route Reflectors (RRs)

If the number of routing peers in the iBGP mesh is large, it is useful to introduce one or more route reflectors (RRs) into the network to offload some of the BGP processing to a dedicated device. Under normal circumstances, the configuration of iBGP in a fully-meshed configuration may require a lot of configuration work each time a new iBGP peer is added. This is because the configuration on all other peers has to be adapted. To avoid this configuration overhead and the large number of sessions per peer, an RR can be added. Instead of peering with all

142   Chapter 6 ▸ Details of MPLS VPNs

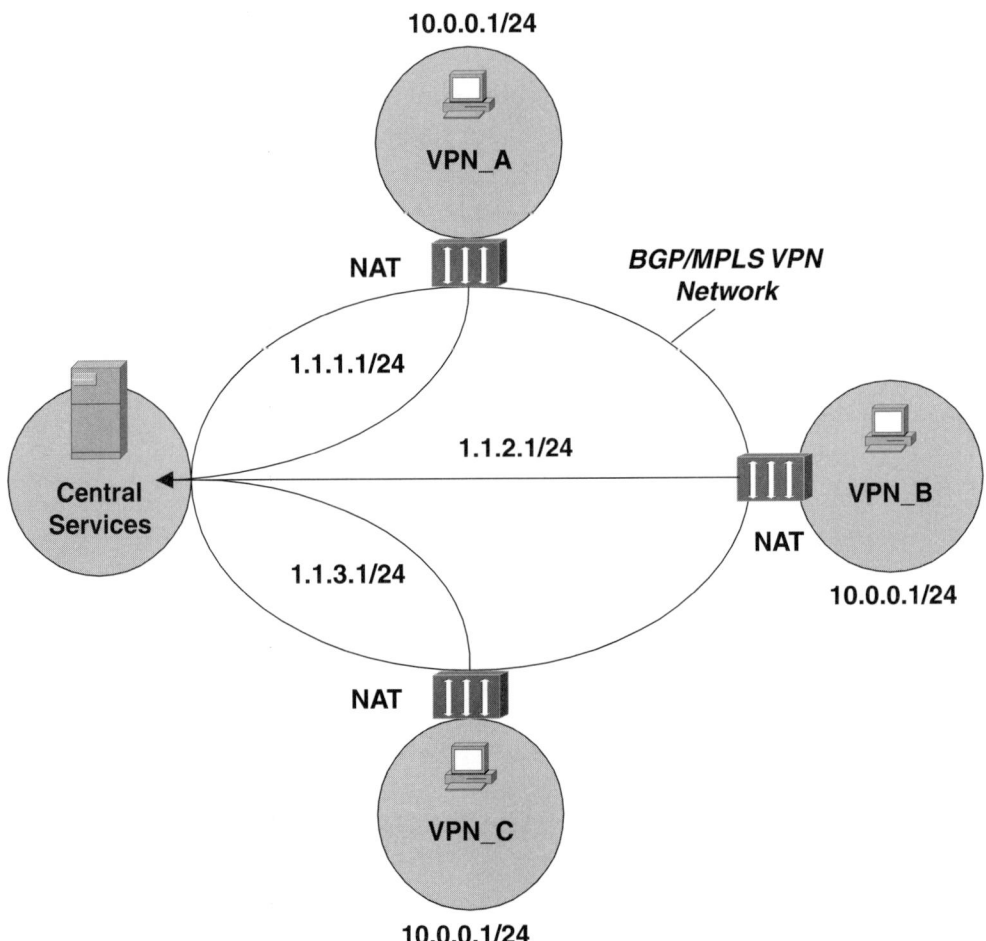

Figure 6–30   NAT between VPNs.

iBGP neighbors, it is possible to peer with just one RR that sends BGP updates to all other iBGP peers. To increase the reliability of the system, two RRs should be physically separated and the logical connections between the RR clients and the RRs should traverse different physical links (see Figure 6–32). It makes no sense to put both RRs in a subnet that is only reachable via one physical link since a single link failure will result in a loss of connectivity to both RRs! The RR can be any router in the network that is capable of handling the required number of sessions. It can also be a PE if there is enough processing power available on the router. This concept is only applicable if all iBGP peers are located in the

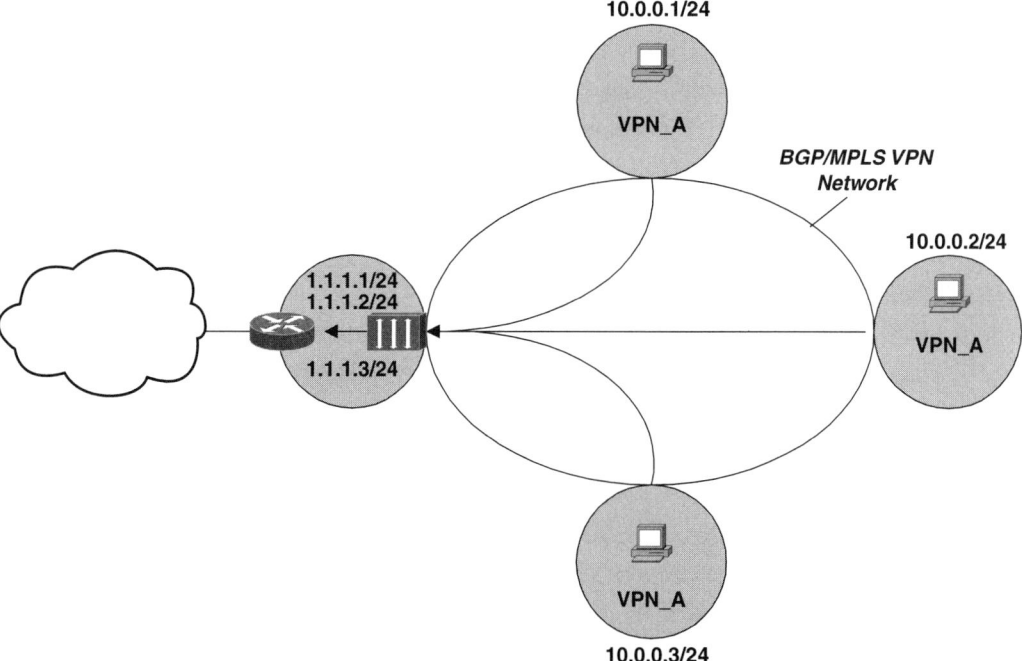

Figure 6–31 Internet access with NAT.

same AS. If there are peers in different ASs, the RRs must maintain eBGP sessions with RRs in other ASs and exchange label information via eBGP.

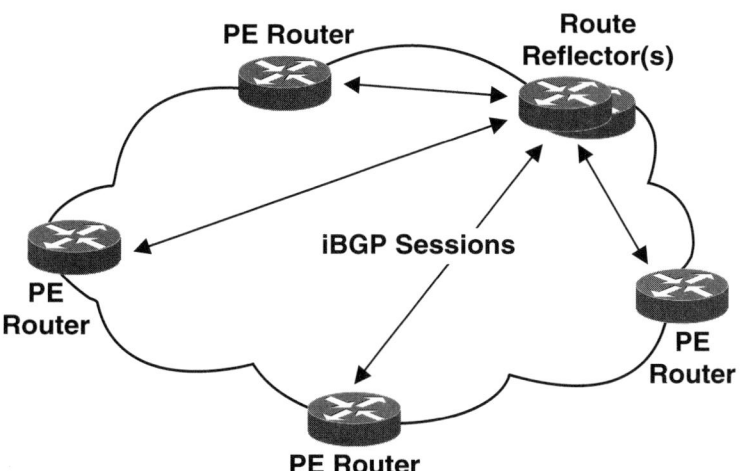

Figure 6–32 Scaling the iBGP mesh with RRs.

Since a single RR is a single point of failure, it should be backed up with at least one secondary RR. RR hierarchies can also be used to improve performance and scalability. It is possible to configure RRs for certain groups of VPNs; this introduces another level of scalability in this architecture (see Figure 6–33). If this is done, there is no need for a central RR that manages all VPN routes.

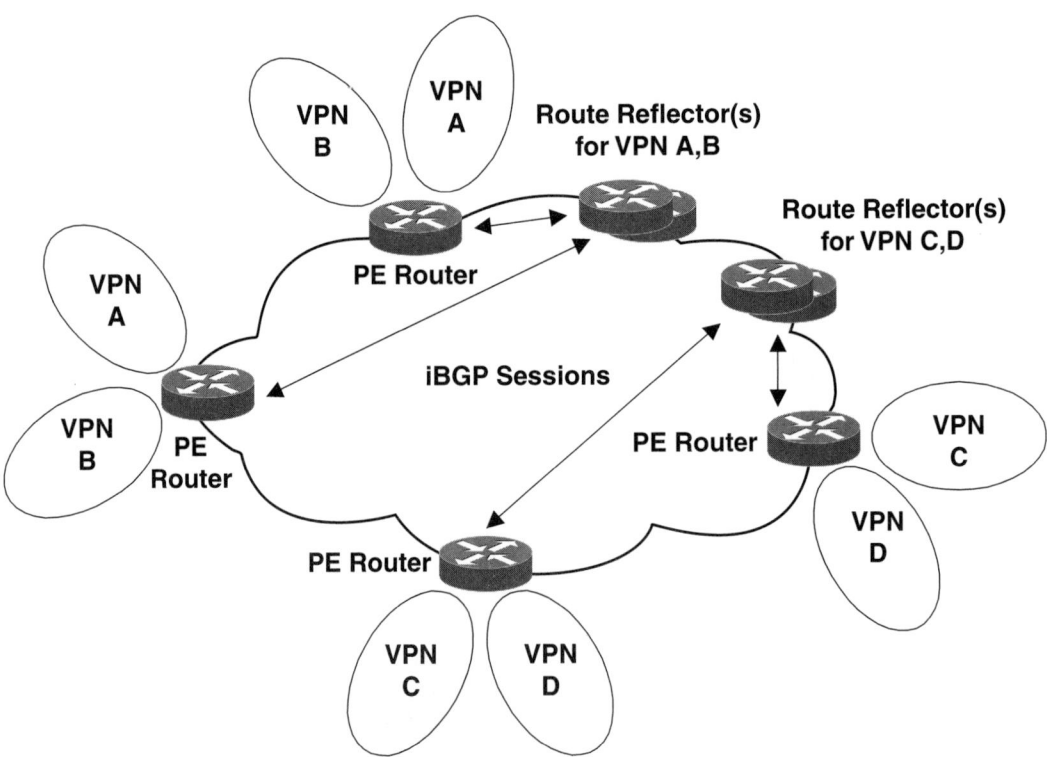

Figure 6-33 RRs for different VPNs.

This scenario can be achieved by setting route filters, called outbound route filters (ORFs), in the RR clients, so that a certain RR only receives routes from a subgroup of all VPNs of the service provider network. These ORFs are configured at the RR and are then applied to the RR clients. The RR sends out a BGP Refresh message to its clients, where all RTs that have to be received by the RR are listed. This mechanism is described in [IETF-6].

If PE routers are located in different ASs, then labels have to be distributed with eBGP as shown in Figure 6–34. This should be done only at private exchange points, and not at public Internet exchanges, to avoid label spoofing and to guarantee a maximum level of security between different VPNs. The ranges of labels that may be announced by different eBGP peers from different ASs should be tightly controlled and filtered at the autonomous system border routers (ASBRs) to prevent breaches in security.

In Figure 6–34, the RR performs the functions of an ASBR in addition to its route reflection duties. Another scenario could be that the ASBR is a client of the RR. Both scenarios are equivalent from a functional perspective.

Adding New Sites to a VPN

One of the major benefits of the BGP/MPLS VPN architecture is the easy configuration of new customer sites. Only the PE where the new site is connected and the CE of the customer site have to be configured. Once this is done, all other sites will automatically receive the routes for the new site as soon as the routing protocols have converged. By contrast, overlay architectures such as GRE, IP over ATM, and IP over Frame Relay require that all customer routers be reconfigured, including the newly added device.

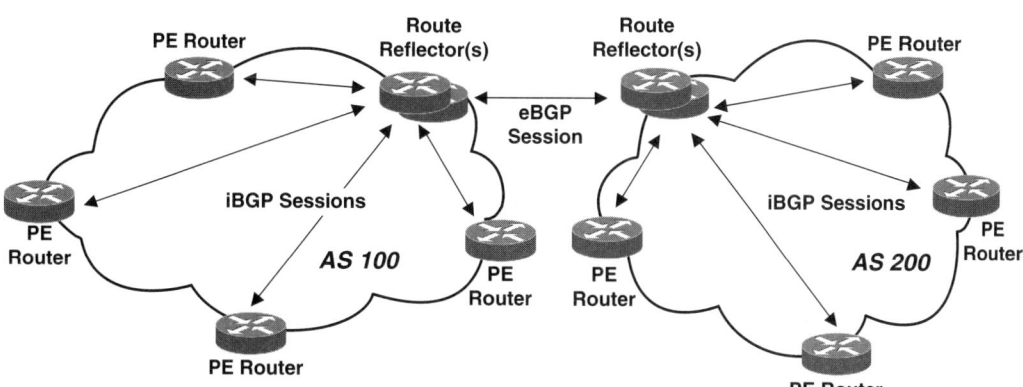

Figure 6–34 Distributing label information with eBGP.

BGP Update Filtering

All PE routers maintain a fully-meshed MP-iBGP session between all other iBGP peers, unless they are connected to an RR. To avoid the situation where all PE routers would have to store all VPN routes, they simply discard every

VPN-IPv4 route with an RT that has not been configured on the PE. Thus, the amount of routing information each PE has to store is on the order of the number of routes to which the VPN is attached. This gives this architecture another element of scalability.

Outbound Route Filters (ORFs)

It would be extremely desirable to avoid the updates other PEs or RRs send to PEs since they have no use for these updates and will discard them. This is achieved by using ORFs [IETF-6]. ORFs can be configured on PEs, and these filters are sent to all other PE peers or to the RRs.

ORFs are sent within BGP Refresh messages. A special Extended Communities ORF type specifies the RTs that should be filtered at the output side of the PE peers or at the RR.

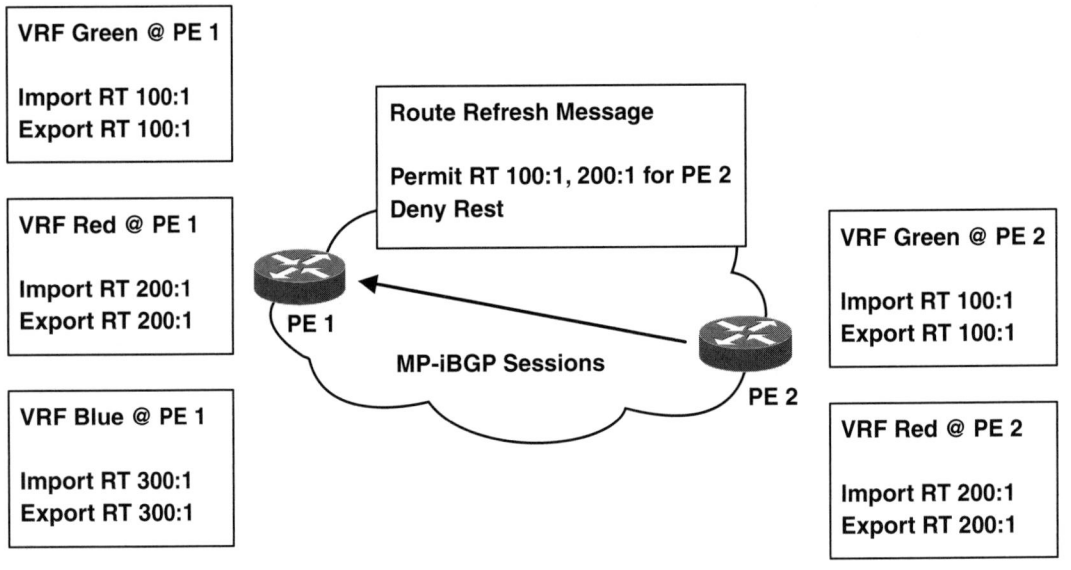

Figure 6-35 ORFs.

In Figure 6-35, router PE 2 sends a BGP Refresh message that contains ORF entries to router PE 1. PE 1 receives the Refresh message and installs ORFs for router PE 2. From this moment on, router PE 1 will send only routing updates that carry RT 100:1 or 200:1 in the Update messages to router PE2.

If at a later point in time PE 2 is reconfigured and VRF Blue is also added to PE 2, then PE 2 has to send another route refresh to PE 1, which clears the filter entry and installs a new filter set.

Carrier's Carrier (CsC)

Imagine a situation where the customer of a service provider who has an MPLS backbone is a service provider itself. Such a configuration is called "Carrier's Carrier," or CsC, in the BGP/MPLS VPN architecture (see Figure 6-36) [IETF-4]. The possibility to provide transit services to other ISPs makes the BGP/MPLS VPN architecture even more powerful and attractive from a service provider's perspective. This section will refer to the provider of the transit service as the "carrier ISP" and the client of this provider as the "client ISP." Clients of the client ISP will be called "client ISP customers."

The main motivation for the CsC additions to the normal BGP/MPLS VPN architecture is the fact that client ISPs may possess the entire Internet routing table in their sites, which may in fact be client ISP PoPs (points of presence). This amount of routing information would have to be carried within the inter-PE MP-iBGP routing updates. This brings up scalability issues since the Internet routing table is very large and has a somewhat dynamic behavior. The Internet routing table consists of several tens of thousands (> 100,000) of routes and often exhibits flapping and transient route changes. The goal of the CsC architecture is to minimize the number of routes the carrier ISP's PEs must exchange. This is achieved by including only internal client ISP routes in the MP-iBGP update process. In addition, external client ISP routes (e.g., the full Internet table) already at the CE router side are labeled. To enable this feature, label distribution is used between the PE-CE link. The carrier ISP's PE routers propagate client ISP site routes to other carrier ISP PEs. The carrier ISP PE routers advertise routes received from other PEs to client ISP CEs. The client ISP CE routers advertise only internal routes and not the full Internet routing table to carrier ISP PE routers.

iBGP multihop sessions are used to advertise external routes between client ISP sites within the same AS; multihop intra-confederation eBGP is used to distribute client ISP external routes between sites within different ASs.

In general, three different cases can be distinguished:

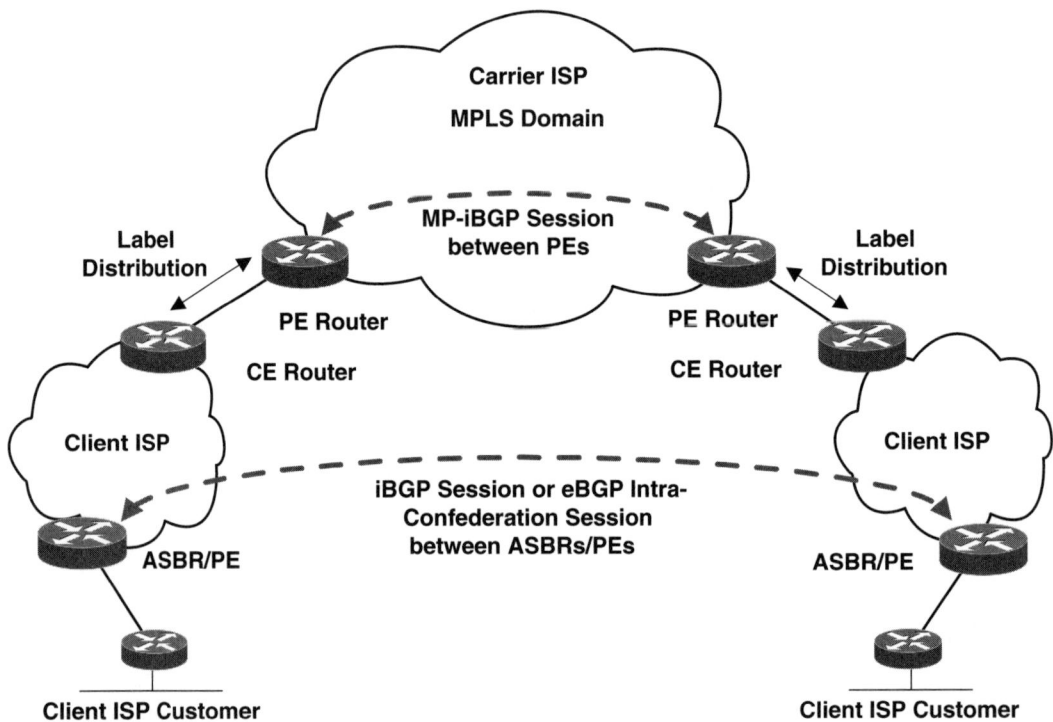

Figure 6–36 CsC architecture.

 i. The client ISP is not running MPLS in its backbone (see Figure 6–37).
 ii. The client ISP is running MPLS in its backbone.
 iii. The client ISP is running MPLS in its backbone and is offering BGP/MPLS VPNs to its customers.

In the first case (i), the client ISP is not running MPLS in its backbone. The sites, which are all in the same AS, establish iBGP sessions between ASBRs on each site in a fully-meshed configuration, or with RRs, to enable the exchange of external routes (e.g., the full Internet routing table). If the sites are not in the same AS, they must use eBGP intra-confederation sessions. Client ISP CE routers receive BGP-4 routes with labels from the carrier's PE router. The client ISP advertises internal site routes without any labels, since the site does not run MPLS. The external routes of the client ISP are not advertised to the carrier's PE routers; hence, the carrier ISP backbone does not need to know any external routes of the client ISP. Packets traveling to an external address from one client ISP site to another client ISP site will be labeled before they enter the carrier

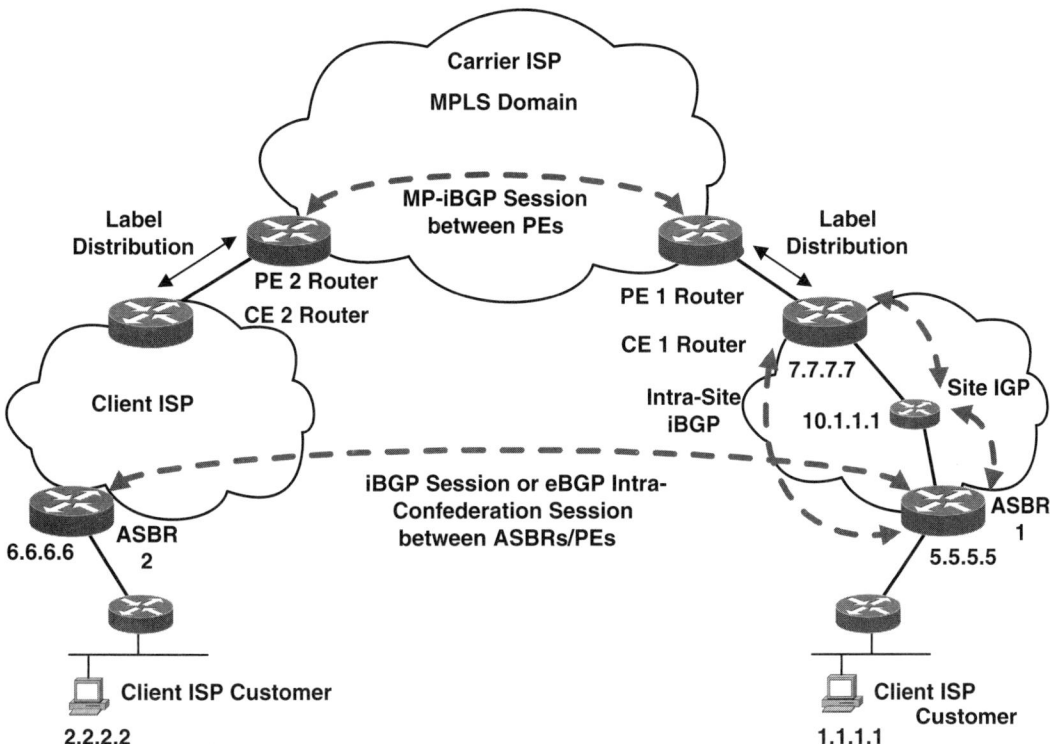

Figure 6-37 Example of CsC (case i).

ISP backbone. The sites have BGP routes for external addresses (from the inter-site BGP session) with next-hop addresses learned by another BGP route, which has been advertised by the carrier ISP PE router. An example demonstrating this follows.

If a packet wants to travel from an external client ISP customer site to another client ISP customer site with external addresses, the lookup procedure is as follows:

>Customer source IP address: [1.1.1.1]
>Customer destination IP address: [2.2.2.2]
>IP packet source [1.1.1.1] destination [2.2.2.2]
>
>Client ISP ASBR 1: [5.5.5.5]
>Client ISP ASBR 2: [6.6.6.6]
>Client ISP CE 1: [7.7.7.7]

The packet arrives at client ISP ASBR 1.
Client ISP ASBR 1 has the following routing table:

2.2.2.2 is reachable via 6.6.6.6 (learned from BGP inter-site session)
6.6.6.6 is reachable via 7.7.7.7 (learned from iBGP intra-site session)
7.7.7.7 is reachable via 10.1.1.1 (learned from client ISP site IGP, e.g., OSPF)

The ASBR learns the route to the destination of the packet from the inter-site BGP session. This route entry has the ASBR of the other site [6.6.6.6] listed as a next hop. Actually, ASBR 2 is only reachable via the carrier's ISP backbone. The intra-site iBGP has propagated that [6.6.6.6] is reachable via router CE 1 [7.7.7.7]. If CE 1 is not directly connected, then the site IGP has to have an entry for the CE 1 router. This procedure represents a double recursive lookup. When the packet arrives at CE 1, it will be labeled and sent out to PE 1, where it gets label switched through the carrier's ISP backbone network and inserted into the destination VPN, where it will be sent to its final destination.

In the second scenario (case ii), the client ISP is running MPLS in its backbone. As in the previous example, iBGP multihop or eBGP intra-confederation sessions are used between client ISP sites to distribute external routes between these sites. There are two possibilities: either the BGP session between the sites distributes label information or it does not. The argument for inter-site label distribution is that the last ASBR the packet traverses does not need to perform an IP lookup if it knows which label is associated with which customer. This can only be accomplished if the labels are distributed via BGP across the different client ISP sites. If the sites do not exchange label information, only one label is needed in the label stack in the client ISP site. If the sites exchange label information, two labels in the client ISP site are needed to switch the packet to its final destination. In an effort to mark the interface, the ASBR has to send out the packet to the customer's network based on applying the top label on a per-interface basis; the bottom label is applied on an end-to-end (ASBR-to-ASBR) basis. The client ISP CE router must distribute all internal routes from the other sites that it has learned from the carrier ISP PE router. All client ISP CE routers and ASBRs have to run iBGP sessions. The client ISP IGP guarantees the reachability of all internal routes within the site, and LDP distributes label information in the site.

In the third case (iii), the client ISP runs MPLS in its backbone and offers BGP/MPLS VPNs to its customers. The mechanisms for this last scenario are similar to the mechanisms discussed in the previous examples (cases i and ii). The main difference is that the client ISP's ASBRs are now PE routers. The client ISP PE router has VRFs configured, and its customer interfaces are assigned to these VRFs. The client ISP maintains MP-iBGP sessions between all its PE routers and exchanges VPN-IPv4 addresses between them. The total number of labels is: three labels in the carrier ISP backbone and two labels in the client ISP backbone.

This chapter discussed the details of MPLS VPNs. We covered how VPNs interact with other routing protocols and how we can access the Internet from within VPNs. We also covered the possibility of offering VPN services to carriers who offer VPN services themselves.

Having described all the mechanisms and protocols that build MPLS VPNs, we will look at typical current and future applications in the next chapter.

7
MPLS VPN Applications

There are various applications for Border Gateway Protocol/Multiprotocol Label Switching Virtual Personal Networks (BGP/MPLS VPNs). A very strong argument for this architecture is that it is not linked to a special access technology because it is by its nature, independent of the data link protocol and access media used. In this chapter, we will look closer at how BGP/MPLS VPNs can be used in different scenarios and network types.

Enterprise VPN Services

Most legacy VPN services rely on Frame Relay or Asynchronous Transfer Mode (ATM) as the access network technology (see Figure 7–1). Both Frame Relay and ATM are still well-suited to build the access network infrastructure for Internet Protocol (IP) VPNs.

The major difference is that Frame Relay or ATM will only be used between customer edge (CE) and provider edge (PE) routers, whereas the backbone technology that runs between the PEs is chosen by the service provider. An alternative to the Frame Relay/ATM service is to skip the access network and just use leased lines as an access medium. Since Frame Relay and ATM are well-understood access network technologies, we will focus on relatively new access methods such as Asymmetric Digital Subscriber Line (ADSL), cable access, and mobile wireless.

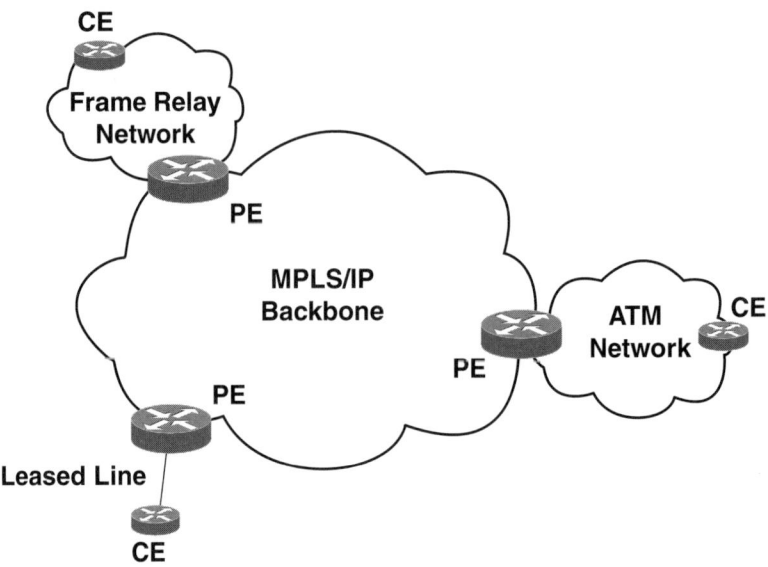

Figure 7-1 Typical enterprise access network technologies.

ADSL VPNs

DSL Technology Overview

Digital Subscriber Line (DSL) is a public network technology that delivers high-speed bandwidth on conventional twisted-pair copper wiring over limited distances. DSL is provisioned via modem pairs, with one modem located at a central office and the other at the customer site. As is the case in legacy dial-in services, modems co-located at the central office site are physically implemented in a single device called the DSL access multiplexer/concentrator. DSL technology is designed to coexist with legacy voice services over the existing copper wire infrastructure. Analog voice services are always supported in this technology, and ISDN services are even supported in most cases. There are four types of DSL available today: ADSL, HDSL, SDSL, and VDSL.

Asymmetric Digital Subscriber Line (ADSL) is designed to deliver more bandwidth downstream (i.e., from the service provider network to the customer site) than in the upstream direction (i.e., from the customer site to the service provider network). Downstream rates range from 1.5 to 9 Mbps, while upstream bandwidth ranges from 16 to 640 Kbps. ADSL transmissions are capable of functioning at distances of up to 5,488 meters over a single copper twisted pair.

High-data-rate Digital Subscriber Line (HDSL) delivers up to 2 Mbps in both directions and is deployed over two twisted pairs of copper cable.

Single-line Digital Subscriber Line (SDSL) and the standardized version, Symmetric High-speed Digital Subscriber Line (G.SHDSL), deliver 2 to 2.3 Mbps of bandwidth both downstream and upstream over a single copper twisted pair.

Very-high-data-rate Digital Subscriber Line (VDSL) delivers 13 to 52 Mbps of bandwidth in the downstream direction and 1.5 to 2.3 Mbps upstream. VDSL offers these data rates over a single twisted-pair connection. The operating range of VDSL is limited to 304.8 to 1,372 meters.

ADSL defines ATM as the underlying data link protocol. Figure 7–2 depicts a very simplified diagram of the salient elements present in the ADSL network architecture.

ADSL is a pure transport technology, and does not define any services.

One way to implement the DSL access multiplexer is to terminate the physical layer at the modems and then switch the ATM traffic according to the ATM service class. The ADSL modem maintains one or more ATM permanent virtual connections (PVCs) to the ADSL access multiplexer integrated with the shelf of modems. ATM cells are transported over ADSL technology using Discrete Multitone (DMT) modulation. The access multiplexer is located at the central office, where all data lines are terminated. The ADSL access multiplexer switches the ATM PVCs it maintains between itself and the IP aggregation device. The IP aggregation device is typically implemented as a router. The main function of the aggregation device is to unpack ATM cells that have been carried over the PVCs and examine the upper-layer information contained therein. The upper-layer information is IP and/or PPP traffic in most cases. Traffic is forwarded to its final destination depending on the Layer 3 (IP) or Layer 2 (PPP) information.

An alternate implementation scenario is to build Layer 3 intelligence into the ADSL access multiplexer. In this case, it is possible to terminate the ATM PVCs that emanate from the modems and unpack their ATM cell payload. The cell payload is either IP and/or Point-to-Point Protocol (PPP). The capability to examine Layer 3 information directly at the ADSL access multiplexer point

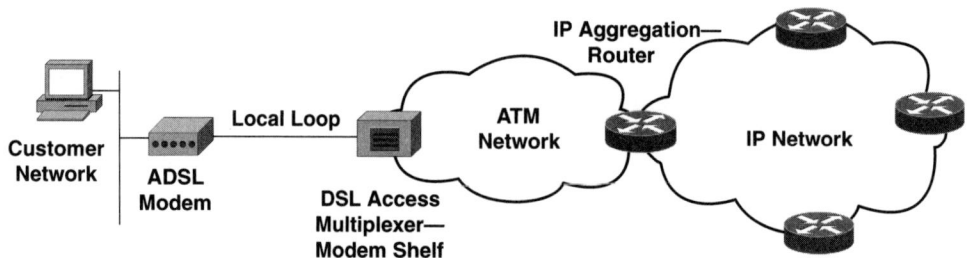

Figure 7-2   ADSL network architecture.

results in greater flexibility for the provider in offering value-added network services such as IP QoS or IP VPNs.

Connection Paradigm

Different vendors use different connection paradigms to connect their customers to the network. The choices available are either bridged PPP over Ethernet (PPPoE) or PPP over ATM (PPPoA). These are both defined in RFC 1483 [IETF-21]. The bridged variant is connectionless, while the PPP variants are connection-oriented. The user or modem must establish a PPP session, which should require the user to authenticate. This is not the case in the bridged configuration.

ADSL IP VPNs

The most scalable way of providing VPN services for large numbers of customers that are spread among numerous customer sites is to migrate to BGP/MPLS VPNs. The question then becomes one of where to locate the PE functionality. If we first consider the modem as a candidate for PE functionality, we soon determine that the capability of such a device is probably not well-suited for this purpose. First, in most cases, the modem has no routing functionality because it would make the device much too expensive. Second, even if the modem supports routing, in our case, we need at least three different routing processes to execute in this device: the PE-CE routing protocol, the PE-PE routing protocol [MP-iBGP], and IGP to the P routers. Finally, if we require a fully-meshed PE to be implemented with MP-iBGP, we encounter problems in terms of minimum routing/forwarding horsepower as well as minimum memory requirements that may be prohibitive in terms of cost constraints. This occurs even if BGP route reflector (RRs) are employed.

The next most logical component to consider as a PE device is the ADSL access multiplexer. This is a very viable solution, assuming this device supports IP functionality since it is often built on legacy ATM switching hardware. The decentralized architecture of this solution, especially if we consider the distribution of the routing tables, makes it very appealing. Being able to "hardwire" modem PVCs into VPN Routing and Forwarding table (VRFs) on the ADSL access multiplexer would be a suitable solution. The provisioning process would require that the appropriate VRF for a certain VPN be pre-instantiated on the device before the customer is connected. This solution requires the VPN service provider to know the exact physical location of the customer to provision the VPN service for this customer. If the customer moves, the configuration must be changed.

If we move further toward the core IP network, the next candidate is the IP aggregation device. This device has routing functionality and is very well-suited to deliver PE functionality for modems in a bridged configuration using RFC 1483 [IETF-21]. Despite these advantages, the service provider must still know the approximate location (i.e., behind which IP aggregation device) of the customer to configure the appropriate VRF on the IP aggregation device.

If we assume that the customer establishes a PPP session directly from its client, we have another choice for the PE device. We can "relay" the PPP session using Layer 2 Tunneling Protocol (L2TP) [IETF-8] on the IP aggregation device or L2TP access server (LAC), and terminate it on an L2TP network server (LNS). The LNS is essentially another IP router that is capable of terminating L2TP sessions. It is also capable of PE functionality. The advantage of this solution is the high level of scalability and flexibility it provides. If the ADSL provider decides to offer a wholesale variant of this service to other alternative service providers, it is possible to even offer BGP/MPLS VPN services.

Based on the domain name, the LAC will decide which LNS it should establish an L2TP tunnel with. The LNS terminates the L2TP session and puts the user in the appropriate VRF (see Figure 7–3).

If L2TP is employed as a connection technology, the location of the PE must be selected. It is possible to build groups of VPNs on one device, and if processing power or memory becomes limited because of the number of routing entries,

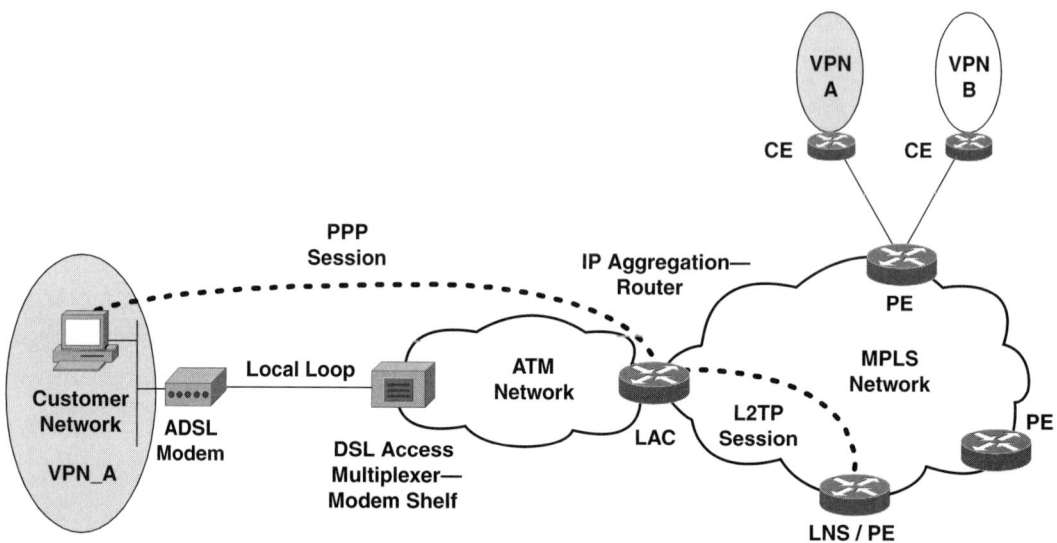

Figure 7-3 ADSL VPNs with L2TP.

it is possible to install another LNS/PE. Thus, each PE keeps track of a group of VPNs and a certain number of users. Additionally, the capability to store locality information for each VPN LNS in a Radius server makes this scenario even more appealing to network designers and administrators.

In Figure 7-4, we see a scenario where the incumbent SP, the PTT, or the incumbent operator offers L2TP access to another service provider (i.e., an ISP). Based on Radius information, the client PPP sessions are tunneled to LNSs that assign clients to the appropriate VRFs. This scenario works well if the ISP wishes to deploy BGP/MPLS VPNs with the prerequisite that the PTT must allow more than one tunnel to each ISP. Each different VPN maintained by the ISP will consume one L2TP tunnel. For example, if an ISP would like to offer a new VPN for customer A, there must be a domain that identifies the tunnel. One such naming convention could be user_x@VPN_A#ISP.COM. The domain name, VPN_A#ISP.COM, must be stored in the PTT's Radius server and must point to the IP address of an LNS in the ISP network. The character "#" is used as delimiter by the PTT; the character "@" is used by the ISP as a delimiter.

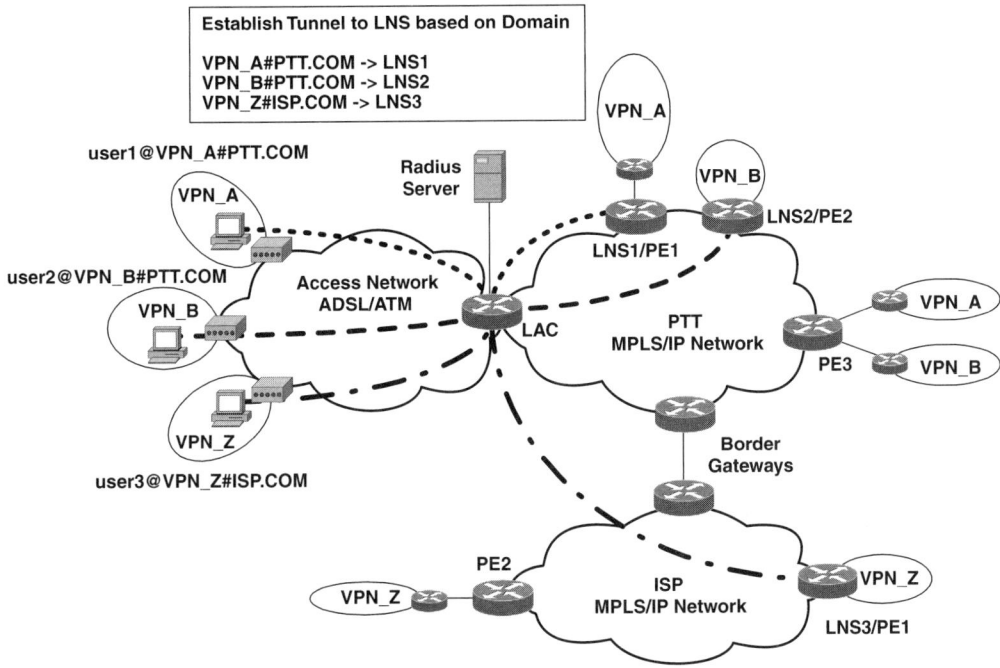

Figure 7-4 PTT provides L2TP access to another ISP.

Routing

If a user initiates a PPP session from a PC, the LNS will simply install a host route for this client at the time the session comes up. To avoid the injection of host routes into the MP-iBGP process, it is possible to configure the network from which the host route is assigned on the LNS ahead of time. If every host route were injected into the MP-iBGP process, this would result in many routing changes, as well as the unnecessary consumption of processor power. Due to the slow convergence of BGP, it could take up to one minute for all PE peers in the network to learn of a new host route. It is therefore preferred to announce the entire network before session initialization. This scenario is very similar to traditional dial-in networking.

If the client initiating the PPP session is an ADSL router, this will result in the whole network being logically "behind" this router. The result is that this network must be announced to the other PE routers. We can use the same protocols that we use between PE and CE routers in a legacy configuration to accomplish this, or we can configure static routing entries on the LNS. Unless the MP-iBGP update timers are updated and dynamic routing between CE (ADSL router) and PE (LNS) is employed, slow convergence times may be experienced. Routing stability and convergence time must be taken into account if this technology is used to create backup network connections.

Cable Access VPNs

Cable Technology Overview

Data over cable is a relatively new technology that uses the existing hybrid fiber coax infrastructure to transport data traffic. There are three major standards currently in use: the Data over Cable Interface Specification (DOCSIS), Euro-DOCSIS, and DVB-RC (Digital Video Broadcast-Return Channel). Euro-DOCSIS is a slight variation of the DOCSIS standard, whereby the upstream frequency range and downstream channel width differ from DOCSIS. All three standards use two different channels (i.e., frequency ranges) for bi-directional data communication between the service provider and customer. In all cases, the downstream channel refers to the connection from the service provider network to the customer, and the upstream channel denotes the connection from the customer to the service provider network. DVB-RC defines an additional channel that transports low-speed data traffic; it is called the out-of-band (OOB) channel. Like the DOCSIS standard, DVB-RC also defines a high-speed in-band (IB) channel within the video channel. Both standards use MPEG framing and QPSK, QAM 16, QAM 64, or QAM 256 as the modulation scheme. DOCSIS uses its own MAC layer format and encapsulates native IP, while DVB-RC uses ATM cells as a transport technology. Table 7–1 depicts the specifics of each standard.

Figure 7–5 demonstrates the basic network architecture and key components of a cable access network.

In this basic architecture, the cable modem typically acts as a Layer 2 bridge between the cable network and the customer's LAN. On one side, the cable modem runs a Layer 2 and, optionally, a Layer 3 protocol such as IP/Ethernet. It then bridges or routes traffic between this interface and the one facing the cable network. The cable network interface modulates and demodulates the

Table 7–1 Cable Access Standards

FEATURE	DOCSIS 1.x	EURO-DOCSIS	DVB-RC
Downstream Rates	64-QAM: 27 Mbps; 256-QAM: 42 Mbps; ITU J83 Annex B FEC; 6-Mhz channelization	64-QAM: 38 Mbps; 256-QAM: 52 Mbps; ITU J83 Annex A FEC; 8-Mhz channelization	64-QAM: 38 Mbps; 256-QAM: 52 Mbps; ITU J83 Annex A FEC; 8-Mhz channelization; OOB
Upstream Rates	.320, .640, 1.280, 2.560, and 5.120 Mbps QPSK; and .640, 1.280, 2.560, 5.120, and 10.24 Mbps 16-QAM 5-42 Mhz	.320, .640, 1.280, 2.560, and 5.120 Mbps QPSK; and .640, 1.280, 2.560, 5.120, and 10.24 Mbps 16-QAM 5-65 Mhz	1.544 Mbps; 3.088 Mbps; Differential QPSK 5-65 Mhz
Performance	>80% efficiency over mixed voice and data services at up to 10.24 Mbps in 3.2 Mhz	>80% efficiency over mixed voice and data services at up to 10.24 Mbps in 3.2 Mhz	50–72% efficiency at 3.088 Mbps in 2 Mhz
Services	Internet access, interactive set-top box, Voice over IP	Internet access, interactive set-top box, Voice over IP	Internet access, interactive set-top box
Basic Protocol	Variable-length, native IP with QoS	Variable-length, native IP with QoS	ATM cell transport, with IP adaptation layer translation

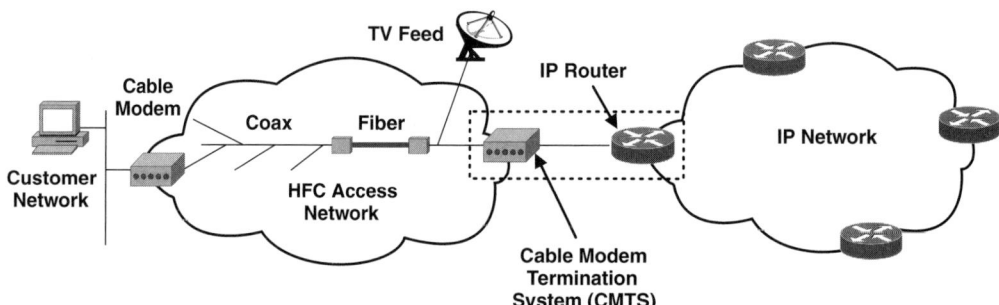

Figure 7–5   Cable access network architecture.

information streams from the Cable Modem Termination System (CMTS) onto the cable RF network. Most cable networks use fiber technology to transport TV and data signals to a point that is physically near the customer's home, while the last mile is typically built with coax cable. The converters from fiber to coax and vice versa are called fiber nodes.

There are two architectures for cable networks: one uses the lower frequencies of the HFC infrastructure to transport the upstream data (two-way networks) and the other uses the public telephony network (telephony return). However, in the discussion that follows, we will focus only on two-way networks since they are widely deployed as compared to telephony return networks.

Connection Paradigm

The cable modem bridges the traffic between the customer's Ethernet and the cable service provider's HFC network. All client PCs connected to the network will receive IP addresses from a centralized DHCP server administered by the cable service provider. The default gateway for client machines is the CMTS, if it has routing functionality built in, or the router attached to the CMTS.

For nearly all cable service providers, the ease of use inherent in the bridged solution makes it far more appealing than a connection-oriented solution such as PPPoE. PPPoE requires that the cable service provider maintain a piece of network driver software at the client PC. However, since PPPoE drivers are not available as standard drivers in most operating systems, this is problematic. Further, the support of such a piece of software is very time-consuming and expensive for the cable operator. Hence, this solution is less attractive for the mass market, but this may change with the ubiquity of PPPoE drivers.

Cable IP VPNs

There are two main drivers behind the deployment of BGP/MPLS VPNs in the cable environment. First, the demand from businesses on cable operators to deploy services has grown over the past few years. Currently, cable access is mainly a consumer technology because of the relatively cheap subscription fees. However, if a service provider could guarantee both service and security, the cable service provider could obtain market share in the business-oriented service provider market segment.

The second driver behind the demand for VPNs in cable networks is a country's regulations regarding circuit services. In some countries, the cable access infrastructure might be viewed as a monopoly by the local regulative authority. It is therefore important for the cable operator to find a way to offer equal access to competing service providers without building a second access infrastructure. BGP/MPLS VPNs are a solution that can be used to achieve both goals: to attract business customers and provide equal access to other ISPs.

Let's now investigate how BGP/MPLS VPNs could be implemented over an existing cable infrastructure and where BGP/MPLS functionality should be implemented (see Figure 7-6). As was the case with DSL modems, full Layer 3 functionality is required within a cable modem to support MP-iBGP and VRFs. As we discussed earlier with ADSL modems, deploying this functionality within the model is quite a challenge in terms of scalability, both from the economic and design perspectives. Thus, Layer 3 support within a cable modem as a PE device is not an attractive option.

The next device to consider is the CMTS. The CMTS is well-suited for PE functionality if it has Layer 3 functionality built-in, that is, if the CMTS is also a router. The CMTS/router needs to have the ability to support the separation of cable modems into different groups to which it can then assign them to an appropriate VRF(s). The mapping of cable modem-to-VPN should be configurable on the centralized cable modem-provisioning server. This will foster the automatic configuration of a MAC address on every CMTS/router.

Since the cable access technology uses the HFC network as a shared access medium, customers may have some security concerns with this technology. Advanced features, such as the ability to prevent clients that are situated behind the cable modems from spoofing their IP addresses, as well as the implementation of access lists at the cable modem, can help prevent security problems. The

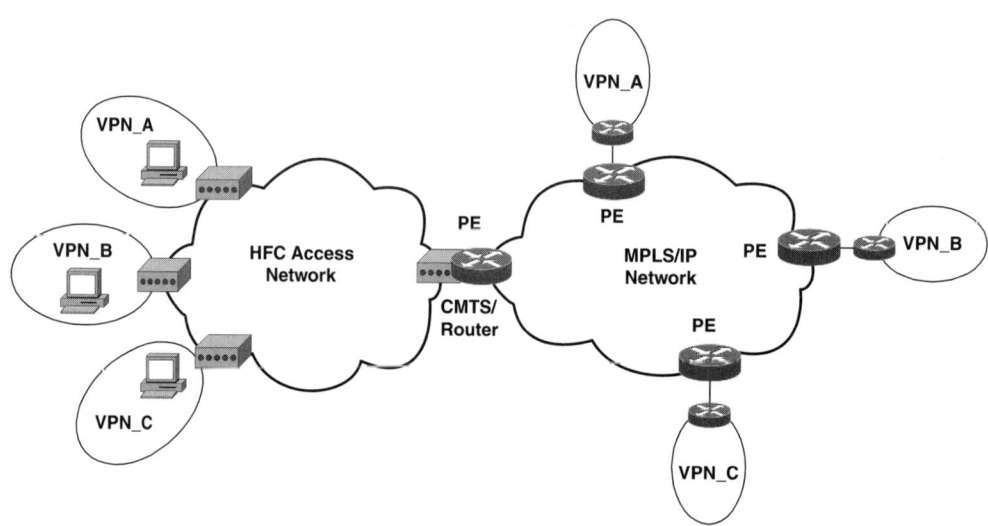

Figure 7-6 Cable access network BGP/MPLS VPNs.

additional use of encryption at the MAC layer and/or at Layer 3 might be appropriate if an even higher level of security in cable network VPNs is desired.

Figure 7-7 demonstrates how BGP/MPLS VPN technology is well-suited for business customers in cable access networks. It also shows how cable operators can successfully provide equal access over cable networks to competing ISPs using BGP/MPLS VPNs (see Figure 7-8). An alternative way to achieve equal access is to use policy-based routing at the CMTS/router or at the router behind the Layer 2 CMTS. This method has the drawback that service providers can only use public IP addresses for the clients and cable modems. If they would use private IP addresses, they would have to agree on certain private address ranges per service provider, which might prove to be difficult to administer. Service providers that share the same access infrastructure often want to offer internal services, which should not be accessible to customers of other service providers on the same HFC network.

Cable modems and clients obtain IP addresses from a service provider's network range. Every modem and every client is known by its MAC address at the DHCP server. If the cable modem or the client behind the cable modem issues a DHCP Request message to the DHCP server, the server checks its database and assigns the correct IP address. The IP address will be taken out of the appropriate service provider network range to which the client is subscribed.

Cable Access VPNs **165**

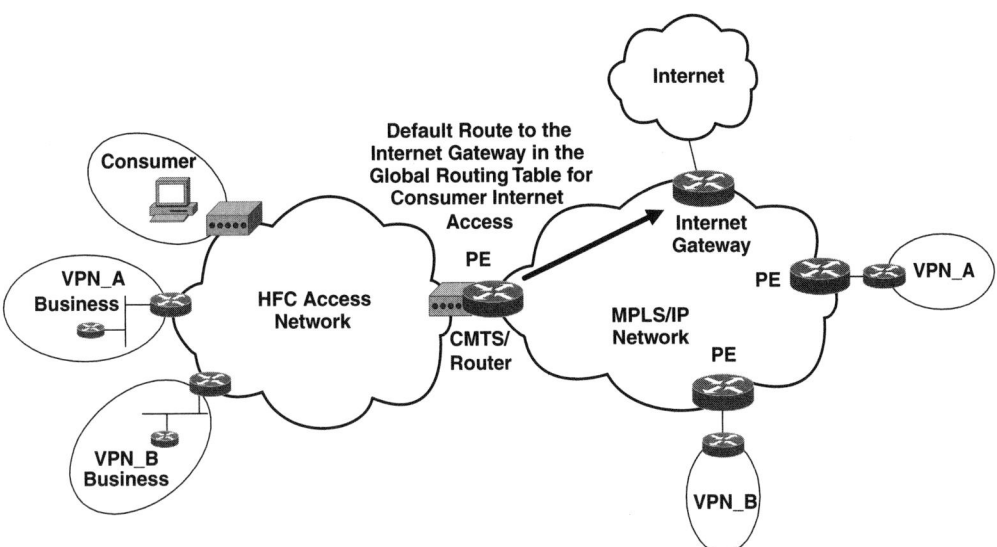

Figure 7-7   Business and consumer customers in a cable access network.

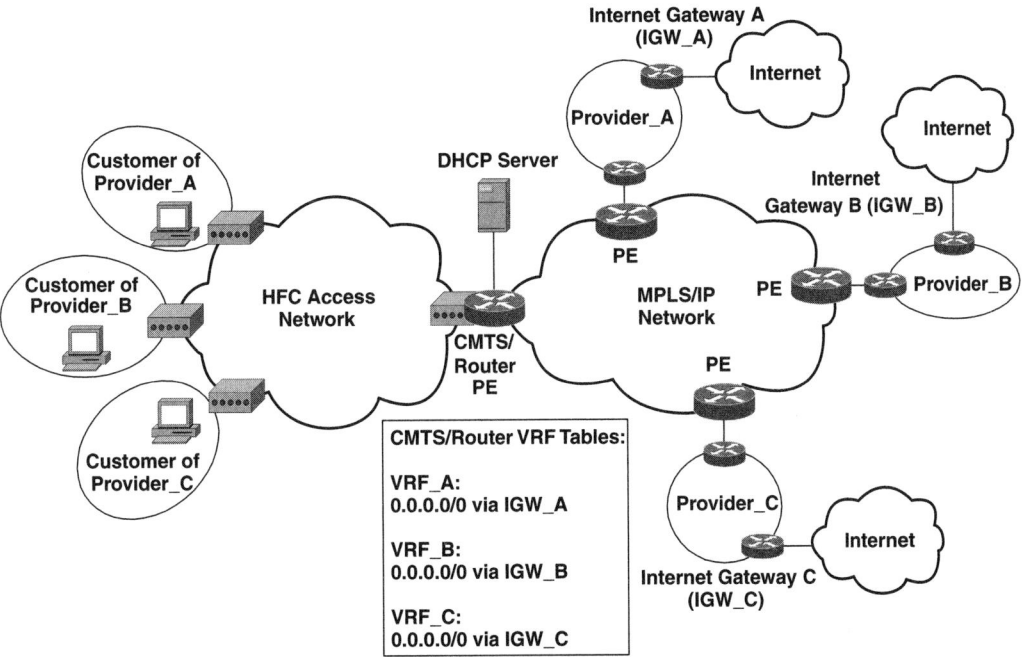

Figure 7-8   Equal access in a cable access network.

The cable modem and client will be assigned to the appropriate VRF based on their IP address. Each VRF should hold a default route for the Internet routes since it is not very scalable to load the full Internet routing table into each VRF. It is possible to end up with n * 100,000 routes at the CMTS/router, where n is the number of service providers that share the cable access network.

Mobile Wireless VPNs

Beginning in the early 1990s, we saw an enormous growth in available mobile wireless voice services, especially in Europe because of the common Global System for Mobile Communications (GSM) standard. While the growth rate for voice services in terms of the number of subscribers is expected to settle down over the next five years, tremendous growth potential in mobile wireless data services still exists. Starting with the General Packet Radio Service (GPRS) for GSM operators and later with IMT-2000 or UMTS, there will be a move toward mobile data services. Mobile terminals capable of processing data traffic will top the number of PCs installed shortly as well. Therefore, one of the major applications of mobile data besides vanilla Internet access is be a mobile intranet service (i.e., provide remote access to VPNs). Imagine a very simple application that lets you access your company's phone directory via your mobile data terminal, which could either be a mobile phone or PDA. There are numerous simple, yet very effective applications of this technology.

GPRS Technology Overview

GPRS is a data overlay network over the legacy GSM cellular voice network. It is designed to provide mobile data access up to 171.2 Kbps (theoretical maximum). Currently, access speeds are typically only about 64 Kbps and depend largely on the radio resource planning of the mobile operator. GPRS is an evolution of GSM. It was developed and designed by the European Telecommunications Standard Institute (ETSI) and has been widely accepted as a worldwide standard for digital mobile communications. The major difference between this technology and legacy mobile data access technologies is the packet-oriented nature of GPRS. Packet switching in the mobile operator network means that the scarce resources of the mobile RF interface are much better utilized than if circuit-switched access like V.110, for example, were being used [FERR-1]. The same is true for the transport network of the mobile operator.

The basic network elements of a cellular wireless voice network are shown in Figure 7–9.

The base transceiver station (BTS) communicates via the mobile RF interface with mobile terminals (MTs). The BTS is attached to the base station controller (BSC), which controls a group of BTSs. The BSCs are connected to mobile switching centers (MSCs). The MSCs are, in essence, legacy central office switches with specific mobile extensions built into their software. The Home Location Register (HLR) and Visitor Location Register (VLR) are databases that store user and mobility information.

With this thumbnail sketch of the mobile wireless network in mind, we will now focus on the data portion of the network and on the GPRS-specific elements shown in Figure 7–10.

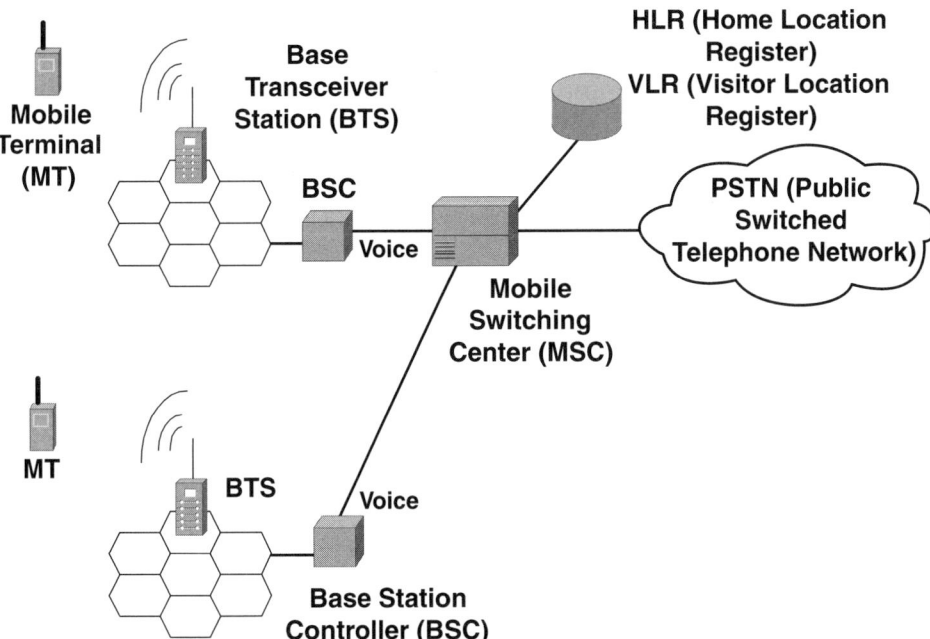

Figure 7–9 Basic elements of a mobile wireless voice network.

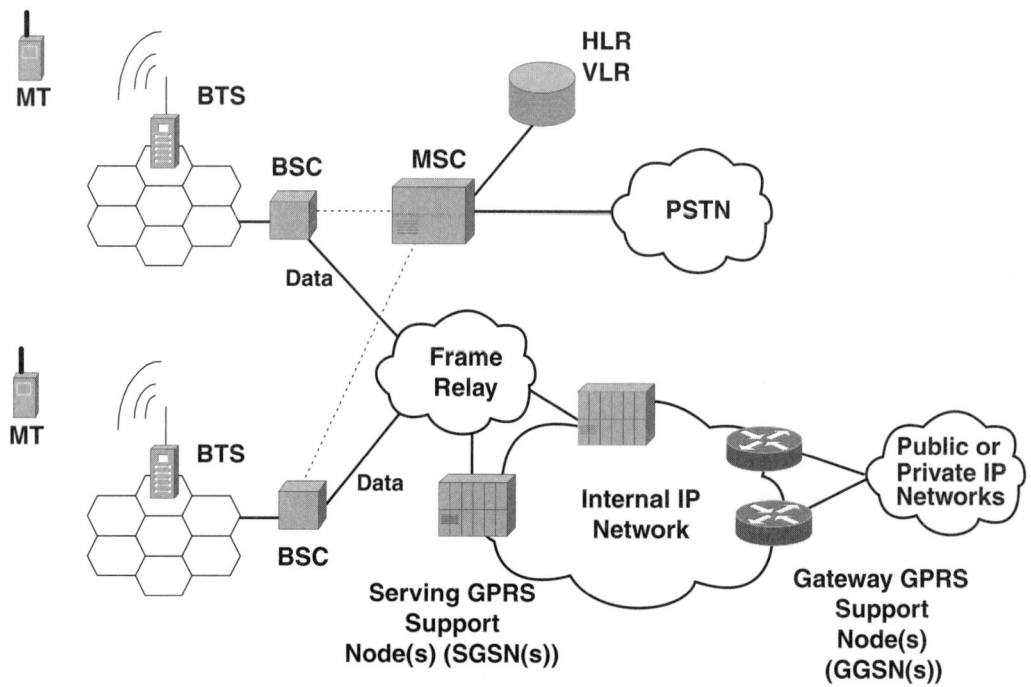

Figure 7–10   GPRS network elements.

The main problem encountered in an environment where the user may roam between subnets is data packet routing. With the static nature of IPv4 addressing, a new technique that enables the network to associate the user with a static IP address and at the same time allow the user to roam around the network has to be employed. The way in which this can be achieved is with tunneling. A router is located at the tunnel head-end. This router advertises the IP address (or the network) of the user, maintains a tunnel with an intermediate device called a serving GPRS support node (SGSN), and knows how to reach the user on the other end of the tunnel. When the client moves from one SGSN to another, the router at the head-end will use another tunnel to reach the client (see Figure 7–11).

Mobile IP is a new technology that is well-suited to support this functionality. In the case of GPRS, the ETSI decided to standardize another protocol, called the GPRS Tunneling Protocol (GTP), for this function. The reason for this decision was mainly the native X.25 support of GTP. This was a factor because X.25 support was also included in the initial specifications of GPRS.

Mobile Wireless VPNs   169

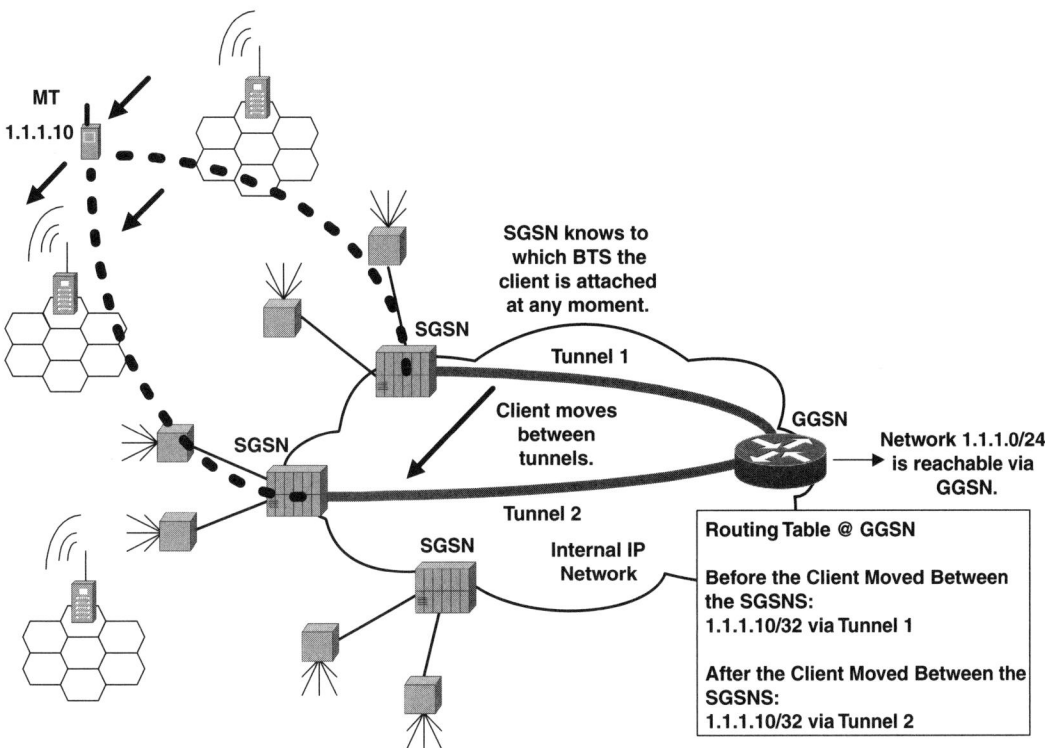

Figure 7–11   GPRS mobility management.

As we can see, it does not make sense to put BGP/MPLS functionality at the SGSNs or at the BTSs because of the possibility of having to move VRFs as clients roam throughout the network. This implies that VPN routes will have to move from one box to another very quickly. That is simply not scalable in mobile networks and it would not provide any benefit. The gateway GPRS support node (GGSN) is much better suited for BGP/MPLS VPN PE functionality. GPRS uses the notion of an access point name (APN) as the logical interface on which a GGSN user terminates its GTP session. The APN, which is often physically located in the HLR and/or in an MT, can be used to identify the network the user wants to attach to. For example, this is useful if the user wants to access the Internet via a mobile operator ISP or access a private company intranet with a mobile terminal. In the case where the user wants to access the public Internet, the appropriate APN (e.g., isp.mobile_operator.gprs) would be used. In the case where the user would like to access intranet resources, another APN (e.g., company_xyz.mobile_operator.gprs) would be used. The APN is then mapped to the appropriate VRF and the user is thus attached to the appropriate VPN service (see Figure 7–12).

This is a viable solution for the initial phases of GPRS. However, if we assume that the number of mobile data users will increase dramatically in the next five years, each GGSN will most likely terminate a large number of users on the order of 100,000–250,000. The number of different VRFs per GGSN could become overwhelming and difficult to handle. The scalability issue could again become an issue in terms of the total number of routes stored in a single box. An alternative approach that offers even more scalability for future growth is to use the GGSN as an aggregation device only. PE functionality would then be pushed further to the edge of the network.

Figure 7–13 shows how an additional layer of PE routers can be introduced within the GPRS network. In this model, users will be terminated on the GGSN, either where the GGSN will maintain a static GRE tunnel to the PE or where the GGSN will establish an L2TP tunnel on-demand. The VRF is no longer located on the GGSN; instead, it will be located on the PE routers.

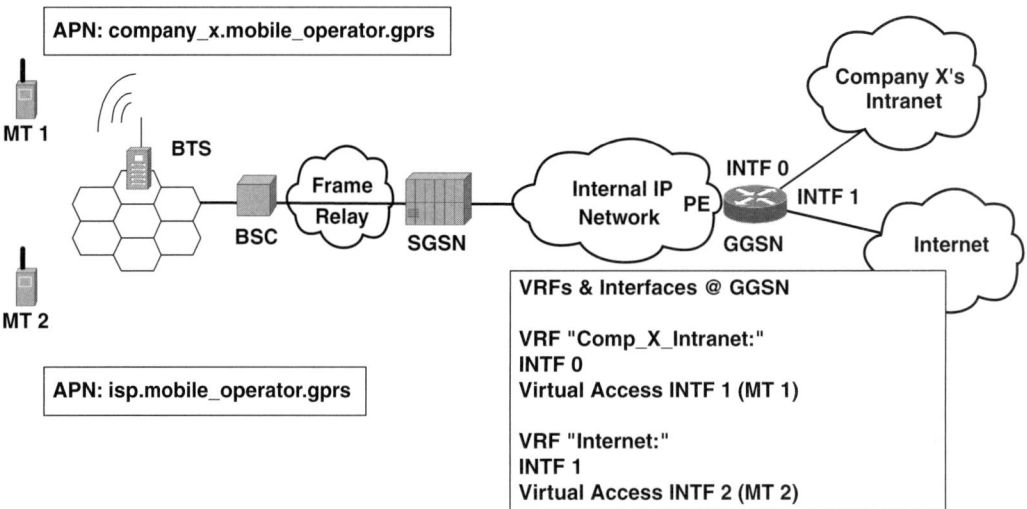

Figure 7–12   GPRS APN-to-VRF mapping.

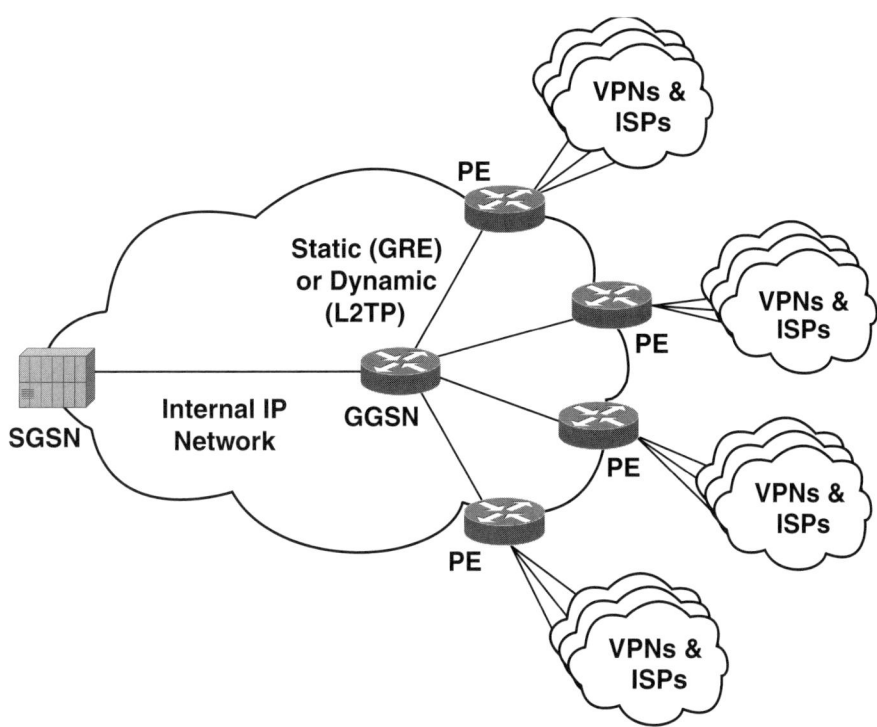

Figure 7–13 GPRS PE scalability.

When the mobile operator has numerous connections to smaller VPN customers, it is useful to separate PE functionality from the GGSN to a separate dedicated aggregation device.

The ETSI defined standard interfaces for GPRS as shown in Figure 7–14. For example, the interface between the SGSN and GGSN is called Gn, and the interface between the GGSN and external packet data networks is called the Gi interface. The Gn and Gi interfaces are separated by the GGSN. It is also useful to deploy firewall functions at this point in the network to prevent hackers from getting access to the internal network resources of the mobile operator. Mobile operators may deploy a single IP network that is able to handle both internal networks (SGSNs, servers, etc.) and external networks (Internet, customer VPNs, etc.).

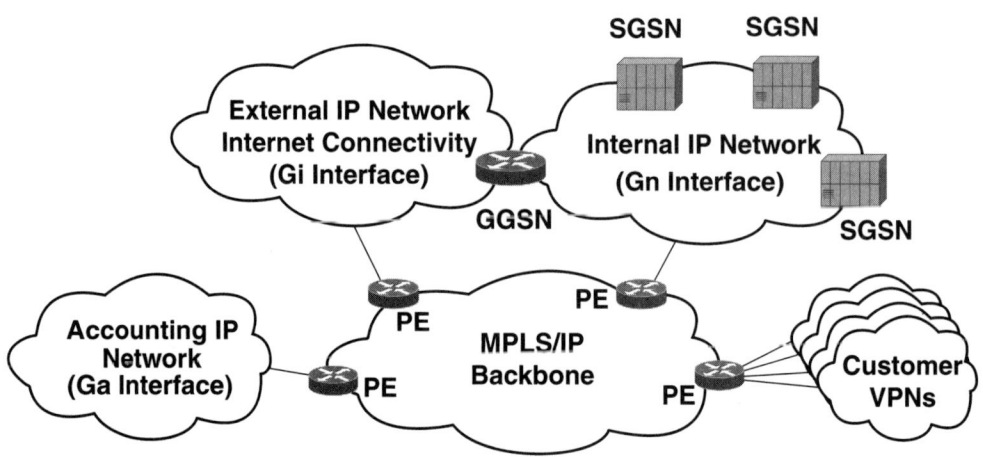

Figure 7–14   GPRS MPLS/IP backbone.

Dial Access IP VPNs

The most popular access service for consumer customers is some form of dial-in service that is used to access the Internet or a corporate intranet. The public switched telephone network (PSTN) is ubiquitous and dial access is possible from just about any telephone line in the world. The network architecture for dial-in service is shown in Figure 7–15.

At first glance, PE functionality directly at the access server appears to be a good idea. However, if we think critically about the nature of dial access, it should be clear that a large number of users dial in to the same access number. After a user is connected, he/she is assigned one or more timeslots in an E1 or T1 trunk, and finally, he/she is terminated on an access server. The user's identity is not known at the time he/she connects to the access server. Therefore, the user is generally required to provide authentication credentials during the establishment phase of the data connection. This is typically accomplished during the PPP authentication phase. Thus, we do not know which VPN the user is a member of at the time the user gets assigned an access server by the telephony system. To accomplish this, all VRFs and all routes of all VPNs of the service provider network would have to be stored in every access server! Another possibility would be the dynamic instantiation of a VRF. This has the drawback that all routes would have to be loaded into the access server whenever a user connects. Both possibilities may be viable in small networks

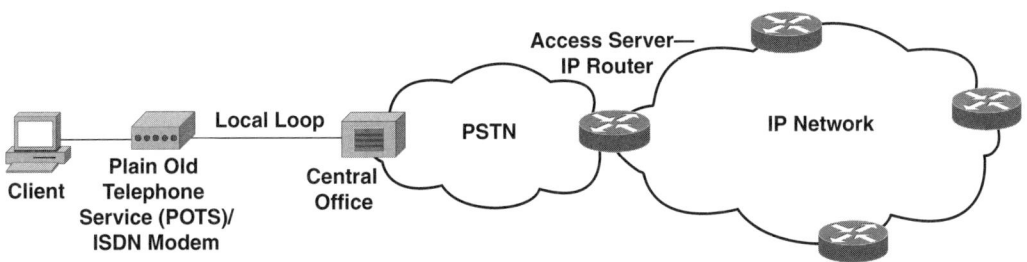

Figure 7–15   Dial service network architecture.

containing a limited number of VPNs, but will definitely lack scalability in medium or large networks.

These problems can be avoided by employing a tunneling method whereby forwarding is based either on the domain name or on the Dialed Number Identification Service (DNIS) on the appropriate PE router. One of the tunneling protocols that supports this feature is Layer 2 Tunneling Protocol (L2TP).

Figure 7–16 demonstrates the dial service IP VPN architecture. In this architecture, a client first dials into the access server, called the L2TP access concentrator (LAC). The access server then challenges the client to provide authentication credentials. The user must provide a username in the following form: dilbert_123@fool.com. The LAC strips off the domain name ("fool.com") and passes it to the authentication, authorization, and accounting (AAA) server, using the Radius protocol, for example. The AAA server next returns the appropriate LNS server IP address and the LAC establishes the L2TP tunnel to the LNS. This tunnel should be secured with passwords to avoid security holes. The LNS authenticates the client a second time with the username-password pair it received from the LAC after tunnel establishment. The user does not recognize, however, that he or she has been authenticated twice.

The LNS passes the username-password to the AAA server. At this point, the server returns an appropriate per-user configuration such as: authentication pass/fail, name of VRF (VRF_fool), and IP address pool. The LNS creates a host route for the client and all members of that VPN subsequently are reachable by the client, and vice versa.

A slightly different scenario is the integration of dial on-demand routing (DDR) services in the BGP/MPLS IP VPN network (see Figure 7–17). DDR can provide a very important backup scenario for a service provider, and should be considered when deploying this technology.

174 Chapter 7 ▸ MPLS VPN Applications

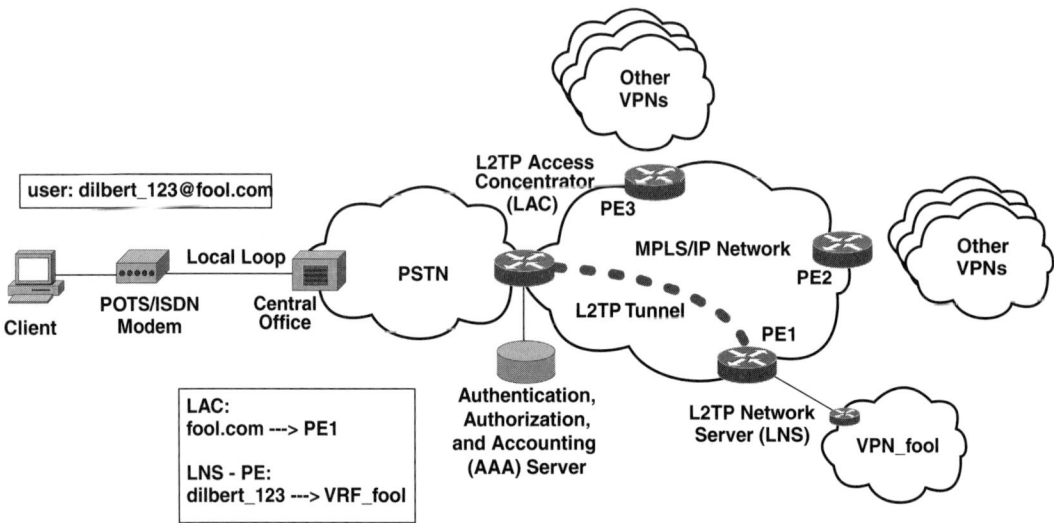

Figure 7–16 Dial service IP VPN architecture.

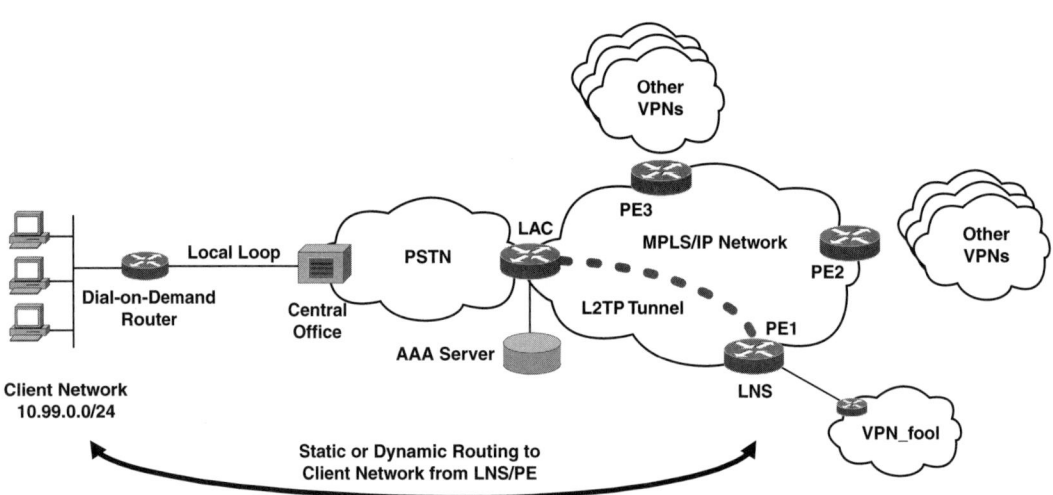

Figure 7–17 DDR service in IP VPN architecture.

In this model, the LNS creates a host route for the WAN interface, but it does not create a route for the LAN interface of the router. To allow this network to become reachable for other clients and routers, either a static route on the PE/LNS to the client network must be defined, or a routing protocol between the dial on-demand router and PE/LNS must be configured and enabled.

This chapter focused on typical applications of MPLS VPNs. There are many areas where MPLS VPNs can be used very efficiently to build different private networks over a shared infrastructure as seen in the examples in this chapter. When we look at the European mobile operators, we see many providers who want to share the costly Universal Mobile Telecommunications System (UMTS) infrastructure. By building mobile virtual network operators (MVNOs), these providers can all use the same infrastructure while actually having logically separated networks. MPLS VPNs can be a good building block to allow these MVNOs to efficiently share the infrastructure. This is only one example of a future application of MPLS VPNs. Many more applications will follow within the next few years.

A

LDP Protocol Structure—Examples

Let's have a detailed look at two messages: the Label Request message and the Label Mapping message.

Label Request Message

When an LSR wants to request a label binding to a particular FEC from its downstream LSR, it will send a Label Request message to its downstream peer. The encoding for this message looks like Figure A–1:

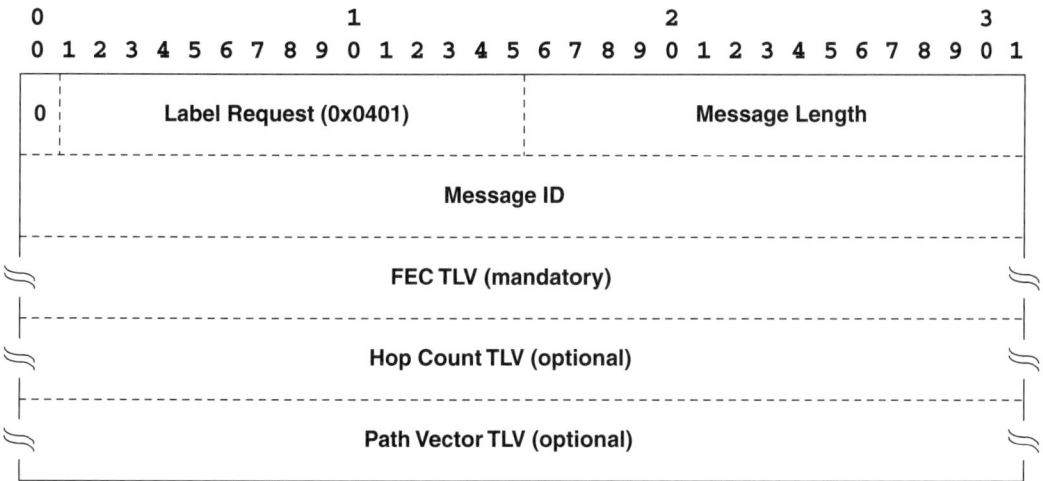

Figure A–1 LDP Label Request message.

Label Request Message (LDP_PDU)

- Message Type (LDP_PDU/label_request_message)—Contains the value 0x0401, which encodes the message type as "Label Request."
- Message Length (LDP_PDU/label_request_message)—Specifies the cumulative length in octets of the Message ID, Mandatory Parameters (FEC TLV), and Optional Parameters (Hop Count TLV and Path Vector TLV).
- Message ID (LDP_PDU/label_request_message)—A 32-bit value used to identify this message.
- FEC TLV (LDP_PDU/label_request_message)—The FEC for which a label is being requested. The format for this TLV looks like the following (Figure A–2).
- FEC Element 1 to FEC Element n (LDP_PDU/label_request_message/FEC_TLV)—There are several types of FEC elements. FEC element encoding depends on the type of the FEC element.

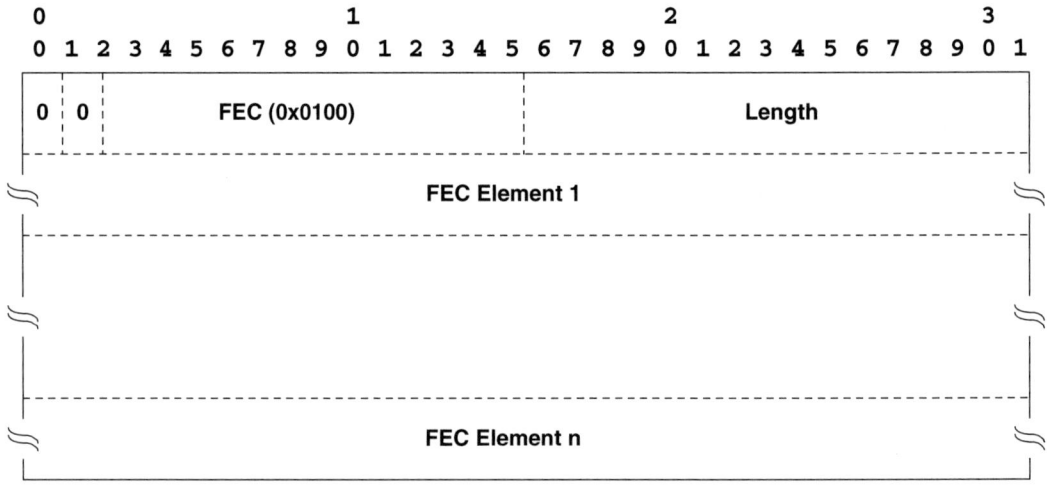

Figure A–2 LDP FEC TLV.

In the specification [IETF-23], three different FEC elements are listed:
- Wildcard FEC Element (LDP_PDU/label_request_message/FEC_TLV/FEC_Element)—This is only used in the Label Withdraw message and in the Label Release messsage. It is always the only FEC element in the FEC TLV.
- Prefix FEC Element (LDP_PDU /label_request_message/FEC_TLV/FEC_Element)—See Figure A–3.
- Address Family (LDP_PDU/label_request_message/FEC_TLV/Prefix_FEC_Element/Prefix_FEC_Element)—A two-octet quantity containing a value from "Address Family Numbers" in RFC 1700 [IETF-24] that encodes the address family for the address prefix in the Prefix field (see Table A–1).

```
 0                   1                   2                   3
 0 1 2 3 4 5 6 7 8 9 0 1 2 3 4 5 6 7 8 9 0 1 2 3 4 5 6 7 8 9 0 1
+-------------------+-------------------------------+---------------+
|   Prefix (0x02)   |        Address Family         | Prefix Length |
+-------------------+-------------------------------+---------------+
|                             Prefix                                |
+-------------------------------------------------------------------+
```

Figure A–3 LDP Prefix FEC Element.

Table A–1 Address Family Numbers

NUMBER	DESCRIPTION
0	Reserved
1	IP (IPv4)
2	IP6 (IPv6)
3	NSAP
4	HDLC (8-bit multidrop)
5	BBN 1822
6	802 (includes all 802 media plus Ethernet "canonical format")

Table A-1 Address Family Numbers *(Continued)*

NUMBER	DESCRIPTION
7	E.163
8	E.164 (SMDS, Frame Relay, ATM)
9	F.69 (Telex)
10	X.121 (X.25, Frame Relay)
11	IPX
12	Appletalk
13	Decnet IV
14	Banyan Vines
65535	Reserved

- Prefix Length (LDP_PDU/label_request_message/FEC_TLV/Prefix_FEC_Element//Prefix_FEC_Element)—A one-octet unsigned integer containing the length in bits of the address prefix that follows. A length of zero indicates a prefix that matches all addresses (the default destination); in this case, the Prefix itself is zero octets.
- Prefix (LDP_PDU/label_request_message/FEC_TLV/Prefix_FEC_Element)—An address prefix encoded according to the Address Family field, whose length, in bits, was specified in the Prefix Length field, padded to a byte boundary.
- Host Address FEC Element (LDP_PDU/label_request_message/FEC_TLV/FEC_Element)—See Figure A-4.
- Address Family (LDP_PDU/label_request_message/FEC_TLV/HostAddr_FEC_Element)—A two-octet quantity containing a value from "Address Family Numbers" in RFC 1700 [IETF-24] that encodes the address family for the address prefix in the Prefix field. For a list of numbers, see Table A-1.

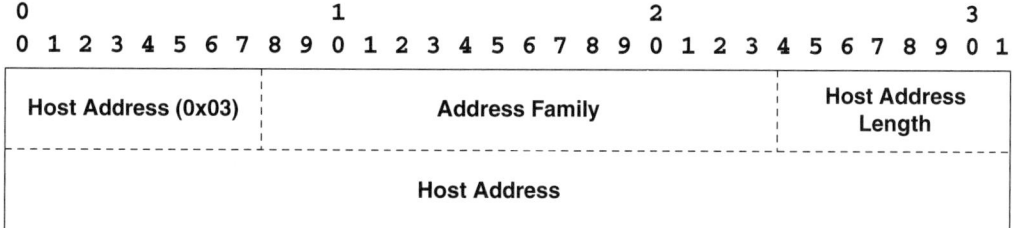

Figure A–4 LDP Host Address FEC Element.

- Host Address Length (LDP_PDU/label_request_message/FEC_TLV/HostAddr_FEC_Element)— The length of the host address in octets.
- Host Address (LDP_PDU/label_request_message/FEC_TLV/HostAddr_FEC_Element)—An address encoded according to the Address Family field.
- Hop Count (LDP_PDU/label_request_message)—This field of the LDP message is an optional parameter and may contain zero or more parameters encoded in the TLV format. This field specifies the running total of the number of LSR hops along the LSP being set up by the Label Request message. See Figure A–5.
- HC Value (LDP_PDU/label_request_message/Hop_Count_TLV)—A one-octet unsigned integer hop count value.
- Path Vector (LDP_PDU/label_request_message)—This field of the LDP message is an optional parameter and may contain zero or more parameters encoded in the TLV format. This field specifies the LSRs along the LSR being set up by the Label Request message. See Figure A–6.

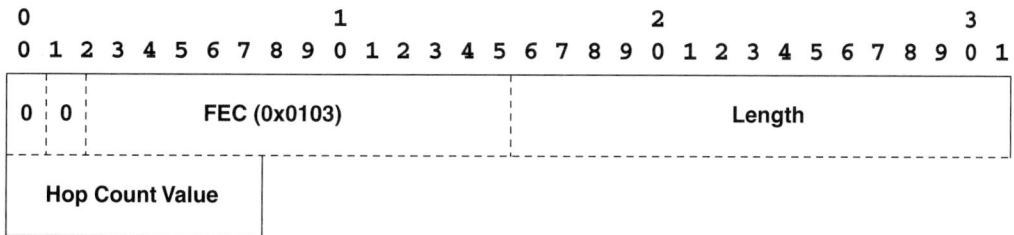

Figure A–5 LDP Hop Count TLV.

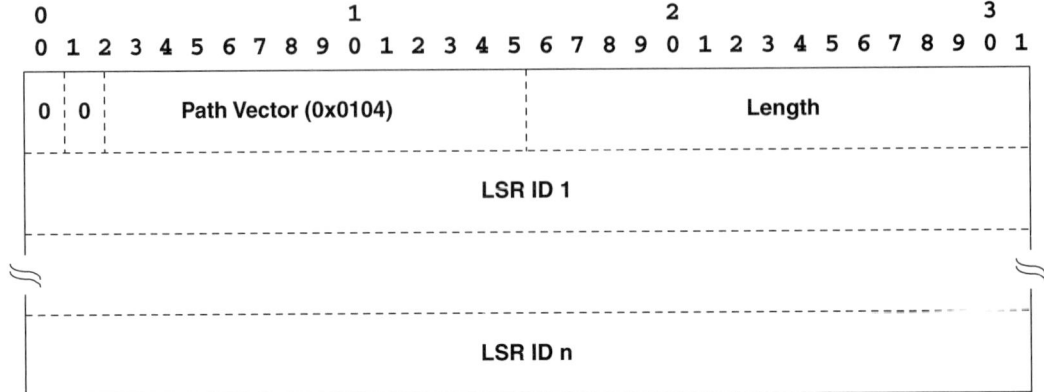

Figure A–6 LDP Path Vector TLV.

- LSR IDs (LDP_PDU/label_request_message/Path_Vector_TLV)—A list of router IDs indicating the path of LSRs the message has traversed. Each LSR ID is the IP address (router ID) component of the LDP identifier for the corresponding LSR. This ensures it is unique within the LSR network.

Label Mapping Message

When an LSR wants to bind a label to a particular FEC, it will send a Label Request message to its upstream peer. This message can be an answer to a Label Request message if the downstream on-demand label binding procedure is used. It can also be sent without a prior request from the upstream peer if the unsolicited downstream procedure is used (see the section in Chapter 3 titled "Label Distribution—Downstream vs. Downstream On-Demand" for further details on binding procedures).

The encoding for this message looks like Figure A–7.

Label Mapping Message (LDP_PDU)

- Message Type (LDP_PDU/label_mapping_message)—Contains the value 0x0400, which encodes the message type as "Label Mapping."
- Message Length (LDP_PDU/label_mapping_message)—Specifies the cumulative length in octets of the Message ID, Mandatory Parameters

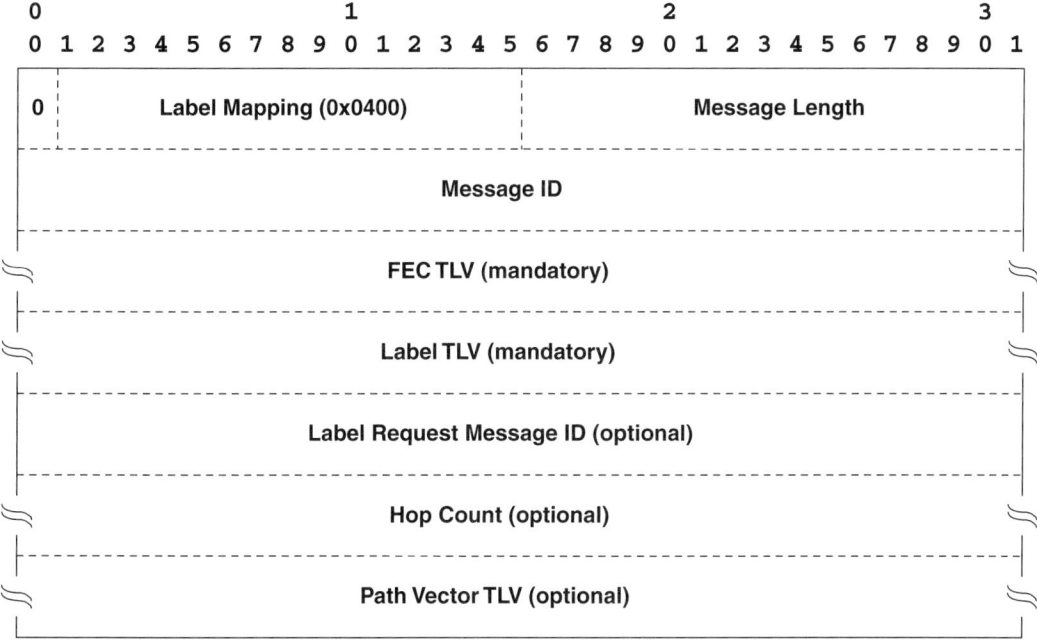

Figure A-7 LDP Label Mapping message.

(FEC TLV), and Optional Parameters (Label Request Message ID, Hop Count TLV and Path Vector TLV).

- Message ID (LDP_PDU/label_mapping_message)—A 32-bit value used to identify this message.
- FEC TLV (LDP_PDU/label_mapping_message)—Specifies the FEC component for which the FEC-label mapping is being advertised. See "Label Request Message" for details on the FEC TLV format.
- Label TLV (LDP_PDU/label_mapping_message)—Specifies the Label component of the FEC-label mapping.

The Label TLV specifies the label value that should be mapped to a particular FEC. As described in Chapter 3 in the section titled "Label Encapsulation," there is more than one method to encapsulate the top labels. According to the different encapsulation techniques, there must be different label TLVs to represent the suitable encapsulation method.

Currently, there are three different label TLVs defined in [IETF-23]:

- Generic Label TLV
- ATM Label TLV
- Frame Relay Label TLV
- Generic Label TLV (LDP_PDU/label_mapping_message/label_TLV)—See Figure A–8.
- Label (LDP_PDU/label_mapping_message/label_TLV/generic_label_TLV)—A 20-bit label value as specified in [REF_ HH], represented as a 20-bit number in a 4-octet field.
- ATM Label TLV (LDP_PDU/label_mapping_message/label_TLV)—See Figure A–9.
- Res (LDP_PDU/label_mapping_message/label_TLV/atm_label_TLV)—This field is reserved. It must be set to zero on transmission and must be ignored on receipt.

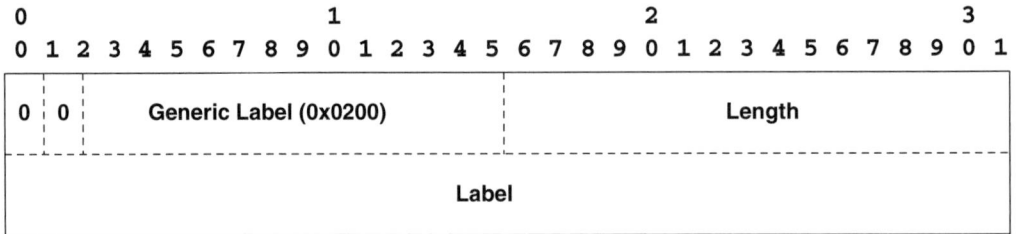

Figure A–8 LDP Generic Label TLV.

Figure A–9 LDP ATM Label TLV.

- V-bits (LDP_PDU/label_mapping_message/label_TLV/atm_label_TLV)—A two-bit switching indicator. If V-bits is 00, both the VPI and VCI are significant; if V-bits is 01, only the VPI field is significant; if V-bit is 10, only the VCI is significant.
- VPI (LDP_PDU/label_mapping_message/label_TLV/atm_label_TLV)—If the VPI (virtual path identifier) is less than 12 bits, it should be right-justified and the preceding bits should be set to 0.
- VCI (LDP_PDU/label_mapping_message/label_TLV/atm_label_TLV)—If the VCI (virtual channel identifier) is less than 16 bits, it should be right-justified and the preceding bits must be set to 0. If virtual path switching is indicated in the V-bits field, this field must be ignored by the receiver and set to 0 by the sender.
- Frame Relay Label TLV (LDP_PDU/label_mapping_message/label_TLV)—See Figure A–10.

```
0                   1                   2                   3
0 1 2 3 4 5 6 7 8 9 0 1 2 3 4 5 6 7 8 9 0 1 2 3 4 5 6 7 8 9 0 1
+-+-+-------------------------------+-------------------------------+
|0|0|   Frame Relay Label (0x0202)  |            Length             |
+-+-+-----------+-------------------+-------------------------------+
      |   Res   |  Len  |                    DLCI                   |
      +---------+-------+-------------------------------------------+
```

Figure A–10 LDP Frame Relay Label TLV.

- Res (LDP_PDU/label_mapping_message/label_TLV/frame_relay_TLV)—This field is reserved. It must be set to zero on transmission and ignored on receipt.
- Len (LDP_PDU/label_mapping_message/label_TLV/frame_relay_TLV)—This field specifies the number of bits in the DLCI. The following values are described in [IETF-23]:

0 = 10 bits DLCI
1 = 17 bits DLCI
2 = 23 bits DLCI

- DLCI (LDP_PDU/label_mapping_message/label_TLV/frame_relay_TLV)—This is the data link connection identifier. Label values and formats are described in detail in [IETF-23].
- Label Request Message ID (LDP_PDU/label_mapping_message)—This field of the LDP message is an optional parameter and may contain zero or more parameters encoded in the TLV format. If this Label Mapping message is a response to a Label Request message, it must include the Request Message ID optional parameter. The value of this optional parameter is the Message ID of the corresponding Label Request message.
- Hop Count (LDP_PDU/label_mapping_message)—Specifies the running total of the number of LSR hops along the LSP being set up by the Label message. See "Label Request Message" for details on the Hop Count TLV format.
- Path Vector (LDP_PDU/label_mapping_message)—Specifies the LSRs along the LSP being set up by the Label message. See "Label Request Message" for details on the Path Vector TLV format.

Glossary

ABR	area border router
ADSL	Asymmetric Digital Subscriber Line
APN	access point name
APNIC	Asia Pacific Network Information Center
ARIN	American Registry for Internet Numbers
AS	autonomous system
ASBR	autonomous system border router
ASIC	Application Specific Integrated Circuits
ASN	autonomous system number
ATM	Asynchronous Transfer Mode
ATM_ARP	an ATM Address Resolution Protocol
ATM-LSR	ATM–label switch routers
BECN	backward explicit congestion notification
BGP	Border Gateway Protocol
BSC	base station controller
BTS	base transceiver station
CCAMP	Common Control and Measurement Plane
CE	customer edge
CES	Circuit Emulation Services
CIR	committed information rate
CLIP	Classical IP

CLP	congestion loss priority
CMTS	Cable Modem Termination System
CPCS	common part convergence sublayer
CPE	customer premise equipment
CRC	cyclic redundancy check
CR-LDP	Contraint-based Routing–Label Distribution Protocol
CR-LSP	Constraint-based Routing–label-switched path
CS	convergence sublayer
CsC	Carrier's Carrier
CSR	Cell Switch Router
DDR	dial-on-demand routing
DF	Don't Fragment (bit)
DiffServ	differentiated services
DLCI	data link connection identifier
DMT	Discrete Multitone
DNIS	Dialed Number Identification Service
DNS	Domain Name Server
DOCSIS	Data Over Cable Interface Specification (also Euro-DOCSIS)
DSCP	DiffServ Code Point
DSL	Digital Subscriber Line
DVB-RC	Digital Video Broadcast-Return Channel
eBGP	external Border Gateway Protocol
EDI	electronic data interchange
ETSI	European Telecommunications Standard Institute
Euro-DOCSIS	see DOCSIS
EXP	experimental (bits)
FEC	forwarding equivalent class
FECN	forward explicit congestion notification
GFC	generic flow control
GGSN	gateway GPRS support node
Gi	interface between GGSN and external packet data networks
GigE	Gigabit Ethernet
GPRS	General Packet Radio System
GRE	generic routing encapsulation

GSM	Global System for Mobile Communications
Gn	interface between SGSN and GGSN
GTP	GPRS Tunneling Protocol
HDSL	High-data-rate Digital Subscriber Line
HEC	header error control
HFC	Hybrid Fiber Coax
HLR	Home Location Register
IANA	Internet Assigned Numbers Association
IB	in-band
iBGP	internal Border Gateway Protocol
ICMP	Internet Control Message Protocol
IETF	Internet Engineering Task Force
IGP	Interior Gateway Protocol
IP	Internet Protocol
IPSec	IP Security Protocol
IS-IS	Intermediate System-to-Intermediate System Protocol
ISP	Internet service provider
L2TP	Layer 2 Tunneling Protocol
LAC	L2TP access concentrator
LAN	Local Area Network
LC-ATMs	label-controlled ATM interface/ATM interface that uses alternative label encapsulation
LCP	Link Control Protocol
LDP	Label Distribution Protocol
LFIB	label forwarding information base
LIB	label information base
LIS	logical IP subnet
LNS	L2TP network server
LSA	link state advertisement
LSP	label-switched path
LSR	label switch router
MAC	media access control
MID	Message Identifier
MSC	mobile switching center
MPEG	Motion Picture Experts Group

MP-BGP	Multiprotocol BGP
MPLS	Multiprotocol Label Switching
MPLS-TE	MPLS Traffic Engineering
MT	mobile terminal
MVNO	mobile virtual network operator
NAT	network address translation
NCP	Network Control Protocol
NLRI	network layer reachability information
OOB	out-of-band
ORF	Outbound Route Filter
OSI	Open Systems Interconnection
OSPF	Open Shortest Path First Protocol
PDA	personal digital assistant
PE	provider edge
PDU	protocol data unit
PIM	Protocol Independent Multicast
PoP	point of presence
POS	Packet over SONET/SDH
POTS	plain old telephone service
PPP	Point-to-Point Protocol
PPPoA	PPP over ATM
PPPoE	PPP over Ethernet
PPVPN	Provider-Provisioned Virtual Private Network
PSTN	public switched telephone network
PT	Payload Type
PTT	Post, Telephone & Telegraph
PVC	permanent virtual connection
PWE3	Pseudo-Wire Emulation Edge-to-Edge
QAM	Quadrature Amplitude Modulation
QPSK	Quadrature Phase-Shift Keying
QoS	Quality of Service
RD	route distinguisher
RF	Radio Frequency
RIPE	Réseaux IP Européens
RR	route reflector

RSVP	Resource Reservation Protocol
RT	route target
SAR	Segmentation and Reassembly
SDSL	Single-line or Symmetric Digital Subscriber Line
SGSN	Serving GPRS support node
SVC	switched virtual connection/circuit
TE	traffic engineering
TLV	Type/Length/Value
TOS	Type of Service
TTL	time to live
UDP	User Datagram Protocol
UMTS	Universal Mobile Telecommunications System
UNI	user-to-network interface
VC	virtual channel
VCI	virtual channel identifier
VCID	virtual connection identifier
VDSL	Very-high-data-rate Digital Subscriber Line
VLANs	virtual LANs
VLR	Visitor Location Register
VPI	virtual path identifier
VPN	Virtual Private Network
VRF	Virtual Routing and Forwarding Instance
WAN	Wide Area Network

Notes

[DAVIE-1] B. Davie, P. Doolan, Y. Rekhter, *Switching in IP Networks*, Morgan Kaufmann Publishers, ISBN: 1 55860 505 3, 1998.

[FERR-1] C. Ferrer, M. Oliver, "Overview and Capacity of the GPRS (General Packet Radio Service)," *Applied Maths & Telematics*, Universitat Politècnica de Catalunya (UPC), 1998.

[HALA-1] B. Halabi, *Internet Routing Achitectures*, Cisco Press, ISBN: 1-56205-652-2, 1997.

[IETF-1] E. Crawley, et. al., RFC 2382, "A Framework for Integrated Services and RSVP over ATM," August 1998.

[IETF-2] S. Blake, et. al., RFC 2475, "An Architecture for Differentiated Services," December 1998.

[IETF-3] M. Laubach, RFC 1577, "Classical IP and ARP over ATM," January 1994.

[IETF-4] Y. Rekhter, E. Rosen, RFC 2547, "BGP/MPLS VPNs," March 1999

[IETF-5] S. Ramachandra, D. Tappan, "BGP Extended Communities Attribute," [draft-ramachandra-bgp-ext-communities-09.txt], work in progress, June 2001.

[IETF-6] E. Chen, Y. Rekhter, "Cooperative Route Filtering Capability for BGP-4," [draft-ietf-idr-route-filter-03.txt], work in progress, April 2001.

[IETF-7] Y. Rekhter, et al., RFC 1918, "Address Allocation for Private Internets," February 1996.

[IETF-8] W. Townsley, et al., RFC 2661, "Layer Two Tunneling Protocol," August 1999.

[IETF-9] Peter Newman, ct al., RFC 1987, "Ipsilon's General Switch Management Protocol Specification," August 1996.

[IETF-10] Bilel Jamoussi, et al., RFC 2340, "Nortel's Virtual Network Switching (VNS) Overview ," May 1998.

[IETF-11] E. Rosen, R. Callon, A. Viswanathan, RFC 3031, "Multiprotocol Label Switching Architecture," January 2001.

[IETF-12] Dino Farinacci, Tony Li, A. Conta, Y Rekhter, Dan Tappan, E. Rosen, G. Fedorkow, RFC 3032, "MPLS Label Stack Encoding," January 2001.

[IETF-13] Francois Le Faucheur, et al., "MPLS Support of Differentiated Services," [draft-ietf-mpls-diff-ext-09.txt], work in progress, April 2001.

[IETF-14] J. Mogul, S. Deering, RFC 1191, "Path MTU Discovery," November 1990.

[IETF-15] A. Conta, S. Deering, RFC 1885, "Internet Control Message Protocol (ICMPv6) for the Internet Protocol Version 6 (IPv6) Specification," December 1995.

[IETF-16] McCann, J., Deering, S., Mogul, J., RFC 1981, "Path MTU Discovery for IP version 6," August 1996.

[IETF-17] Simpson, W., Editor, RFC 1661, STD 51, "The Point-to-Point Protocol (PPP)," July 1994.

[IETF-18] Bruce Davie, et al., RFC 3035, "MPLS using LDP and ATM VC Switching," January 2001.

[IETF-19] Ken-ichi Nagami, et al., RFC 3038, "VCID Notification over ATM link for LDP," January 2001.

[IETF-20] A. Conta, P. Doolan, A. Malis, RFC 3034, "Use of Label Switching on Frame Relay Networks," January 2001.

[IETF-21] Juha Heinanen, RFC 1483, "Multiprotocol Encapsulation over ATM Adaptation Layer 5," July 1993.

[IETF-22] I. Widjaja, A. Elwalid, RFC 2682, "Performance Issues in VC-Merge Capable ATM LSRs," September 1999.

[IETF-23] Andersson, et al., RFC 3036, "LDP Specification," January 2001.

[IETF-24] J. Reynolds, J. Postel, RFC 1700, STD 2, "Assigned Numbers," October 1994.

[IETF-25] D. Ooms, et al., "Framework for IP Multicast in MPLS," [draft-ietf-mpls-multicast-05.txt], work in progress, January 2001.

[IETF-26] Bilel Jamoussi, et al., "Constraint-Based LSP Setup using LDP," [draft-ietf-mpls-crldp-05.txt], work in progress, January 2001.

[IETF-27] R. Braden, et al., RFC 2205, "Resource ReSerVation Protocol (RSVP) - Version 1, Functional Specification," September 1997.

[IETF-28] R. Braden, D. Clark, S. Shenker, RFC 1633, "Integrated Services in the Internet Architecture: an Overview," June 1994.

[IETF-29] G. Swallow, et al., "Extensions to RSVP for LSP Tunnels," [draft-ietf-mpls-rsvp-lsp-tunnel-08.txt], work in progress, February 2001.

[IETF-30] D. O. Awduche, et al., "Applicability Statement for Extensions to RSVP for LSP-Tunnels," [draft-ietf-mpls-rsvp-tunnel-applicability-02.txt], work in progress, April 2001.

[IETF-31] Y. Rekhter, T. Li, RFC 1771, "A Border Gateway Protocol 4 (BGP-4)," March 1995.

[IETF-32] Yakov Rekhter, Eric Rosen, RFC 3107, "Carrying Label Information in BGP-4," May 2001.

[IETF-33] T. Bates, et al., RFC 2858, "Multiprotocol Extensions for BGP-4," June 2000.

[IETF-34] K. Nichols, et al., RFC 2474, "Definition of the Differentiated Services Field (DS Field) in the IPv4 and IPv6 Headers," December 1998.

[MET2-1] Chris Metz, "MSS and IP Switching," IBM Whitepaper.

[NEWM-1] P. Newman, T. Lyon, G. Minshall, "Flow Labelled IP: Connectionless ATM Under IP," Ipsilon Networks Inc. Whitepaper, 1996.

Index

A

AAA 90, 173
Address Family Identifier 124, 127
ADSL 88
any to any 119
ARIS 15, 16
AS number 101, 102, 116
ATM 9, 10, 11, 14, 48, 50
autonomous system 5, 36, 101

B

BGP/MPLS VPN 1, 107, 147
Border Gateway Protocol (BGP-4) 101

C

Cable Modem Termination System (CMTS) 162

Carrier ISP 147, 149, 151
Carrier's Carrier 139, 147
CE Router 109, 130
Cell Switched Routing (CSR) 14
Classical IP over ATM (CLIP) 9
Client ISP 147
community attributes 102, 131
connectionless 10, 156
connection-oriented 10, 69, 90, 156, 162
control process 18, 19
CPE 129, 132
Customer Network (C Network) 112

D

Data over Cable Interface Specification (DOCSIS) 160
data-driven 1, 15
Diffserv Code Point 33, 90
Digital Subscriber Line 155
Digital Subscriber Line (DSL) 154
DLCI 5, 32, 185, 186
DOCSIS 160

DSL 154
DVB-RC 160

E

eBGP 36, 104, 145, 148
encapsulation 1, 32, 33, 36, 38, 43, 47, 51, 53, 55
encryption 88, 89, 164
Enterprises 3
ESCON 188
Extended Community 118
extranet 81, 85, 109

F

flow-based 15
Forwarding Equivalency Class 20
forwarding process 13, 18, 27, 28, 30
Frame Relay 5, 32, 48, 60, 89, 90
full-mesh 6, 122

G

G.SHDSL 155
Gateway GPRS Support Node 169
GGSN 169
GPRS 140, 166, 194
GRE 34, 86, 109, 145, 170
GSM 166

H

HDSL 154, 155
HFC 162
Hub and Spoke 87, 89, 133, 134, 135, 136

I

iBGP 104, 122, 141
IETF 9, 16, 88, 107, 122
IGP 4, 27, 96, 114, 134, 137, 149, 151, 156
IMT-2000 166
Internet 2, 15, 73, 101, 114, 124, 137, 141, 147, 166, 172
Internet Assigned Numbers Association (IANA) 101
IP Precedence 90
IP routing table 27
IP Switch 13
IP switching 1, 13, 14, 15, 16
IPSec 6, 88
IPv6 44, 73, 77, 105, 195

L

L2F 88
L2TP 88, 91, 157, 158, 159, 170, 173
label distribution 1, 26, 28, 31, 35, 59, 65, 66, 67, 75, 76, 147, 150
Label Distribution Protocol 26, 51, 59
Label Forwarding Information Base (LFIB) 24, 27

Label Information Base (LIB) 26
label stack 31, 32
Label Switched Path 67, 68, 74
label switched path 20, 30, 41, 75
Label Switched Path (LSP) 34
LAN 2, 14, 47, 123, 160, 174, 194

M

Maximum Transmission Unit (MTU) 43
MP-BGP 4, 7, 115
MP-iBGP 137, 159
MPLS 190
MPLS EXP 90
Multiprotocol Border Gateway Protocol 122
multicast 24, 47, 67, 73, 77, 97, 196
Multiplexer 187
Multiprotocol Extensions 105, 115, 123, 124, 196

N

Network Address Translation 140, 142, 143
Network Layer Reachability Information 123, 124, 127, 128

O

OSPF 20, 27, 50, 96, 129, 135, 149
Outbound Route Filters 146
Overlay Model 1, 11, 89, 90

P

P Router 109
packet switching 3, 4, 5
partial mesh 5
Path Attribute 118, 124, 127
path vector 41, 69, 70, 102
PE Router 109
PE-CE Link 109
Peer Model 1, 13, 95
Penultimate Hop Popping 25, 30, 31
PNNI 191
point-to-point 46, 47, 82, 86
PPP 46, 47, 88, 90, 109, 155, 172, 195
PPPoA 156
PPPoE 156, 162
PPTP 88
privacy 5
protocol 191
Provider Network (P Network) 109
provisioning 190

Q

QoS 4, 20, 22, 73, 90, 94, 156, 161
quality of service 88, 94

R

Radius 90, 158, 173
Resouce Reservation Protocol 26
RIPv2 129, 134, 135
Route Distinguisher 115, 127
Route Reflectors 141, 144, 145, 146, 148
Route Target 119, 122, 127, 134, 146

routing loops 16, 70, 102, 131
routing policies 101, 102, 124
routing updates 11, 94, 96, 104, 118, 129, 147

S

Scalability 6, 10, 89, 93, 141, 167, 168, 169, 170,
SDSL 155
security 5, 88, 89, 95, 115, 132, 145, 163, 173
Service Providers 3, 81
Serving GPRS Support Node 168
SGSN 168
shim header 32, 36, 43, 47, 55
Static Routes 129
SVC 12, 14, 53

T

Tag Switching 15, 47
Time to Live field (TTL) 37

topology-driven 1, 20
traffic engineering 3, 18, 20, 34, 51, 72, 74, 77, 88
Type of Service 22, 33, 90

U

UMTS 140, 166, 175

V

VCI 5, 14, 32, 41, 48, 50, 65, 185
VDSL 155
video 15, 85, 95, 97, 160
Virtual Circuits 10, 12, 54
voice 22, 85, 95, 154, 166
VPN-IPv4 115, 122, 127, 128, 146, 151
VRF 112, 114, 115

Solutions from experts you know and trust.

| Articles | Free Library | eBooks | Expert Q & A | Training | Career Center | Downloads | MyInformIT |

Login   Register   About InformIT

Topics
Operating Systems
Web Development
Programming
Networking
Certification
and more...

www.informit.com

Expert Access

Free Content

✓ Free, in-depth articles and supplements

✓ Master the skills you need, when you need them

✓ Choose from industry leading books, ebooks, and training products

✓ Get answers when you need them - from live experts or InformIT's comprehensive library

✓ Achieve industry certification and advance your career

Visit *InformIT* today and get great content from PH PTR

Prentice Hall and InformIT are trademarks of Pearson plc / Copyright © 2000 Pearson

PRENTICE HALL
Professional Technical Reference
Tomorrow's Solutions for Today's Professionals.

Keep Up-to-Date with
PH PTR Online!

We strive to stay on the cutting edge of what's happening in professional computer science and engineering. Here's a bit of what you'll find when you stop by **www.phptr.com**:

@ Special interest areas offering our latest books, book series, software, features of the month, related links and other useful information to help you get the job done.

☞ Deals, deals, deals! Come to our promotions section for the latest bargains offered to you exclusively from our retailers.

$ Need to find a bookstore? Chances are, there's a bookseller near you that carries a broad selection of PTR titles. Locate a Magnet bookstore near you at www.phptr.com.

! What's new at PH PTR? We don't just publish books for the professional community, we're a part of it. Check out our convention schedule, join an author chat, get the latest reviews and press releases on topics of interest to you.

✉ Subscribe today! Join PH PTR's monthly email newsletter!

Want to be kept up-to-date on your area of interest? Choose a targeted category on our website, and we'll keep you informed of the latest PH PTR products, author events, reviews and conferences in your interest area.

Visit our mailroom to subscribe today! **http://www.phptr.com/mail_lists**